TWENTIETH CENTURY VIEWS

The aim of this series is to present the best in
contemporary critical opinion on major authors,
providing a twentieth century perspective on
their changing status in an era of profound
revaluation.

Maynard Mack, *Series Editor*
Yale University

MELVILLE

MELVILLE

A COLLECTION OF CRITICAL ESSAYS

Edited by

Richard Chase

A SPECTRUM BOOK

Prentice-Hall, Inc., *Englewood Cliffs, N.J.*

Current printing (last digit):

18   17

© 1962 BY PRENTICE-HALL, INC.

ENGLEWOOD CLIFFS, N.J.

LIBRARY OF CONGRESS CARD NO.: 62-14917

Printed in the United States of America

57429-C

Table of Contents

MELVILLE

Introduction

by Richard Chase

I

Although some of the essayists who contribute to this volume have reservations of various kinds about the art of Melville or the quality of his thought, none of them thinks it necessary to defend his greatness. To the literary historian, who perhaps has an eye for cultural ironies, this will seem remarkable, in view of the long time it took Melville to gain even half the recognition he deserved, not to mention the apparently unshakable reputation he now has. He now seems to most readers to be pre-eminent among the American "classic" writers whose genius for prose fiction flowered before the Civil War, such as James Fenimore Cooper, Edgar Allan Poe, and Nathaniel Hawthorne. His writings are not so voluminous as those of Cooper, but they are more readable. He has something of Poe's talent for the macabre, but in Melville the macabre is only a part of a larger view of life and seldom becomes obsessive. He is not so graceful a writer as Hawthorne, but his range is greater and his imagination is more powerful and diverse. In *Moby-Dick* we see one of those unique productions into which have been drawn all of its epoch's significant and freshening currents of mind and imagination. Only Melville was able to perform this culminating act of vision in our classic literary period.

Perhaps this is easy enough to see as we read and ponder *Moby-Dick* in relation to the literature of the time. But we have come to see also that Melville and his writings occupy a more central position in the history of our culture than was formerly thought. The radical, realist critics of a former generation made no such provision for the importance of Melville. Vernon Lewis Parrington's *Main Currents in American Thought* (published during the late 1920's and early '30's) was for many years and perhaps still is for an older generation the overwhelmingly influential account of American literature. Its impress can be seen on dozens of lesser critical and scholarly works and on dozens of anthologies. Yet Parrington regarded Melville as an eccentric figure, an exotic plant among healthier organisms like Whitman, Emerson, William Cullen Bryant, and Horace Greeley. Parrington calls Melville without qualification a "pessimist." He speaks of the futility of his dreams and calls him "an arch romantic who vainly sought to erect his romantic dreams as a defense against reality, and suffered disaster." Melville, we are told, "was in love with the ideal," and Parrington continues by comparing him with James Branch Cabell! It strikes the modern reader as odd that Melville should be thought a mere escapist unable to face life, and that the author of *Mardi, Billy Budd,* and the Civil-War poems called *Battle-Pieces* should be charged with having no sense of the political facts of life. Nor do Melville's democratic convictions get in "by the back door" of his despair, as Parrington thought; rather they are forthrightly, sometimes even exuberantly, proclaimed. One can hardly imagine an exquisite and mannerist like Cabell having a profound affinity with Shakespeare. Yet this affinity is one of the signs of Melville's centrality as a thinker and moralist, in spite of his undeniable extremism and occasional eccentricity. It was not Cabell but Melville who wrote:

> No utter surprise can come to him
> Who reaches Shakespeare's core;
> That which we seek and shun is there—
> Man's final lore.

Van Wyck Brooks had laid the ground for the Parrington conception of our literature in such early essays as "America's Coming-of-Age" (1915). Much of this long, eloquent, epoch-making essay is devoted to a reassessment of the nineteenth century authors, and it is indicative of the state of Melville's reputation at the time that he is not even mentioned. Brooks's argument is that the great tradition of American literature stems from Whitman, who was the "focal center" of American thought and feeling. Whitman he believed to be the "precipitant" who brought together in a glorious prophetic affirmation the various currents of the American experience. In *Democratic Vistas* Whitman had said that one of the signs by which we know the great American writer is the "absence in him of the idea of the covert, the lurid, the maleficent, the devil, the grim estimates inherited from the Puritans, hell, natural depravity, and the like." Yet Melville had written in praise of "the great power of blackness" in Hawthorne's imagination and supposed that it derived "its force from its appeals to that Calvinistic sense of Innate Depravity and Original Sin, from whose visitations, in some shape or other, no deeply thinking mind is always and wholly free." Melville, himself a religious sceptic, is thinking here of that dark side of the American imagination which has always been and continues to be as powerful as the impulse toward optimistic prophecy and a serene acceptance of the essential good luck of democratic conditions in a benign universe. The confident "Yea" of Whitman and the Transcendentalists has always been balanced by the sceptical "Nay" of the darker imagination. "There is the grand truth about Nathaniel

Hawthorne," writes Melville. "He says No! in thunder; but the Devil himself cannot make him say *yes*. For all men who say *yes*, lie." This is rhetorically overstated of course. Even less than Hawthorne was Melville a Nay-sayer pure and simple. His writings are sometimes joyously affirmative, and certain passages in *Moby-Dick* sound like democratic hosannas out of Whitman. Nor are Whitman and Emerson exclusively Yea-sayers. Both have enough of the sense of evil in human life to keep them in adequate balance as moralists, and both are capable of saying an uncompromising No to some aspects of American democracy.

These facts suggest that there is no "focal center" in the American mind and that there is, instead, a dialectic or continuing dialogue between the Yea-sayers and the Nay-sayers. They suggest furthermore that with whatever degree of imbalance, this dialogue goes on within the mind of each of our most interesting and characteristic writers. This view, advanced by critics like R. W. B. Lewis and deriving, perhaps, from Lionel Trilling's essay "Reality in America," is clearly superseding Parrington and Brooks. We may be sure, at any rate, that the attempt to relegate Melville and others with whom we associate the "power of blackness" to a position of eccentricity or irrelevance can never again be successfully made.

II

In the years shortly after Melville returned from his wanderings in the South Seas, he published two volumes based upon his experiences, *Typee* and its sequel *Omoo*. Both books are semi-romanticized although both contain a wealth of authentic personal observation. Their peculiar mixture of realism and romance made them popular with readers, and Melville quickly became something of a literary celebrity. But the first fine glow of his success soon grew dim. *Mardi*, which begins as another adventure story and then abruptly transforms itself into the genre of the imaginary voyage (such as *Gulliver's Travels*), is not a very satisfactory book from any point of view. But it seems to us who have the whole of Melville's work before us a moderately interesting experiment in allegory, symbol, and satire—the first book in which the author's true capacities begin to assert themselves openly. To most readers of the day, who doubtless expected another *Typee*, it was a disappointing performance, bordering on incomprehensibility if not outright lunacy. By 1851, while he was finishing *Moby-Dick*, Melville (still only thirty-two) regarded himself as a writer without an audience and without the possibility of an adequate income from his writings. Yet we find that in the famous letters to Hawthorne of that year he is defiantly determined to follow the bent of his own genius, which, of course, had already taken him a long way beyond the relatively easy-going South-Seas romances with which he had opened his career. He is determined to tell the "Truth" as he sees it. "Dollars damn me," he exclaims; "and the malicious Devil is forever grinning in upon me, holding the door ajar." And again, "Try to get a living by the Truth—and go to the Soup Societies." And he adds, "What I feel most moved to write, that is banned,—it will not pay. Yet, altogether, write the *other* way I cannot." He was right; not even *Moby-Dick* "paid."

Melville's reputation was blurred by *Mardi*, not ransomed by *Moby-Dick*, and nearly annihilated by *Pierre*, which outraged most readers with its theme of love, incest, and death. He was never to regain his early audience, nor to find another. True, he found a number of sympathetic readers both here and in England in his later years, but his fame remained so sporadic and unconsolidated that he became the very type of the isolated artist in America, to whom our cultural critics have paid so much fascinated attention. The spectacle of the author of *Moby-Dick* enduring nearly twenty years of drudgery as a customs inspector in New York has become one of the memorable, and humiliating, archetypes of American culture.

The quiet heroism of his later life does not hide the fact that Melville felt his isolation keenly. See for example the plea in his essay "Hawthorne and His Mosses" for that "shock of recognition" which should unite genius all over the world. It has often been conjectured that such a story as "Bartleby the Scrivener" mirrors Melville's own isolation. "Bartleby," one of the world's great short stories, is not to be understood simply as masked autobiography—its meanings are rich and various, reminding us alternately of Melville's kinship with Dickens, Dostoyevski, Kafka, and the author of the Book of Job. Its dark probings into the spirit of man and its delineation of "sickness unto death" clearly go beyond a merely introspective self-assessment. Nevertheless one cannot help thinking of Melville himself as we watch the law-office copyist gradually resist and recede from the conventional, workaday, commercialized world around him. Melville had in effect answered the literary demands made upon him by the going concern of conventional life in Bartleby's tragi-comic refrain: "I would prefer not to." Add to this the fact that Melville's brothers Gansevoort and Allan, like Bartleby's employer, practiced law in Wall Street and that Melville's father-in-law was a judge who sometimes helped the author's family financially. Clearly, there is an autobiographical dimension to the story, more so than in "Benito Cereno," where some readers have seen an overburdened and recessive Melville in the portrait of the Spanish captain and "conventional society" in Captain Delano. The fact remains, however, that Melville's isolation was not sickness unto death. He continued throughout a long life to write, and in his last years produced *Billy Budd*, one of his best works. Melville died leaving the manuscript of *Billy Budd* among his papers. It was not published until 1924, when Raymond Weaver, who three years earlier had published the first full-scale biography of Melville, brought out an edition. These events mark the beginning of the modern appreciation of the long neglected author.

III

Despite Melville's eloquence, his humor, his tragic sense of life, his often successful use of myth, symbol, and allegory counterbalanced with a solid realism, his art has distinct limitations. He was not superbly a fictional inventor. Particularly the voyage books, including *Moby-Dick*, depend a good deal on Melville's own experiences of knocking around the world as a sailor; and they show a considerable dependence on his readings of books by ship captains and explorers. So that at least one of his troubles after 1851 was that in a rapid series of volumes he had come close to exhausting the main well-spring of his imagination, his experiences as a sailor, especially in the South Seas—for the voyage in the South Seas did as much to give Melville's imagination its essential form as did the Mississippi River Mark Twain's imagination or the "international scene" Henry James' imagination.

Even in *Moby-Dick* the style is sometimes too full of words for its own good; it occasionally becomes stilted or inscrutable. Melville could often catch the cadences of American speech in his dialogue sequences, and yet at other times he could write dialogue as if he had never heard *anyone* actually speak—this is painfully so in *Pierre*. Like Cooper, but unlike Faulkner or Mark Twain, he sometimes gives us the impression that his dialogue is written according to a literary convention we cannot quite identify.

Melville's humor enlivens many of his pages, but like the popular humor of his time (whose gambits he often employed), it sometimes deteriorates into mere jocosity rather than concentrating itself into authentic wit. His deepest sense of life is genuinely tragic. But this sense of life also shows traces of a romantic nihilism. It can become neurotically disoriented, as in *Pierre*, and it can become black pessimism, as in *The Confidence-Man*.

Melville was not a master of "the art of fiction," as we have conceived of this art since the novels and essays of Henry James. *Pierre* is the closest Melville came to writing a novel in the Jamesian sense, and it is certainly a botched book, though not by that token without interest. The contributors to the present volume, except for R. P. Blackmur, testify to all this by not thinking of Melville as a novelist at all. They are content to take him as a writer of romance—that particular kind of poetic fiction which we associate with Cooper, Hawthorne, Poe, Mark Twain, and even a modern writer like Hemingway. More than any of Melville's other works *Pierre*, because of its subject, its would-be characters, its projected action, and its settings, demanded to be written novelistically. Mr. Blackmur's essay shows us what Melville lost by being a "condemned" rather than a "convicted" novelist, but he also shows us from an unusual angle (unusual in Melville criticism, that is) the gains that went with the losses. Even less than his fellow classic American fictionists did Melville have the characteristic equipment of the novelist—the ability to create fully rounded characters who think, act, and feel in relation to each other as our common knowledge of life tells us people think, act, and feel. In the novel continuity is of the essence, James tells us—the continuity, that is, between what people feel and think and what they do; the continuity between what one character does and what the others do; the continuity of the central dramatic action; the continuity between a character's fate and his past or the social class he comes from; the continuity among character, setting, and action; the continuity, finally, between what happens to a character and his sense of what happens to him. Melville's deficiency, or lack of interest, in these novelistic qualities is pointed up by Mr. Blackmur when he calls Captain Ahab of *Moby-Dick* a "great figure, not a great character" and goes on to say that "Ahab is as solitary in the book as he was in his cabin."

But despite the fact that Melville was in some sense condemned by his time, because the novel had become *the* great mode of fictional narrative, to write as if he were a novelist, his assumptions about the fictional art, like those of Cooper, Hawthorne, and many other American writers, were quite different from those to which James was later to give authoritative definition. He wrote "romances," not of course the merely exotic or escapist fictions this word is likely to call to mind, but fictions that have a characteristic light-and-dark poetry and range freely (all too freely from the Jamesian point of view) among the extremes of human thought and experience. Ahab is indeed a "figure." He has the two-dimensional, legendary quality of most of Melville's imagined people, though on a larger, epic scale. Melville is a creator of figures also in the sense of figures of speech, of grandly conceived, epic, mythic, or symbolistic metaphors like the pursuit of the white whale—or on a scale less grand, the valley of Typee, the retreat of Bartleby, the confrontation of Benito Cereno and Captain Delano, the river voyage of the confidence man, the hanging of Billy Budd. These are all elements of plot, setting, and character, and of recognizable reality, and, given his idea of fiction, Melville usually treats them adequately as such. But they interest him more as metaphors, poetic conceptions which he brought to bear upon questions of the moral and intellectual life. He is content to sacrifice continuity or even credibility as long as he can establish a significant poetic action. He is content to leave things unexplained that common sense wants to know about. If it suits his purpose, he will unexpectedly abandon a character who he had led us to suppose would have a central role, as he abandons Bulkington in *Moby-Dick*. A novel, properly so called, contains all the data the reader needs for a full understanding of the motives and events that shape the fate of the characters. Not so a romance. Often the sequence of events is unexplained; the fate of men is made mysteriously; motives, if they are shown at all, are simplified and rendered abstract.

Moral values are derived from a purely personal sense of honor or virtue; or else they are derived from abstract and intellectualized conceptions. They do not derive, as tends to be true in a novel, from the manners, assumptions, laws, and conventions of society. His bias toward romance places Melville in the great tradition of American fiction, which extends from Charles Brockden Brown to Faulkner, Hemingway, and beyond. It is a tradition which far outshines the "novelistic" tradition of James (who is nevertheless our greatest writer of fiction) and Howells.

IV

As compared with many American writers, Melville had an unusually reflective and philosophical mind. Despite his lack of formal education (his Harvard and Yale were the fo'c'sle of a whale ship, as he remarks in *Moby-Dick*), he was a resourceful and thoughtful reader and, as F. O. Matthiessen points out in his essay on *Billy Budd,* a tireless underliner of striking passages and annotator of page margins. His love of speculative thought is plain to every reader of his works and is memorably attested to by Hawthorne, who recalled a visit from Melville in Liverpool in 1856, on which occasion Melville talked eloquently and with characteristic vehemence about the ultimate problems of knowledge, truth, and belief and impressed Hawthorne as being a man who could neither believe "nor be comfortable in his unbelief." Unlike Hawthorne, who seems to have been relatively serene in his unbelief, Melville spent a lifetime in an unsuccessful pursuit—alternately agonized and humorous, always ardent —of a metaphysical conception which would explain to him the nature of our universe of reality and thought, and a moral conception that would make some sense out of the bewildering inequities, injustices, and ambiguities which form the context of human action and human motive. Melville seems to have given up the hope of believing in God early in life. To be sure, his works often display Christian feeling and employ Christian allusion. But Melville's "religion" must finally be called something like "skeptical humanism"—although Leslie Fiedler in *Love and Death in the American Novel* prefers to call it "tragic humanism." This "religion" is so complex, at any rate, that it persuaded one critic (see Lawrance Thompson's *Melville's Quarrel with God*) to argue that Melville's works are a concerted, embittered, and deeply veiled attack on God from an atheist or perhaps diabolist point of view.

Melville is fascinated above all with the contradictions and ambiguities which, as no one ever felt more keenly than he, inhere in the condition of being human and which confront and baffle the mind of man whenever he tries to go beyond the conventional evasions which the unthinking man is content to substitute for thought. It is this which engages his mind in one way or another from *Typee* to *Billy Budd* and which determines more than anything else the quality of his imagination. *Typee* is not overtly a philosophical book. Yet the actions that occur, the symbols Melville employs, and the emotional undercurrents of *Typee* are the matrix out of which more philosophical utterances emerge in later books. Apparently light-hearted and aimed at entertainment of a slightly shocking kind, *Typee* is nevertheless a serious book, and it establishes Melville as an author whose mind is perplexed and whose imagination is stirred by the contradictoriness of human experience. The very rhythms of the action suggest this—consisting as they do of alternate imprisonments and escapes, of painful ascents of mountains and precipitous descents into valleys. In this context of symbolic action, galling questions present themselves to the hero. Why should there be cannibalism in Paradise? Why in such an idyllic place should there be an ambiguous hint of evil and danger? Why the malignancy of the infection in the hero's leg, an infection which is in part a symbolic sickness? What has happened to Western man in the process of forming a high civilization that makes it impossible to "get back to nature"? D. H. Lawrence, who has no doubt that *Typee* is more than mere entertainment, says that the hero finds it necessary to go back to Home and Mother (which Melville disastrously does in *Pierre*) and that what Melville was seeking was a perfect love or friendship, a quest that becomes more and more desperate the longer a man refuses to admit that there is no such thing. This interpretation is true and enlightening, and is borne out by the later works. But it is somewhat limited by Lawrence's own preoccupations. It serves, however, to remind us of the personal anguish that underlay Melville's flights of thought and imagination—the anguish of a powerful need for love which he never found. There is no question but that even within his own family (there were four children) he remained what he calls in *Moby-Dick* an "isolato."

As I have suggested, the underlying emotional and intellectual ferment of *Typee* finds, or tries to find, overt expression in *Mardi*. Like *Typee,* *Mardi* ends with the flight of the hero to undiscovered realms. But Taji's imaginary travels about the imaginary archipelago of Mardi are much more consciously a quest than were the hero's adventures in *Typee,* and his flight at the end is much more consciously a pursuit of something he has not yet found. It is not always easy to tell what Taji is pursuing through the pages of Melville's rather bizarre medley of genres and intentions. Newton Arvin is surely right, however, when he tells us that Taji (Melville) is in quest of "emotional security . . . a just and happy sociality . . . an absolute and transcendent Truth." This manifold quest, the hero comes to see, must be made, even in such a blithesome place as Mardi, amidst ambiguities and irreconcilable polarities. The polarities are symbolized by the significant if slightly ridiculous characters called Yillah and Hautia—examples of the angelic fair woman and the sinister dark woman who figure so much as symbols and so little as woman in our classic fiction from Cooper to Hawthorne. Yillah, one may hazard, suggests innocence, happiness, enlightenment, and untroubled sexuality (if any). Hautia suggests evil, the vortex of darkness and falsity, and a guilty and devouring sexuality.

In *Redburn* and *White-Jacket* Melville turns to more conventional narrative, with a minimum of the speculative and symbolic. Yet broadly speaking he is in both books constantly aware of the tensions created by the exposure of the youthful innocence of the hero to a corrupt and evil world and aware, too, of the necessity of shedding innocence in order to survive in a world of evil, or at best a world of moral ambiguity. When the hero of the second of these books sheds the white jacket that symbolizes his innocence, he does so at the last moment in a nearly fatal situation.

Moby-Dick, too enormous and rich a book to discuss here, is, in the words of R. W. B. Lewis, "an elaborate pattern of countercommentaries, the supreme instance of the dialectical novel—a novel of tension without resolution." The essay on *Moby-Dick* by the present editor, reprinted below, may serve to follow out, among other things, some of the implications of Mr. Lewis's observation, and thus complement the appreciative humanism of Alfred Kazin's approach and the archetypal, psychiatric approach of Henry A. Murray and the political-theological approach of Marius Bewley.

In *Pierre* the angelic girl, now called Lucy, and the dark woman, Isabel, again are emblematic of the irreconcilable. The "ambiguities" mentioned in the subtitle are manifold—the mixed love and aggressiveness of the mother's feeling for the son; the incest which occurs between Pierre and his half-sister Isabel; the spectacle of Pierre, the "Fool of Truth," dashing himself against an adamant world wherein the easy compromiser and the outright sinner flourish; the difference between "horological" and "chronometrical" time. If *Pierre* is a book that tries to be a novel of manners and turns into a ranting melodrama, *The Confidence-Man* is a kind of nondramatic comedy that sometimes reminds us of Molière and Ben Jonson and turns into a sort of grim masquerade demonstrating the contrast between appearance and reality and showing the absurdity of the attempt to lead the moral life where meaning and value shift ground as readily as the wily confidence man assumes a new disguise. Despite its nihilism, its lack of unity, and the fact that it is too long for what Melville wants to do, *The Confidence-Man* is still a misunderstood and underestimated book—a situation Daniel G. Hoffman does much to remedy in his essay on the subject.

In his later years Melville gradually modulated his powerful and sometimes despairing reaction to the cruel irreconcilables of life. A new mood appears in his poetry, for example, and as Robert Penn Warren points out, some of the Civil-War poems assert, tentatively at least, that conflict can be assuaged or even absorbed into harmony by the passage of time, by the curative powers of nature, or by the human capacity for transfiguring reality into legend. Similar assertions are made in *Billy*

Budd, where, for example, the truth about the hanged sailor is perpetuated in the popular legends of his shipmates. In contrast to some of Melville's more violent works, *Billy Budd* is elegiac and tender; it displays a certain serenity which suggests that in his latest years Melville could derive solace from the idea that man might yet find his way through the "ambiguities" by depending upon a principle of grace or spiritual health that still has a marginal place in a "man-of-war world." Mr. Matthiessen says this all but definitively, erring only by making *Billy Budd* a more dedicatedly Christian book than it really is.

Notwithstanding the modulations of thought and feeling which occurred in Melville's later years, the unity and hallmark of his writing as a whole (even, as it seems to me, including *Billy Budd*) stem from his preoccupation with the contradictoriness of experience. This is perforce an abstract assertion, and as a key to understanding Melville in detail and in context from book to book it is far from capable of opening all the doors there are to open. The following essays open many of these doors. The rest the reader must open for himself.

NOTE: I have found no occasion in the above remarks to notice two works of considerable interest, *Israel Potter* and *Clarel.* Nor, except in passing, are these discussed by the essayists who follow. *Israel Potter* is a lively, bumptious tale in the picaresque manner concerning the adventures of a rustic American who becomes embroiled in clandestine politics and spy activities in Europe during the American Revolution. The book contains vivid portraits of Ethan Allen, John Paul Jones, and Benjamin Franklin, the last of whom Melville depicts good-humoredly as a charlatan, almost, indeed, a confidence man. *Clarel* is a very long poem, or rather, a kind of intellectual novel in verse. It has to do with the pilgrimage to Palestine of a young American divinity student who has been worried by an inner doubt about the validity of religious revelation. He is joined by various characters representing different intellectual positions and cultural backgrounds. The book has its arid stretches and the verse rises to true poetry only in spots. But it has the same kind of interest as do other thoughtful works of the Age of Victorian Doubt, such as those of Matthew Arnold (whose writings Melville read with some thoroughness). For the American reader *Clarel* has the added virtue of presenting among its characters certain perennial American types.

Herman Melville's *Typee* and *Omoo*

by D. H. Lawrence

The greatest seer and poet of the sea for me is Melville. His vision is more real than Swinburne's, because he doesn't personify the sea, and far sounder than Joseph Conrad's, because Melville doesn't sentimentalize the ocean and the sea's unfortunates. Snivel in a wet hanky like Lord Jim.

Melville has the strange, uncanny magic of sea-creatures, and some of their repulsiveness. He isn't quite a land animal. There is something slithery about him. Something always half-seas-over. In his life they said he was mad—or crazy. He was neither mad nor crazy. But he was over the border. He was half a water animal, like those terrible yellow-bearded Vikings who broke out of the waves in beaked ships.

He was a modern Viking. There is something curious about real blue-eyed people. They are never quite human, in the good classic sense, human as brown-eyed people are human: the human of the living humus. About a real blue-eyed person there is usually something abstract, elemental. Brown-eyed people are, as it were, like the earth, which is tissue of bygone life, organic, compound. In blue eyes there is sun and rain and abstract, uncreate element, water, ice, air, space, but not humanity. Brown-eyed people are people of the old, old world: *Allzu menschlich*. Blue-eyed people tend to be too keen and abstract.

Melville is like a Viking going home to the sea, encumbered with age and memories, and a sort of accomplished despair, almost madness. For he cannot accept humanity. He can't belong to humanity. Cannot.

The great Northern cycle of which he is the returning unit has almost completed its round, accomplished itself. Balder the beautiful is mystically dead, and by this time he stinketh. Forget-me-nots and sea-poppies fall into water. The man who came from the sea to live among men can stand it no longer. He hears the horror of the cracked church-bell, and goes back down the shore, back into the ocean again, home, into the salt water. Human life won't do. He turns back to the elements. And all the

vast sun-and-wheat consciousness of his day he plunges back into the
deeps, burying the flame in the deep, self-conscious and deliberate. Like
blue flax and sea-poppies fall into the waters and give back their created
sun-stuff to the dissolution of the flood.

The sea-born people, who can meet and mingle no longer: who turn
away from life, to the abstract, to the elements: the sea receives her own.

Let life come asunder, they say. Let water conceive no more with fire.
Let mating finish. Let the elements leave off kissing, and turn their backs
on one another. Let the merman turn away from his human wife and
children, let the seal-woman forget the world of men, remembering only
the waters.

So they go down to the sea, the sea-born people. The Vikings are
wandering again. Homes are broken up. Cross the seas, cross the seas,
urges the heart. Leave love and home. Leave love and home. Love and
home are a deadly illusion. Woman, what have I to do with thee? It is
finished. *Consummatum est.* The crucifixion into humanity is over. Let
us go back to the fierce, uncanny elements: the corrosive vast sea. Or Fire.

Basta! It is enough. It is enough of life. Let us have the vast elements.
Let us get out of this loathsome complication of living humanly with
humans. Let the sea wash us clean of the leprosy of our humanity and
humanness.

Melville was a northerner, sea-born. So the sea claimed him. We are
most of us, who use the English language, water-people, sea-derived.

Melville went back to the oldest of all the oceans, to the Pacific. *Der
Grosse oder Stille Ozean.*

Without doubt the Pacific Ocean is æons older than the Atlantic or the
Indian Oceans. When we say older, we mean it has not come to any
modern consciousness. Strange convulsions have convulsed the Atlantic
and Mediterranean peoples into phase after phase of consciousness, while
the Pacific and the Pacific peoples have slept. To sleep is to dream; you
can't stay unconscious. And, oh, heaven, for how many thousands of
years has the true Pacific been dreaming, turning over in its sleep and
dreaming again: idylls: nightmares.

The Maoris, the Tongans, the Marquesans, the Fijians, the Polyne-
sians: holy God, how long have they been turning over in the same sleep,
with varying dreams. Perhaps, to a sensitive imagination, those islands
in the middle of the Pacific are the most unbearable places on earth. It
simply stops the heart, to be translated there, unknown ages back, back
into that life, that pulse, that rhythm. The scientists say the South Sea
Islanders belong to the Stone Age. It seems absurd to class people according to their implements. And yet there is something in it. The heart of
the Pacific is still the Stone Age; in spite of steamers. The heart of the
Pacific seems like a vast vacuum, in which, mirage-like, continues the life
of myriads of ages back. It is a phantom-persistence of human beings who

should have died, by our chronology, in the Stone Age. It is a phantom, illusion-like trick of reality: the glamorous South Seas. Even Japan and China have been turning over in their sleep for countless centuries. Their blood is the old blood, their tissue the old soft tissue. Their busy day was myriads of years ago, when the world was a softer place, more moisture in the air, more warm mud on the face of the earth, and the lotus was always in flower. The great bygone world, before Egypt. And Japan and China have been turning over in their sleep, while we have "advanced." And now they are starting up into nightmare.

The world isn't what it seems.

The Pacific Ocean holds the dream of immemorial centuries. It is the great blue twilight of the vastest of all evenings: perhaps of the most wonderful of all dawns. Who knows.

It must once have been a vast basin of soft, lotus-warm civilization, the Pacific. Never was such a huge man-day swung down into slow disintegration, as here. And now the waters are blue and ghostly with the end of immemorial peoples. And phantom-like the islands rise out of it, illusions of the glamorous Stone Age.

To this phantom Melville returned. Back, back, away from life. Never man instinctly hated human life, our human life, as we have it, more than Melville did. And never was a man so passionately filled with the sense of vastness and mystery of life which is nonhuman. He was mad to look over our horizons. Anywhere, anywhere out of *our* world. To get away. To get away, out!

To get away, out of our life. To cross a horizon into another life. No matter what life, so long as it is another life.

Away, away from humanity. To the sea. The naked, salt, elemental sea. To go to sea, to escape humanity.

The human heart gets into a frenzy at last, in its desire to dehumanize itself.

So he finds himself in the middle of the Pacific. Truly over a horizon. In another world. In another epoch. Back, far back, in the days of palm trees and lizards and stone implements. The sunny Stone Age.

Samoa, Tahiti, Raratonga, Nukuheva: the very names are a sleep and a forgetting. The sleep-forgotten past magnificence of human history. "Trailing clouds of glory."

Melville hated the world: was born hating it. But he was looking for heaven. That is, choosingly. Choosingly, he was looking for paradise. Unchoosingly, he was mad with hatred of the world.

Well, the world is hateful. It is as hateful as Melville found it. He was not wrong in hating the world. *Delenda est Chicago.* He hated it to a pitch of madness, and not without reason.

But it's no good *persisting* in looking for paradise "regained."

Melville at his best invariably wrote from a sort of dream-self, so that events which he relates as actual fact have indeed a far deeper reference to his own soul, his own inner life.

So in *Typee* when he tells of his entry into the valley of the dread cannibals of Nukuheva. Down this narrow, steep, horrible dark gorge he slides and struggles as we struggle in a dream, or in the act of birth, to emerge in the green Eden of the Golden Age, the valley of the cannibal savages. This is a bit of birth-myth, or rebirth myth, on Melville's part— unconscious, no doubt, because his running underconsciousness was always mystical and symbolical. He wasn't aware that he was being mystical.

There he is then, in Typee, among the dreaded cannibal savages. And they are gentle and generous with him, and he is truly in a sort of Eden.

Here at last is Rousseau's Child of Nature and Chateaubriand's Noble Savage called upon and found at home. Yes, Melville loves his savage hosts. He finds them gentle, laughing lambs compared to the ravening wolves of his white brothers, left behind in America and on an American whale-ship.

The ugliest beast on earth is the white man, says Melville.

In short, Herman found in Typee the paradise he was looking for. It is true, the Marquesans were "immoral," but he rather liked that. Morality was too white a trick to take him in. Then again, they were cannibals. And it filled him with horror even to think of this. But the savages were very private and even fiercely reserved in their cannibalism, and he might have spared himself his shudder. No doubt he had partaken of the Christian Sacraments many a time. "This is my body, take and eat. This is my blood. Drink it in remembrance of me." And if the savages liked to partake of their sacrament without raising the transubstantiation quibble, and if they liked to say, directly: "This is thy body, which I take from thee and eat. This is thy blood, which I sip in annihilation of thee," why surely their sacred ceremony was as awe-inspiring as the one Jesus substituted. But Herman chose to be horrified. I confess, I am not horrified. Though of course I am not on the spot. But the savage sacrament seems to me more valid than the Christian: less side-tracking about it.—Thirdly he was shocked by their wild methods of warfare. He died before the great European war, so his shock was comfortable.

Three little quibbles: morality, cannibal sacrament, and stone axes. You must have a fly even in Paradisal ointment. And the first was a lady-bird.

But Paradise. He insists on it. Paradise. He could even go stark naked, like before the Apple episode. And his Fayaway, a laughing little Eve, naked with him, and hankering after no apple of knowledge, so long as he would just love her when he felt like it. Plenty to eat, needing no clothes to wear, sunny, happy people, sweet water to swim in: everything a man can want. Then why wasn't he happy along with the savages?

Because he wasn't.

He grizzled in secret, and wanted to escape.

He even pined for Home and Mother, the two things he had run away from as far as ships would carry him. HOME and MOTHER. The two things that were his damnation.

There on the island, where the golden-green great palm-trees chinked in the sun, and the elegant reed houses let the sea-breeze through, and people went naked and laughed a great deal, and Fayaway put flowers in his hair for him—great red hibiscus flowers, and frangipani—O God, why wasn't he happy? Why wasn't he?

Because he wasn't.

Well, it's hard to make a man happy.

But I should not have been happy either. One's soul seems under a vacuum, in the South Seas.

The truth of the matter is, one cannot go back. Some men can: renegade. But Melville couldn't go back: and Gauguin couldn't really go back: and I know now that I could never go back. Back toward the past, savage life. One cannot go back. It is one's destiny inside one.

There are these peoples, these "savages." One does not despise them. One does not feel superior. But there is a gulf. There is a gulf in time and being. I cannot commingle my being with theirs.

There they are, these South Sea Islanders, beautiful big men with their golden limbs and their laughing, graceful laziness. And they will call you brother, choose you as a brother. But why cannot one truly be brother?

There is an invisible hand grasps my heart and prevents it opening too much to these strangers. They are beautiful, they are like children, they are generous: but they are more than this. They are far off, and in their eyes is an easy darkness of the soft, uncreate past. In a way, they are un-create. Far be it from me to assume any "white" superiority. But they are savages. They are gentle and laughing and physically very handsome. But it seems to me, that in living so far, through all our bitter centuries of civilization, we have still been living onward, forward. God knows it looks like a *cul-de-sac* now. But turn to the first negro, and then listen to your own soul. And your own soul will tell you that however false and foul our forms and systems are now, still, through the many centuries since Egypt, we have been living and struggling forward along some road that is no road, and yet is a great life-development. We have struggled on in us that on we must still go. We may have to smash things. Then let us smash. And our road may have to take a great swerve, that seems a retrogression.

But we can't go back. Whatever else the South Sea Islander is, he is centuries and centuries behind us in the life struggle, the consciousness-struggle, the struggle of the soul into fulness. There is his woman, with her knotted hair and her dark, inchoate, slightly sardonic eyes. I like her, she is nice. But I would never want to touch her. I could not go back on myself so far. Back to their uncreate condition.

She has soft warm flesh, like warm mud. Nearer the reptile, the Saurian age. *Noli me tangere.*

We can't go back. We can't go back to the savages: not a stride. We can be in sympathy with them. We can take a great curve in their direction, onward. But we cannot turn the current of our life backward, back toward their soft warm twilight and uncreate mud. Not for a moment. If we do it for a moment, it makes us sick.

We can only do it when we are renegade. The renegade hates life itself. He wants the death of life. So these many "reformers" and "idealists" who glorify the savages in America. They are death-birds, life-haters. Renegades.

We can't go back. And Melville couldn't. Much as he hated the civilized humanity he knew. He couldn't go back to the savages. He wanted to. He tried to. And he couldn't.

Because, in the first place, it made him sick. It made him physically ill. He had something wrong with his leg, and this would not heal. It got worse and worse, during his four months on the island. When he escaped, he was in a deplorable condition. Sick and miserable. Ill, very ill.

Paradise!

But there you are. Try to go back to the savages, and you feel as if your very soul was decomposing inside you. That is what you feel in the South Seas, anyhow: as if your soul was decomposing inside you. And with any savages the same, if you try to go their way, take their current of sympathy.

Yet, as I say, we must make a great swerve in our onward-going life-course now, to gather up again the savage mysteries. But this does not mean going back on ourselves.

Going back to the savages made Melville sicker than anything. It made him feel as if he were decomposing. Worse even than Home and Mother.

And that is what really happens. If you prostitute your psyche by returning to the savages, you gradually go to pieces. Before you can go back, you *have* to decompose. And a white man decomposing is a ghastly sight. Even Melville in Typee.

We have to go on, on, on, even if we must smash a way ahead.

So Melville escaped. And threw a boat-hook full in the throat of one of his dearest savage friends, and sank him, because that savage was swimming in pursuit. That's how he felt about the savages when they wanted to detain him. He'd have murdered them one and all, vividly, rather than be kept from escaping. Away from them—he must get away from them—at any price.

And once he has escaped, immediately he begins to sigh and pine for the "Paradise."—Home and Mother being at the other end even of a whaling voyage.

When he really was Home with Mother, he found it Purgatory. But Typee must have been even worse than Purgatory, a soft hell, judging from the murderous frenzy which possessed him, to escape.

But once aboard the whaler that carried him off from Nukuheva, he looked back and sighed for the Paradise he had just escaped from in such a fever.

Poor Melville! He was determined Paradise existed. So he was always in Purgatory.

He was born for Purgatory. Some souls are purgatorial by destiny.

The very freedom of his Typee was a torture to him. Its ease was slowly horrible to him. This time *he* was the fly in the odorous tropical ointment.

He needed to fight. It was no good to him, the relaxation of the non-moral tropics. He didn't really want Eden. He wanted to fight. Like every American. To fight. But with weapons of the spirit, not the flesh.

That was the top and bottom of it. His soul was in revolt, writhing forever in revolt. When he had something definite to rebel against—like the bad conditions on a whaling ship—then he was much happier in his miseries. The mills of God were grinding inside him, and they needed something to grind on.

When they could grind on the injustice and folly of missionaries, or of brutal sea-captains, or of governments, he was easier. The mills of God were grinding inside him.

They are grinding inside every American. And they grind exceeding small.

Why? Heaven knows. But we've got to grind down our old forms, our old selves, grind them very very small, to nothingness. Whether a new somethingness will ever start, who knows. Meanwhile the mills of God grind on, in American Melville, and it was himself he ground small: himself and his wife, when he was married. For the present, the South Seas.

He escapes on to the craziest, most impossible of whaling ships. Lucky for us Melville makes it fantastic. It must have been pretty sordid.

And anyhow, on the crazy *Julia* his leg, that would never heal in the paradise of Typee, began quickly to get well. His life was falling into its normal pulse. The drain back into past centuries was over.

Yet, oh, as he sails away from Nukuheva, on the voyage that will ultimately take him to America, oh, the acute and intolerable nostalgia he feels for the island he has left.

The past. The Golden Age of the past. What a nostalgia we all feel for it. Yet we won't want it when we get it. Try the South Seas.

Melville had to fight, fight against the existing world, against his own very self. Only he would never quite put the knife in the heart of his paradisal ideal. Somehow, somewhere, somewhen, love should be a fulfilment, and life should be a thing of bliss. That was his fixed ideal. Fata Morgana.

That was the pin he tortured himself on, like a pinned-down butterfly.

Love is never a fulfilment. Life is never a thing of continuous bliss.

There is no paradise. Fight and laugh and feel bitter and feel bliss: and fight again. Fight, fight. That is life.

Why pin ourselves down on a paradisal ideal? It is only ourselves we torture.

Melville did have one great experience, getting away from humanity: the experience of the sea.

The South Sea Islands were not his great experience. They were a glamorous world outside New England. Outside. But it was the sea that was both outside and inside: the universal experience.

The book that follows on from *Typee* is *Omoo*.

Omoo is a fascinating book: picaresque, rascally, roving. Melville as a bit of a beachcomber. The crazy ship *Julia* sails to Tahiti, and the mutinous crew are put ashore. Put in the Tahitian prison. It is good reading.

Perhaps Melville is at his best, his happiest, in *Omoo*. For once he is really reckless. For once he takes life as it comes. For once he is the gallant rascally epicurean, eating the world like a snipe, dirt and all baked into one *bonne bouche*.

For once he is really careless, roving with that scamp, Doctor Long Ghost. For once he is careless of his actions, careless of his morals, careless of his ideals: ironic, as the epicurean must be. The deep irony of your real scamp: your real epicurean of the moment.

But it was under the influence of the Long Doctor. This long and bony Scotsman was not a mere ne'er-do-well. He was a man of humorous desperation, throwing his life ironically away. Not a mere loose-kneed loafer, such as the South Seas seem to attract.

That is good about Melville: he never repents. Whatever he did, in Typee or in Doctor Long Ghost's wicked society, he never repented. If he ate his snipe, dirt and all, and enjoyed it at the time, he didn't have bilious bouts afterwards. Which is good.

But it wasn't enough. The Long Doctor was really knocking about in a sort of despair. He let his ship drift rudderless.

Melville couldn't do this. For a time, yes. For a time, in this Long Doctor's company, he was rudderless and reckless. Good as an experience. But a man who will not abandon himself to despair or indifference cannot keep it up.

Melville would never abandon himself either to despair or indifference. He always cared. He always cared enough to hate missionaries, and to be touched by a real act of kindness. He always cared.

When he saw a white man really "gone savage," a white man with a blue shark tattooed over his brow, gone over to the savages, then Herman's whole being revolted. He couldn't bear it. He could not bear a renegade.

He enlisted at last on an American man-of-war. You have the record in *White-Jacket*. He was back in civilization, but still at sea. He was in

America, vet loose in the seas. Good regular days, after Doctor Long Ghost and the *Julia*.

As a matter of fact, a long thin chain was round Melville's ankle all the time, binding him to America, to civilization, to democracy, to the ideal world. It was a long chain: and it never broke. It pulled him back.

By the time he was twenty-five his wild oats were sown; his reckless wanderings were over. At the age of twenty-five he came back to Home and Mother, to fight it out at close quarters. For you can't fight it out by running away. When you have run a long way from Home and Mother, then you realize that the earth is round, and if you keep on running you'll be back on the same old doorstep. Like a fatality.

Melville came home to face out the long rest of his life. He married and had an ecstasy of a courtship and fifty years of disillusion.

He had just furnished his home with disillusions. No more Typees. No more paradises. No more Fayaways. A mother: a gorgon. A home: a torture box. A wife: a thing with clay feet. Life: a sort of disgrace. Fame: another disgrace, being patronized by common snobs who just know how to read.

The whole shameful business just making a man writhe.

Melville writhed for eighty years.

In his soul he was proud and savage.

But in his mind and will, he wanted the perfect fulfilment of love. He wanted the lovey-doveyness of perfect mutual understanding.

A proud savage-souled man doesn't really want any perfect lovey-dovey fulfilment in love. No such nonsense. A mountain-lion doesn't mate with a Persian cat. And when a grizzly bear roars after a mate, it is a she-grizzly he roars after. Not after a silky sheep.

But Melville stuck to his ideal. He wrote *Pierre* to show that the more you try to be good the more you make a mess of things: that following righteousness is just disastrous. The better you are, the worse things turn out with you. The better you try to be, the bigger mess you make. Your very striving after righteousness only causes your own slow degeneration.

Well, it is true. No men are so evil today as the idealists: and no women half so evil as your earnest woman, who feels herself a power for good. It is inevitable. After a certain point, the ideal goes dead and rotten. The old pure ideal becomes in itself an impure thing of evil. Charity becomes pernicious, the spirit itself becomes foul. The meek are evil. The pure in heart have base, subtle revulsions: like Dostoevsky's Idiot. The whole Sermon on the Mount becomes a litany of white vice.

What then?

It's our own fault. It was *we* who set up the ideals. And if we are such fools, that we aren't able to kick over our ideals in time, the worse for us.

Look at Melville's eighty long years of writhing. And to the end he writhed on the ideal pin.

From the "perfect woman lover" he passed on to the "perfect friend." He looked and looked for the perfect man friend.

Couldn't find him.

Marriage was a ghastly disillusion to him, because he looked for perfect marriage.

Friendship never even made a real start in him—save perhaps his half-sentimental love for Jack Chase, in *White-Jacket*.

Yet to the end he pined for this: a perfect relationship: perfect mating: perfect mutual understanding. A perfect friend.

Right to the end he could never accept the fact that *perfect* relationships cannot be. Each soul is alone, and the aloneness of each soul is a double barrier to perfect relationship between two beings.

Each soul *should* be alone. And in the end the desire for a "perfect relationship" is just a vicious, unmanly craving. *"Tous nos malheurs viennent de ne pouvoir être seuls."*

Melville, however, refused to draw his conclusion. *Life* was wrong, he said. He refused Life. But he stuck to his ideal of perfect relationship, possible perfect love. The world *ought* to be a harmonious loving place. And it *can't* be. So life itself is wrong.

It is silly arguing. Because after all, only temporary man sets up the "oughts."

The world ought *not* to be a harmonious loving place. It ought to be a place of fierce discord and intermittent harmonies: which it is.

Love ought *not* to be perfect. It ought to have perfect moments, and wildernesses of thorn bushes. Which it has.

A "perfect" relationship ought *not* to be possible. Every relationship should have its absolute limits, its absolute reserves, essential to the singleness of the soul in each person. A truly perfect relationship is one in which each party leaves great tracts unknown in the other party.

No two persons can meet at more than a few points, consciously. If two people can just be together fairly often, so that the presence of each is a sort of balance to the other, that is the basis of perfect relationship. There must be true separatenesses as well.

Melville was, at the core, a mystic and an idealist.

Perhaps, so am I.

And he stuck to his ideal guns.

I abandon mine.

He was a mystic who raved because the old ideal guns shot havoc. The guns of the "noble spirit." Of "ideal love."

I say, let the old guns rot.

Get new ones, and shoot straight.

Mardi, Redburn, White-Jacket

by Newton Arvin

Mardi has several centers, and the result is not a balanced design.
There is an emotional center, an intellectual center, a social and political
center; and though they are by no means utterly unrelated to one another,
they do not occupy the same point in space. The emotional center of the
book is the relation between Taji and Yillah, between the "I" and the
mysterious blonde maiden he rescues from the priest Aleema, at the cost
of slaying him; the maiden with whom he dwells for a short time in
perfect felicity on a little islet off the coast of Odo, but who then vanishes
as mysteriously as she has appeared. Taji sets out in quest of her throughout Mardi; he fails to find her on one island after another; he fails, in
the end, to find her at all, but he discovers that she has fallen a victim
to the witchcraft of the enchantress Hautia, and in ultimate despair, convinced that life without Yillah would be "a life of dying," he turns his
prow at last toward the open sea of self-destruction.

In the poetic sense the whole allegory of Yillah is too tenuous and too
pretty to be anything but an artistic miscarriage. In the personal and
biographical sense, and in connection with the rest of Melville's work, it
is extremely revealing. The blonde and bloodless Yillah, who in the language of flowers is associated with the lily, is an embodiment of the
pure, innocent, essentially sexless happiness which, given his relations
with his mother, Melville longed to find in his relations with some other
woman, and which he had some reason to feel he had at one time
fleetingly enjoyed. Even then—we do not know why—he had enjoyed it
only at the expense of some act of emotional violence, of injury to
another; and such happiness as he had had was soon destroyed by the
intrusion of the sensual, the carnal, the engrossingly sexual, of which
Hautia, symbolized by the dahlia, is the embodiment. With all of this the
most intense and anguished emotions of remorse are associated: they
drove Melville, in *Mardi*, to an act of symbolic suicide. It is possible that

"*Mardi, Redburn, White-Jacket.*" (Original title, "The Author of *Typee, Omoo,* etc.")
From *Herman Melville* (New York: William Morrow & Co., Inc., 1950; Viking Press,
Inc., 1957, Compass C20) by Newton Arvin. Copyright 1950 by William Sloane Associates,
Inc. Reprinted by permission of William Sloane Associates. The title has been supplied
by the editor.

he was expressing thus the emotional history of his marriage to Elizabeth Shaw, which took place during the summer of 1847, perhaps after he had written the first, seagoing chapters of *Mardi,* but certainly before he had written the greater part of the book. It may be that the abrupt break at the end of the thirty-eighth chapter occurred at the time of the wedding and honeymoon, and in any case the allegory of Yillah and Hautia is strongly suggestive of the passage from an idealized courtship to the fleshly realities of marriage. What is not open to doubt is that physical sexuality was charged through and through for Melville with guilt and anxiety.

Meanwhile the middle portion of *Mardi* is mainly occupied by a series of forays in social and political satire, and by quasi-metaphysical speculations, that are at the best only loosely and uncertainly related to the quest for Yillah: the attempt to weave them together into a unified fabric was almost as quixotic as the attempt would be to find a common frame for *Endymion* and *A Connecticut Yankee.* If the fabric of *Mardi* holds together at all, it is only because there is a certain congruity among the various more or less frustrated quests it dramatizes—the quest for an emotional security once possessed, the quest for a just and happy sociality once too easily assumed possible, and the quest for an absolute and transcendent Truth once imagined to exist and still longed for.

The social and political strictures which are so explicitly expressed in *Mardi* are sometimes astonishingly sweeping and severe: they force us to remember that, though the deep centers of his work lie elsewhere, Melville was all along, among other things, a writer of the critical and protestant order to which Carlyle, Thoreau, and Tolstoy belonged. Partly under the sway of writers like this, no doubt, but much more under the bombardment of his own harshly instructive experience— "bowed to the brunt of things," as he says, "before my prime"—Melville had conceived an attitude toward the civilization of his age that mingled in quite special and personal fusion the ingredients of skepticism, humorous contempt, and the anger of an outraged sense of right. It is not great passion, for example, but it is a real enough disdain that inspires his treatment of the fashionable world in *Mardi*—in the allegory of the silly Tapparians and their insipid, formalized life on the island of Pimminee. There is a much deeper note in the satire on militarism as one sees it in the sanguinary war games constantly being played on the Isle of Diranda. There is a deeper note still in the glimpse one has, behind the charming fore-scene on Odo, of the broken serfs and helots who labor in the *taro* trenches and dwell in noisome caves; of the horrors of industrialism on the island of Dominora, which is the England of Dickens and Engels; and of the collared people, toiling under the eyes of armed overseers, in the extreme south even of republican Vivenza.

Vivenza is of course Melville's own country, and *Mardi* expresses, with no attempt at a forced consistency, both the pride he always felt in being an American—"in that land seems more of good than elsewhere"—and the skeptical reservations with which he contemplated America's present and future. It is not that these reservations leave one in any uncertainty where Melville's feelings as a democratic writer lay: the indictment of arbitrary political power and an inhumane or rigidified inequality is unambiguous enough. What he rejects is not the profounder moralities of democracy—they were in his blood—but a cluster of delusions and inessentials that, as he felt, had got themselves entangled with the idea of democracy in American minds; the delusion that political and social freedom is an ultimate good, however empty of content; that equality should be a literal fact as well as a spiritual ideal; that physical and moral evil are rapidly receding before the footsteps of Progress. All this Melville rejects, and he counters it with a group of insights that are by no means always sharp and strong; they are sometimes feeble and sometimes capricious; but in their wiser expressions they take the form of a political and social pessimism that was for him wholly reconcilable with a democratic humanism, though certainly not with an optimistic one. "For evil is the chronic malady of the universe."

So reads, in part, a scroll which the travelers find fixed against a palm tree in Vivenza: it is Melville's somber retort not only to the overweening political hopefulness of his time and place but to its optimistic ethics and metaphysics as well; to the unmodulated affirmations to which Emerson had given the most exaggerated expression: "Through the years and the centuries . . . a great and beneficent tendency irresistibly streams." Melville saw no such tendency in nature or in history; on the contrary, he had failed to find in nature any warrant for the aspirations of humanity ("nature is not for us") and he had failed to find in history—or in his own experience—any warrant for a belief in human perfectibility. Man he had very generally found to be a "pugnacious animal," "but one member of a fighting world," and his discovery had not filled him with confidence in the human outlook. On the whole, experience and reflection had confirmed the dark view of the natural man which his Calvinist nurture had implanted in him. They had not, however, confirmed the metaphysical absolutes of Calvinism, or indeed absolutes of any sort; and the philosophical plot of *Mardi* is furnished by the interaction—which, to tell the truth, is too largely a vacillation—between the longing for certainty, a longing at least as intense as that for Yillah, and the painfully recurring suspicion that, on all the great questions, "final, last thoughts you mortals have none; nor can have."

"Faith is to the thoughtless, doubts to the thinker," says one of Melville's spokesmen in *Mardi,* and in the end Taji himself cannot find spiritual assurance even in the pristine, purified, undogmatic Christianity of Serenia. Meanwhile, however, it is clear that Melville is struggling to avoid "a brutality of indiscriminate skepticism," as he calls it, and no doubt—divided and confused as he was, when he wrote the book, among a host of contradictory emotions and ideas—he came nearest to expressing his basic thought in a speech of Babbalanja's as he "discourses in the dark": "Be it enough for us to know that Oro"—God—"indubitably is. My lord! my lord! sick with the spectacle of the madness of men, and broken with spontaneous doubts, I sometimes see but two things in all Mardi to believe:—that I myself exist, and that I can most happily, or least miserably exist, by the practice of righteousness."

It is not a very trumpet-tongued conclusion, nor even philosophically a very remarkable one, and indispensable though *Mardi* is to a study of Melville's developing powers—fine, even, as a few passages in it are—the book suffers irremediably, as a work of art, from the intellectual pre-cipitateness and prematurity out of the midst of which it was palpably written. If Melville could have brought himself, at that period, to con-fide his crowding thoughts to the pages of a personal journal, the result might well have been a gradual burning up of his own smoke and, in the end, the pure lucidity of tragic insight that is consistent with dramatic and poetic wholeness. As it is, what one mostly finds in *Mardi* is not the clarifying solemnity of tragic acceptance; it is the drifting and eddying fog of intellectual worry, vacillation, and indecision, and in consequence there is no imaginative purification in reading it. Doubt and repudiation are great themes, and great books have been written on them; mere indecisiveness is strictly speaking not a theme for a work of art at all, and despite the violent termination of *Mardi,* its general movement is that of indecision rather than of strong denial.

This is what essentially keeps the personages, the narrative, and the symbols themselves from really enlisting our imaginative interest and taking a sure hold on our imaginative attention; most readers will end by agreeing with T. E. Lawrence that *Mardi,* as a whole, is a dull book. A remark of Eliot's may also occur to some of them: "We cannot afford to forget that the first—and not one of the least difficult—requirements of either prose or verse is that it should be interesting." Melville was quite capable of remembering just this, and doubtless it is with a momentary flash of self-criticism that he remarks in *Mardi* itself: "Genius is full of trash." If *Mardi* is a mixture of trash and genuineness, however, it is the sort of mixture of which only genius is capable. The unalloyed metal still remained to be run into the molds.

In both the intellectual and the literary senses *Mardi* had turned out, despite its undeniable qualities, to be a great detour for Melville; in the end it brought him back to his own route but in an oblique and rather wasteful way. His mind was still developing too rapidly and too intensely for him to be long content with the kind of skepticism, impatient and even intemperate, which *Mardi* ended by expressing. There is a lesser skepticism and a larger one, and the skepticism of this book is not yet the latter. In its form and texture, too, *Mardi* was evidently not what Melville was struggling to arrive at; he made no second use of its characteristic manner, and years later he was to voice his true feeling about the book when he remarked that the worst thing he could say about Richter's *Titan* was that "it is a little better than *Mardi*." His central problem as a writer was to find a fictional style in which there would be a particular kind of dynamic balance between fact and form, between concept and symbol, between the general and the particular—"the whole problem is there," as Gide once observed—and Melville had by no means found his solution in transcendental allegory of the Early Romantic type or even in the ancient mode of satirical burlesque he had inherited from Rabelais and Swift. Just how flimsy Yillah and Hautia are as vehicles for Melville's meaning is evident when one reflects for a moment on the essential unnaturalness and unspontaneity, for him, of the flower images that accompany them, the un-Melvillean verbenas and vervain; and as for the Rabelaisian tour of the archipelago of Mardi, it grows more and more perfunctory and essayistic as the book wears on.

Manqué though it was, however, *Mardi* had been written, we may be sure, at the cost of a heavy drain on Melville's psychological resources, and he was not yet ready to move on to another effort of comparable scope and difficulty: time would have to elapse before his highest energies could accumulate their full weight and force. Meanwhile it was a question of lowering his sights a degree or two, and what he did when he went on to write *Redburn* and *White-Jacket* had superficially the air of a return upon himself, a lapse back to the vein he had already worked in *Typee* and *Omoo*, the vein not of metaphysical allegory but of unpretentious reminiscent narrative, vibrating again between the poles of literal autobiography and free fictional improvisation. *Redburn* and *White-Jacket* take us back once more to the ship and the sea voyage, to "real" ships and "real" seas: in the one case, to the deck of an American merchant vessel making an ordinary trip across the North Atlantic; in the other, to the deck of an American man-of-war on its cruise from the port of Callao in Peru, around the Horn, back to its home port on the eastern seaboard. Both books abound in information, in factuality, in solid objects and practical activities, and in all this they recall *Typee* and *Omoo*. But the movement Melville was describing, it need hardly be said, was not a retrograde but a spiral one, and *Redburn* and *White-Jacket*, though they have lost the youthful charm of the earlier books, are denser in substance, richer in feeling, tauter, more complex, more connotative in texture and imagery. Whatever imperfections they may have, they give us the clear sense that the man who wrote them was again on his own track.

The prose, for one thing, is that of a much more mature person and more expert writer. One easily sees how much ground Melville has gained, partly as a result of writing *Mardi*, when one turns from almost

any page of the first two books to almost any page of the later ones. Here
is a characteristic passage from *Omoo:*

> Toward morning, finding the heat of the forecastle unpleasant, I ascended
> to the deck, where everything was noiseless. The Trades were blowing with
> a mild, steady strain upon the canvas, and the ship heading right out into
> the immense blank of the Western Pacific. The watch were asleep. With one
> foot resting on the rudder, even the man at the helm nodded, and the
> mate himself, with arms folded, was leaning against the capstan.
>
> On such a night, and all alone, revery was inevitable. I leaned over the
> side, and could not help thinking of the strange objects we might be sailing
> over.

Certainly the nocturnal picture here is pleasantly rendered; the effect of
contrasted motion and stillness (the advancing ship, the nodding helms-
man, and the like) is quickly and agreeably achieved; the rhythms are
easy; the forward movement of the sentences is steady and effortless; the
plain, low-pitched diction surges a little, at one moment, to a kind of
grandeur in the phrase, "the immense blank of the Western Pacific." But
rhythmically the passage achieves little more than easiness; the language
is almost neutral and without idiosyncrasy; and the sense of a missed
opportunity in the last sentence is acute. There are finer passages in
Typee and *Omoo,* but virtually nowhere in those books does Melville
write as he repeatedly writes in *Redburn* or *White-Jacket.* Is it possible,
in such a passage as the following, from *Redburn,* to mistake the gain in
rhythmical variety and intricacy, in sharpness of diction, in syntactical
resource, in painterly bravura and the fusing of image and emotion into
a unity of strangeness, beauty, and dread? It is part of the chapter in
which Melville describes his ascent of the mainmast to loosen a skysail at
midnight:

> For a few moments I stood awe-stricken and mute. I could not see far out
> upon the ocean, owing to the darkness of the night; and from my lofty
> perch the sea looked like a great, black gulf, hemmed in, all round, by
> beetling black cliffs. I seemed all alone; treading the midnight clouds; and
> every second, expected to find myself falling—falling—falling, as I have felt
> when the nightmare has been on me.
>
> I could but just perceive the ship below me, like a long narrow plank in
> the water; and it did not seem to belong at all to the yard, over which I was
> hanging. A gull, or some sort of sea-fowl, was flying round the truck over my
> head, within a few yards of my face; and it almost frightened me to hear it;
> it seemed so much like a spirit, at such a lofty and solitary height.

It is not only the spectral sea-fowl here, flying round the masthead in the
darkness, which tells one that, in the progress from *Typee* to *Moby-Dick,*
Melville has already passed the middle point.

If this holds for *Redburn* stylistically, it holds no less truly for its substance and spirit. The outward subject of the book is a young boy's first voyage as a sailor before the mast; its inward subject is the initiation of innocence into evil—the opening of the guileless spirit to the discovery of "the wrong," as James would say, "to the knowledge of it, to the crude experience of it." The subject is a permanent one for literature, of course, but it has also a peculiarly American dimension, and in just this sense, not in any other, *Redburn* looks backward to a book like Brockden Brown's *Ormond* as well as forward to *The Marble Faun* and to so much of James himself. Wellingborough Redburn sets out from his mother's house in a state of innocence like that before the Fall, a state like that of Brown's Constantia Dudley or James's Maisie Farange, but he has hardly gone a mile from home before the world's wickedness and hardness begin to strip themselves before him. Man, Redburn quickly finds, is a wolf to man. On the river boat his shabby indigence elicits no compassion from the comfortable passengers, but only coldness and disdain. He reaches the city and is very soon victimized by a rascally pawnbroker, a pawnbroker who might have stepped out of *David Copperfield* or *Cousin Pons*. He takes himself aboard the *Highlander* and begins at once to be sworn at, pushed around, humiliated, and persecuted by mates and sailors alike; and the dapper Captain Riga, who had appeared so friendly in his cabin while the ship lay at anchor, now, when poor unsophisticated Redburn attempts to address him as man to man, flies into a rage and flings his cap at him.

Blows and hard words are mostly Redburn's lot on the *Highlander,* yet he suffers not only from the inhumanity of men but from the spectacle of their depravity generally. His feelings about the sailors vacillate, it is true; as individuals he finds some of them generous and friendly; but taking them in the lump, he is conscious chiefly of their drunkenness, their profanity and obscenity, their indurated cynicism and sneering misanthropy. All this accumulated evil, indeed, is focused so concentratedly in the figure of one man, the sailor Jackson, as to raise him to something like heroic stature, the stature at any rate of one of Schiller's Majestic Monsters. The first of Melville's full-length studies of "depravity according to nature," Jackson is stricken, symbolically, with a fatal disease —the penalty for his "infamous vices," as Redburn learns—but this does not keep him from being a pitiless bully and exercising an unchallenged and almost preternatural sway over the rest of the crew, who thus, in their pusillanimity, pay tribute to the principle of pure evil in him. He for his part feels nothing but malevolence toward them; nothing but malevolence toward Redburn, if only because he is young, handsome, and innocent; and indeed "he seemed to be full of hatred and gall against everything and everybody in the world." His enmity toward the boy sets the rest of the crew against him too, and Redburn begins to feel a compensatory hatred growing up in himself against them all; but meanwhile, day by day, his ears are assailed by the bitter talk of a man who is "spontaneously an atheist and an infidel," and who argues through the long night watches that there is "nothing to be believed; nothing to be loved, and nothing worth living for; but everything to be hated, in the wide world."

There is a touch of Svidrigailov or old Karamazov in this Jackson, and there is a touch of the Dostoyevskian also in Redburn's feeling that there was "even more woe than wickedness about the man." He is so impressive a figure, one sees, partly because so much of Melville's own bitterness and disbelief entered into his composition. Jackson is easily first among the personal embodiments of evil in this book, but in addition to him and to all the personages, and more overpowering than any of them, there is the infernal city of Liverpool, a near neighbor of the City of Destruction itself. That older allegory is bound to occur to one's mind in thinking of *Redburn* and Liverpool, but even so it was not until the nineteenth century that the great city, any great city, the great city *an sich,* could become just the kind of symbol it did become of human iniquity. In imagining Liverpool as he did, Melville was wholly at one with the deepest sensibility of his age, and in his wonderful series of Hogarthian evocations—in the dark, begrimed, polluted streets, the great prisonlike warehouses, the squalid dwellings, the loathsome haunts of vice and crime, and the beggars, the quacks, the crimps, the peddlers who populate these infested purlieus like moral grotesques—in all this there is a power quite comparable to that with which Balzac's Parisian Inferno is rendered, or Baudelaire's *fourmillante cité,* the London of *Bleak House* and *Our Mutual Friend,* or the Dublin of *Ulysses.* Melville's Liverpool, too, like his Lima, is a City of the Plain.

In such a setting as this there is no mere enigma even in the one chapter of *Redburn* in which Melville seems to be indulging in deliberate mystification—the chapter in which he represents Redburn as being carried off to London on an unexplained errand by his new friend Harry Bolton and taken by him to "Aladdin's Palace." This is an Orientally luxurious pleasure-house of some ill-defined sort, where they spend a melo-dramatic night, and where Harry appears to lose most of his remaining funds at the tables. Aladdin's Palace is the opulent counterpart of the "reeking" and "Sodom-like" dens in Liverpool where Redburn's ship-mates indulge their squalid vices; the walls of one room are hung with pornographic paintings to which Melville suggests various learned paral-lels, but most of these he himself invented as he composed the passage; and their real purpose, like that of the whole chapter, is to dramatize the horrified Redburn's feeling that "this must be some house whose foundations take hold on the pit," and that "though gilded and golden, the serpent of vice is a serpent still." He fails to see another stick or stone of London, and one more drop is thus added to his cup of disappoint-ment; but his experience of evil has been extended in still another direction, and by the engaging Harry, too. The conflict between wishfulness and revulsion is evident enough. For the rest, though the chapter is not without a genuine vein of dreamlike intensity, it is vitiated as a whole by the kind of unnaturalness into which Melville so easily fell with such themes.

Meanwhile, *Redburn* abounds in the imagery not only of moral evil but of disease, disaster, and death. The voyage itself, here as elsewhere, is a metaphor of death and rebirth, of the passage from childhood and innocence to experience and adulthood; the crossing, to and fro, of a sea in the waters of which one dies to the old self and puts on a new. As if to enforce this intention irresistibly, the *Highlander*'s voyage outward and the voyage home are both initiated by a scene of violent death. During the first long night watch that Redburn stands with his mates on the voyage out, he is terrified when all at once a sailor, suffering from delirium tremens, dashes up the scuttle of the forecastle and flings himself to his death over the bows of the vessel. The boy Redburn is then poetically identified with this sailor when he is made to occupy the dead man's bunk. Still more ghastly than this is the discovery, in the first dogwatch of the voyage homeward, that a Portuguese sailor who had been thrown, apparently dead drunk, into a bunk as they left port, is literally dead, and that his corpse is now flickering with a hideous phosphorescence. Neither incident, it appears, occurred on the actual voyage that the young Melville made; both are inventions, and all the more eloquent for being so.

Inventions, too, no doubt, are at least some of the other disastrous episodes of the voyage and of the stay in Liverpool: the collision between the *Highlander* and another vessel, in the darkness, which just fails to be fatal; the sighting of a dismantled, waterlogged schooner in the Irish Sea, with dead men lashed to the taffrail, the victims of storm and starvation (an echo, possibly, of *Arthur Gordon Pym*, but not an improvement on it); the murder of a prostitute at a bar in Liverpool by a drunken Spanish sailor; and the epidemic that, on the homeward voyage, destroys many of the inmates of the overcrowded, unwholesome steerage, and throws the refined cabin passengers into a cowardly panic of terror and selfishness. In these last scenes, as nowhere else in his work, Melville resorts to the symbolism of plague and pestilence that had proved, or was to prove, so expressive for a long series of modern writers, from Defoe and Poe to Thomas Mann; and though for him, as for most of them, the literal pestilence has a moral or spiritual reference, it is characteristic that for him, almost alone among such writers, it has a democratic and humanitarian reference also.

All these elements in *Redburn*, at any rate, are "symbolic" in the sense that, at their best, they are imagined and projected with an intensity that constantly pushes them beyond mere representation, and that makes them reverberate with a more than prosaic force in the reader's own imagina-

tion. Nothing like this had been true of *Typee* or *Omoo:* if there are
symbols in those books, they are there only in the loose sense in which
one would find them in any piece of writing that lifted itself even a little
above the level of a mere record. The sense of symbol in *Redburn* is
unmistakably more acute than in anything of Melville's that preceded
Mardi, and moreover there are two or three points in the book at which
one sees Melville moving toward an even franker and more direct form
of symbolism, one which he himself would doubtless have called "allegorical," but which is far from being allegorical in the sense in which Yillah
and Hautia had been. It is a question now, not of bodying forth emotional
and intellectual experiences in deliberately poetic characters and fables,
of elaborating dramatic symbols that have obvious analogies in the realm
of thought and feeling. It is a question of endowing ordinary objects,
ordinary incidents, with a penumbra of feeling and suggestion that im-
parts to them a symbolic character. One might describe these as antiro-
mantic or shrunken symbols; they have something of the quality of what
is called witty imagery, and they were to become more and more idiosyn-
cratic for Melville.

One of them, here, is the old-fashioned glass ship which Redburn's
father had brought home from France and which the boy's imagination
had hovered over until the object converted his vague longings into a
definite purpose of going to sea. On the very day on which he actually left
home for his voyage, the little glass figurehead of a warrior had fallen
from the bows of the ship into the waves below it, and there he still
lies: "but I will not have him put on his legs again, till I get on my own."
In very much the same vein of feeling is the old guidebook to Liverpool
which, as we have seen already, had proved so help ul to Redburn's
father in his perambulations about the city, but which now proves as mis-
leading and even pervertive as every guidebook is that has had its day.
Most striking of all, however, and happiest in its imaginative quality is
the old gray shooting-jacket that Redburn's elder brother gives him as he
sets out from home; the moleskin shooting-jacket with big horn buttons,
long skirts, and many pockets, that brings down upon Redburn so much
derision from fellow-passengers, shipmates, and Englishmen; which
shrinks day by day, particularly after a rain, until he finds it more and
more uncomfortable to wear; and which comes to be for him an obsessive
emblem of his lost gentility and social humiliation. Redburn's shooting-
jacket puts one in mind of that other shabby garment, the old clerk's
overcoat in Gogol's famous tale, and indeed, in his characteristic preoccupation with clothing, especially shabby and uncomfortable clothing, Melville suggests the Russians more than any other English or American
writer quite does. For the "insulted and injured" there is of course a
natural metaphor in old, cheap, and ill-fitting clothes.

Bitter as the feeling in this is, however, and despite the underlying
gravity of the symbolism generally, *Redburn* is anything but a lugubrious

book as a whole, and it has probably never made any such impression on its readers: the current of animation and vivacity on which it is sustained is purely inspiriting; if this is "pessimism," it is pessimism of the most tonic sort. The book abounds in self-pity, certainly, but distinctions have to be made even here, and there is a kind of self-pity that is more bracing than what passes for restraint and austerity: on the whole, the self-pity in *Redburn* is clearly of that order. Melville's feeling, moreover, for light and shade did not fail him in the writing of *Redburn* as it had done in the writing of *Mardi*. There is the familiar ballast of prosaic information, for one thing—the chapter, for example, on the furniture of the quarter-deck—and there is a good deal of Melville's characteristically smiling and low-toned humor. The account of Max the Dutchman, who has a sober and respectable wife in New York and an equally sober and respectable one in Liverpool, and whose wardrobe is kept in order by the launderings of both spouses—Max the Dutchman is in Melville's happiest vein. He had always had a taste for the burgherlike humor of the little Dutch masters—Teniers, Brouwer, Jan Steen—and in passages like this he approximates it, though in a softened form. In its richness of emotion and variety of tone, *Redburn* generally is the most likable of Melville's secondary books; and it is only because he was so rebelliously conscious how much higher he was capable of going that Melville could have spoken of it contemptuously as "beggarly *Redburn*."

Taken as a whole, *White-Jacket*, which he now went on to write, is something of a drop in quality after *Redburn;* it bears somewhat the same relation to that book as *Omoo* bears to *Typee*. Neither *Redburn* nor *White-Jacket*, and especially not the latter, was written with the concentrated conviction of Melville's whole nature: increasingly he was resentful of the necessities that forced him to write in what seemed to him an inferior strain. Both these books, he said in a letter, he had done simply as jobs, for the sake of making money, as other men are forced to saw wood, and at a time when what he earnestly desired was to write "those sort of books which are said to 'fail'." This, naturally, is a biographical fact, not a critical one, and we cannot be affected by Melville's own feeling in judging either *Redburn* or *White-Jacket;* but the biographical fact has an explanatory interest nevertheless. The earnest desire Melville expressed in his letter was soon to be fulfilled; meanwhile, he seems to have been writing at a murderous rate of speed, and *White-Jacket* itself appears to have been dashed off in the incredible space of two and a half months. It is little wonder that, in writing it, Melville should have lifted from other books not only information (as he had always done) but whole scenes and episodes, without always justifying the theft by improving on what he took. In at least one case he did so, but the symptoms of hurry and fatigue are all too evident elsewhere.

Hitherto he had intuitively succeeded in finding pretty much the true

balance between narrative and factuality, between the imaginative and
the informative, and in *White-Jacket* he continues to alternate the two
—but now in what seems a relatively perfunctory and even wearied
manner. The current of personal narrative is simply not full enough or
strong enough to buoy up and float along the solid and sometimes rather
lumpish blocks of straight exposition and description—straight information about the American navy generally and the individual battleship in
particular. Not quite for the first time, but for the first time oppressively,
one is conscious of the slight streak of pedantry that was always latent in
Melville's passion for facts, and that when his imagination was not deeply
engaged betrayed him into dullness and jejuneness. In proportion to the
whole, one hears too much, in *White-Jacket*, about the gundeck and the
berthdeck, the starboard watch and the larboard watch, the quarter-deck
officers and the warrant-officers, and so on. In matters of organization and
routine such as these Melville was not genuinely interested, or was interested only with the least creative facet of his imagination, and the
result is that he largely fails to endow these things with imaginative life.

The book suffers too, more than the earlier books had done, from the
humanitarian note that dominates it as it dominates no other work of
Melville's. It is hardly worth saying that, on ethical grounds, one cannot
fail to share Melville's indignation. Whatever the personal basis for it,
he could not have taken firmer ground than he did when he cried out
against "the social state in a man-of-war," the atrocious evil of flogging,
and the like. All of it does the utmost credit to Melville's humanity.
What was amiss was not this, certainly, but for the time being Melville's
sense of form, his literary instinct. In speaking of *White-Jacket* one is
tempted to paraphrase Flaubert's remark about *Uncle Tom's Cabin* and
Negro slavery, and to ask: "Is it necessary to make comments on the
iniquities of the Navy? Show them to me; that is enough." *White-Jacket*
is not a novel, to be sure, but it is not a mere pamphlet either; it is an
imaginative work of a very special and precarious sort, and it would have
gained incalculably if Melville had made his protests far less insistent and
less explicit, and if he had dramatized them much more. At least one of
the flogging scenes, for example, seems terribly true, but none of them is
comparable in repellent power to the one scene with which Dana, in *Two
Years*, contents himself; and Melville dilutes the force of his protest partly
by his repetitions of the shocking image and partly by his detailed comments on the evil. His moral passion, as so often happens, had asserted
itself overaggressively at the expense of his inventive and dramatic gift.

It did not keep him, however, from continuing in *White-Jacket* the
search for a right symbolic method that he had carried on in the two
books that came before it. This search now led him, confusedly enough,
in two directions, one of them a sterile, one a fruitful direction. It was
an unhappy inspiration, as it was very probably an afterthought, that

induced him to transform the man-of-war itself into the particular kind
of symbol that the subtitle, "The World in a Man-of-War," indicates.
From time to time as the book advances there are hints that the battleship
Neversink is a kind of Microcosm of the universe; in one of the later
chapters it is specifically remarked that "a man-of-war is but this old-
fashioned world of ours afloat"; and finally Melville appends a short
epilogue in which the analogy between a battleship and the Macrocosm is
explicitly enforced. Just as the *Neversink* sails through the sea, so the
earth sails through the air, "a fast-sailing, never-sinking world-frigate, of
which God was the shipwright." But the port from which the Macrocosm
sails is forever astern; unlike most battleships, that frigate sails under
sealed orders, "yet our final haven was predestinated ere we slipped from
the stocks at Creation." There are parallels, too, between the social
arrangements on a man-of-war and the state of society itself, and though
"we the people," like the common seamen in the Navy, suffer many abuses,
the worst of our evils we blindly inflict on ourselves.

There are fine touches in this epilogue, like the strangely Kafkaesque
suggestion that an abused sailor would appeal in vain, during this life,
"to the indefinite Navy Commissioners, so far out of sight aloft." Yet
on the whole the macrocosmic symbolism of the man-of-war world is as
infelicitous in its way as the allegory of *Mardi* is in its. It is not only
hackneyed in itself—the thought of Longfellow's Ship of State is danger-
ously near at hand—but treated just as Melville treats it, it is far too
simply pictorial and its ethical bearing is made far too ponderously explicit. What is it indeed but a curiously belated, anachronistic example of
what the sixteenth and seventeenth centuries would have called an Emblem—a highly pictorial allegory with a significance that is frankly and
unequivocally enforced? Ships under full sail on calm or stormy seas
appear from time to time in the sometimes charming cuts that illustrate
the old emblem books, and there is an allegorical ship, allegorical of the
soul and its destiny, in the third book of Quarles's *Emblems*. Melville felt
a natural affinity, as some other writers of his time did, for the literature
of the Baroque era, and sometimes it proved to have a genuinely quicken-
ing influence on him. But the emblem in a nineteenth-century literary
setting was as inappropriate as a sixteenth-century woodcut would have
been as an illustration; it was not in those terms that Melville's problem
would find its proper solution.

He was much closer to his own true vein in inventing the symbol that
gives the book its title, the white jacket that, in lieu of a genuine pea
jacket or grego, he represents his young hero, or rather "himself," as
concocting out of an old duck shirt before the *Neversink* sets sail from
Callao. He does so in order to protect himself from the boisterous weather
they are sure to encounter as they round Cape Horn. "An outlandish
garment of my own devising," the jacket is ample in the skirts, clumsily

full about the wristbands, and of course white—"yea, white as a shroud."
He darns and quilts the inside of it in the hope of making it truly water-
proof; but, in spite of this, in rainy weather it proves to be as absorbent
as a sponge, and thus "when it was fair weather with others, alas! it was
foul weather with me." It is such an ungainly, eccentric garment that it
brings down constant ridicule on the wearer's head, and worse than that,
evokes a kind of superstitious hatred on the part of the other sailors. On
one occasion they take White-Jacket himself to be the ghost of the cooper,
lost overboard the day before, when they see him lying on the main-
royalyard in the darkness; as time goes on, some of them are convinced
that other deaths in the crew can be laid to the jacket, and White-Jacket
himself begins to feel that the accursed garment has "much to answer for."

He has tried to persuade the first lieutenant to let him have some black
paint to cover it with, but in vain. And this is a great part of his misery,
for most monkey jackets are of a dark hue and keep their wearers from
being too easily visible, especially at night. When, on the other hand, an
officer wants a man for some particularly hard job, "how easy, in that mob
of incognitoes, to individualize '*that white jacket*,' and dispatch him on
the errand!" White-Jacket tries to free himself of the wretched thing by
swapping it with a messmate and even by putting it up at auction, but
no one will have it, and he begins to imagine that he will never be free
of it until he rolls a forty-two-pound shot in it and commits it to the
deep. This thought, however, is too much like the thought of his own
death, and he refrains. But when the cruise is almost over, the jacket very
nearly proves to be his death after all. White-Jacket is sent up the mainmast one night to reeve the halyards of a stun-sail, and while he is trying
to do this he loses his balance and, entangled about the head by his jacket,
falls rushingly from the yard-arm into the sea. Down he plunges, down
into the deathlike waters of the deep. After some seconds, however, he
shoots up again to the surface, and attempts to strike out toward the ship,
but the fatal jacket, looped about him as it is, almost destroys him. He
saves himself only by cutting himself out of it with a knife and ripping
it up and down "as if I were ripping open myself." It sinks slowly before
his eyes, and White-Jacket returns to life. He does so because he has in
fact ripped open an aspect of himself, thrown it off, and allowed it to
sink in the sea; the aspect of himself that is mere uniqueness and differ-
entness, mere protective-unprotective self-assertion, easy to identify and
individualize in any mob, and white, fatally white, as white as a shroud.

It is a magnificent symbol of the lesser Self, the empirical Self, the Ego; a
far finer symbol for its purpose than that of the man-of-war for its, and it is
so partly because it is homely and unhackneyed, partly because it is
inexplicit, and partly because, though it has an interpretable meaning,
that meaning remains elusive and slightly equivocal. The jacket was
probably sheer invention on Melville's part, though he alleged in a letter

to Dana that it was a real jacket. It does not matter in the least. In its setting the thing has the air of the only kind of reality that counts. Sheer invention, however, so far as Melville's external experience went, is certainly the great scene just alluded to, in which the jacket plays so nearly fatal a role. In literal fact no such mishap befell Melville on the *United States*. The ship's log is silent on the affair, and besides it has long been known that the whole scene is a rewriting of a passage in a little volume called *A Mariner's Sketches* by an old Yankee sailor named Nathaniel Ames, which had been published in Providence twenty years earlier.

It was a passage that was bound to catch Melville's attention as he read the book: the nightmarish image of falling to one's destruction from a high place had appeared before in his own writing, and what psychiatrists call hypsophobia was as characteristic for him as it was for Poe. He had reached the head of Taipi-Vai, according to his own story, by a series of horrifying falls from ledge to ledge of a dreamlike precipice; and in *Redburn*, in the passage already quoted, he represents his horror of "falling—falling—falling" when he is sent up to loosen the skysail. Harry Bolton on the voyage home suffers so terribly from this phobia that he refuses ever to climb the mast a second time, though he is per-manently disgraced for it. And even earlier in *White-Jacket*, Melville or his fictional persona has nearly fallen to his death from the main-royalyard when the superstitious sailors below him suddenly lower the halyards. It takes no great penetration to detect in this recurring image the unconscious impulse to suicide, and the great scene in *White-Jacket* owes its inescapable power, as the scene of White-Jacket's near-flogging does, to the fact that, though it never occurred in the physical world, it did certainly occur in the inner one. The self-destructiveness in Melville expressed itself thus as well as in other ways.

Meanwhile, for all its limitations, *White-Jacket* has stretches of admi-rable writing in it, of which this scene of the fall from the yardarm is one. It is already a famous case, but it remains an especially illuminating one, of Melville's genius for transmuting an uninspired model into something greatly expressive. Nathaniel Ames's own account of his fall from the futtock shrouds—oddly enough, it was on the same frigate, the *United States*—though it has several touches of strong realistic truth, is essen-tially as pedestrian as one would expect it to be if one heard it from the lips of the old seaman himself. Melville transformed it as Shakespeare sometimes transformed Holinshed or North's Plutarch: keeping the facts and the narrative order and even some of the details of feeling, but imparting rhythmicality, and a wonderfully connotative one, to what had had no rhythm at all; working small miracles of linguistic expressiveness ("the strong shunning of death shocked me through"); and intensifying the whole emotional value of the incident through an accompaniment of powerful images—"the speechless profound of the sea," "the maelstrom air," and "some inert, coiled fish of the sea." When he finds in Ames a matter-of-fact sentence like this:

> I kept going down, down, till it appeared to me that the seven fathoms and a half, (the depth of water at our anchorage,) had more than doubled since we let go our anchor;

Melville remakes it thus:

> The blow from the sea must have turned me, so that I sank almost feet foremost through a soft, seething, foamy lull. Some current seemed hurrying me away; in a trance I yielded, and sank deeper down with a glide. Purple and pathless was the deep calm now around me, flecked by summer light-rings in an azure afar.

Much of the effect of this extraordinarily hypnotic passage is due to the delicate skill with which Melville avails himself of phonetic color—the color, here, of labials and sibilants especially and the closed sound of long *e*—but much also to the subtly responsive rhythms (conveying the delicious sense of movement downward through a liquid medium, in such gently protracted phrases as "through a soft, seething, foamy lull"), as well as to the synaesthetic use of a word like "lull" for an experience of the sense of touch, and the sudden shift from the sense of motion to the perception of color in the fine words, "purple" and "azure."

Admittedly this whole scene of the descent into the sea and the re-emergence from it is a rare peak in Melville's early prose; it is the finest writing in the ornate style that he did before *Moby-Dick,* and one can account for it only by remembering that it sprang from a profound inward experience of life and death in conflict. But it is not the only passage of brilliant narrative writing in *White-Jacket,* despite the dead calm of many chapters. In an entirely different key, the key of relaxed and indulgent humor, the scene called "A Man-of-War College," in which the schoolmaster of the *Neversink* lectures to his flock of restless midshipmen on the refinements of naval strategy, is written with admirable ease and charm. In still another and a darker style, that of indignant, satirical caricature, Melville never went beyond the great scene of "The Operation"; the scene in which the pompous and unfeeling surgeon of the *Neversink,* Dr. Cadwallader Cuticle, performs an unnecessary amputation upon an injured foretopman, under which the wretched man dies. There is an inevitable suggestion of Smollett both in the name and in the character of the surgeon, as there is in the whole chapter; yet after all Melville did not write with the particular kind of harsh, brilliant, indefatigable speed and vigor one associates with the author of *Roderick Random.* Indeed, the passage has an essentially different quality from any of the scenes aboard the *Thunder* in that novel, a quality not so much of choleric energy as of mingled pity and detestation, revulsion and ruthlessness, humor and hatred. It would be easy, too, to say that Melville was writing in much the same style in which, for example, Rowlandson drew when he made his monstrous print of "The Amputation"; but the real feeling in Melville is in fact no more that of Rowlandson—board, gross, and grotesque—than it is that of Smollett. It is a feeling in which anger at the spectacle of cruelty is underlain by a still stronger sorrow at the spectacle of evil generally.

On these more intangible grounds *White-Jacket* represents no retreat from or palliation of the insights expressed in *Redburn*. One must confess, in fact, that the later book is the more richly counterpointed, in a moral sense, of the two. The World in a Man-of-War is, at the one extreme, quite as black a world as that in a merchant vessel or a great seaport; it is a world, on the whole, "charged to the combings of her hatchways with the spirit of Belial and all unrighteousness." A world of which the ferocious Articles of War form the domineering code could hardly be other than a basically brutal and un-Christian one, and brutal and un-Christian, with its ultimate dedication to purposes of bloodshed and destruction, the microcosm of the *Neversink* is. What follows morally is what could be predicted: overbearing arrogance on the part of most of the officers, genteel rascality on the part of others, petty insolence even in the boyish midshipmen, and cringing subservience or sullen vindictiveness on the part of many of the sailors—for Melville, committed as he is to the rank and file as over against their superiors, cannot and will not represent the human reality as different from what he has found it in experience. He does not spare himself the task, painful though he obviously finds it, of hinting at "other evils, so direful that they will hardly bear even so much as an allusion"; evils that involve some of the common seamen in "the sins for which the cities of the plain were overthrown."

The portrait of Bland, the knavish master-at-arms, though it is less completely dramatized than that of Jackson, is at least as subtle analytically; and his well-bred, unvulgar, "organic" scoundrelism is both more inexplicable and more profound than Jackson's understandable black-guardliness. Yet morally speaking, despite all this, *White-Jacket* has a higher *relièvo* and a more complex truth than *Redburn*. There is the moral relief of goodness in *Redburn* but it is too largely associated with passiveness and even effeminacy; Redburn himself remains too much the mere victim, embittered but not very resistant, and Harry Bolton is a more extreme case than he. The stage in *White-Jacket* is occupied by a much more richly representative cast of characters. Not all the officers are bullies or martinets. Mad Jack, a junior lieutenant, is a paragon of generous, manly seamanship, and Colbrook, the handsome and gentlemanly corporal of marines, has the extraordinary courage to intercede for White-Jacket when he comes so close to a flogging. Some of the midshipmen are "noble little fellows," and as for the common seamen, there is the self-respecting old Ushant, there is Nord the silent and meditative, and above and beyond all there is of course the "incomparable" and "ever-glorious" Jack Chase, the heroic captain of the maintop, a far more masculine image of virtue than the pathetic Harry. It is quite in keeping with his love for Jack Chase, moreover, that we should feel the vein of iron in White-Jacket as we never quite feel it in Redburn. Melville, as he wrote the book, had at least for the time recovered from the despairing mood of *Mardi* and from the largely resentful mood of *Redburn*. White-Jacket, it is true, would have gone to his death rather than submit to a flogging, but he would have done so in an act of protest; and in a later scene, when death by water would have come so easily, he has the still greater courage to cut himself out of his fatal garment and return to life.

"Introduction" to *Moby-Dick*

by *Alfred Kazin*

I

Moby-Dick is not only a very big book; it is also a peculiarly full and rich one, and from the very opening it conveys a sense of abundance, of high creative power, that exhilarates and enlarges the imagination. This quality is felt immediately in the style, which is remarkably easy, natural and "American," yet always literary, and which swells in power until it takes on some of the roaring and uncontainable rhythms with which Melville audibly describes the sea. The best description of this style is Melville's own, when he speaks of the "bold and nervous lofty language" that Nantucket whaling captains learn straight from nature. We feel this abundance in heroic types like the Nantucketers themselves, many of whom are significantly named after Old Testament prophets and kings, for these, too, are mighty men, and the mightiest of them all, Captain Ahab, will challenge the very order of the creation itself. This is the very heart of the book—so much so that we come to feel that there is some shattering magnitude of theme before Melville as he writes, that as a a writer he had been called to an heroic new destiny.

It is this constant sense of power that constitutes the book's appeal to us, that explains its hold on our attention. *Moby-Dick* is one of those books that try to bring in as much of life as a writer can get both hands on. Melville even tries to create an image of life itself as a ceaseless creation. The book is written with a personal force of style, a passionate learning, a steady insight into our forgotten connections with the primitive. It sweeps everything before it; it gives us the happiness that only great vigor inspires.

If we start by opening ourselves to this abundance and force, by welcoming not merely the story itself, but the manner in which it speaks to us, we shall recognize in this restlessness, this richness, this persistent atmosphere of magnitude, the essential image on which the book is founded.

"'Introduction' to *Moby-Dick*." From the Riverside Edition of *Moby-Dick* (Boston: Houghton Mifflin Company, 1950, Riverside A9), edited by Alfred Kazin. Copyright © 1956 by Alfred Kazin. Reprinted by permission of the author and Houghton Mifflin Company.

For *Moby-Dick* is not so much a book *about* Captain Ahab's quest for the whale as it is an experience *of* that quest. This is only to say, what we say of any true poem, that we cannot reduce its essential substance to a subject, that we should not intellectualize and summarize it, but that we should recognize that its very force and beauty lie in the way it is conceived and written, in the qualities that flow from its being a unique entity.

In these terms, *Moby-Dick* seems to be far more of a poem than it is a novel, and since it is a narrative, to be an epic, a long poem on an heroic theme, rather than the kind of realistic fiction that we know today. Of course Melville did not deliberately set out to write a formal epic; but half-consciously, he drew upon many of the traditional characteristics of epic in order to realize the utterly original kind of novel *he* needed to write in his time—the spaciousness of theme and subject, the martial atmosphere, the association of these homely and savage materials with universal myths, the symbolic wanderings of the hero, the indispensable strength of such a hero in Captain Ahab. Yet beyond all this, what distinguishes *Moby-Dick* from modern prose fiction, what ties it up with the older, more formal kind of narrative that was once written in verse, is the fact that Melville is not interested in the meanness, the literal truthfulness, the representative slice of life, that we think of as the essence of modern realism. His book has the true poetic emphasis in that the whole story is constantly being meditated and unravelled through a single mind.

"Call me Ishmael," the book begins. This Ishmael is not only a character in the book; he is also the single voice, or rather the single mind, from whose endlessly turning spool of thought the whole story is unwound. It is Ishmael's contemplativeness, his *dreaming*, that articulates the wonder of the seas and the fabulousness of the whale and the terrors of the deep. All that can be meditated and summed up and hinted at, as the reflective essence of the story itself, is given us by Ishmael, who possesses nothing but man's specifically human gift, which is language. It is Ishmael who tries to sum up the whole creation in a single book and yet keeps at the center of it one American whaling voyage. It is Ishmael's gift for speculation that explains the terror we come to feel before the whiteness of the whale; Ishmael's mind that ranges with mad exuberance through a description of all the seas; Ishmael who piles up image after image of "the mightiest animated mass that has survived the flood." It is Ishmael who, in the wonderful chapter on the masthead, embodies for us man as a thinker, whose reveries transcend space and time as he stands watch high above the seas. And of course it is Ishmael, both actually and as the symbol of man, who is the one survivor of the voyage. Yet utterly alone as he is at the end of the book, floating on the Pacific Ocean, he manages, buoyed up on a coffin that magically serves as his life-buoy, to give us the impression that life itself can be honestly confronted only in the loneliness of each human heart. Always it is this emphasis on Ishmael's personal vision, on the richness and ambiguity of all events as the skeptical, fervent, experience-scarred mind of Ishmael feels and thinks them, that gives us, from the beginning, the new kind of book that *Moby-Dick* is. It is a book which is neither a saga, though it deals in large natural forces, nor a *classical* epic, for we feel too strongly the individual who wrote it. It is a book that is at once primitive, fatalistic, and merciless, like the very oldest books, and yet peculiarly personal, like so many twentieth-century novels, in its significant emphasis on the subjective individual consciousness. The book grows out of a single word, "I," and expands until the soul's voyage of this "I" comes to include a great many things that are unseen and unsuspected by most of us. And this material is always tied to Ishmael, who is not merely a witness to the story—someone who happens to be on board the *Pequod*—but the living and germinating mind who grasps the world in the tentacles of his thought.

The power behind this "I" is poetical in the sense that everything comes to us through a constant intervention of language instead of being presented flatly. Melville does not wish, as so many contemporary writers do, to reproduce ordinary life and conventional speech. He seeks the marvellous and the fabulous aspects that life wears in secret. He exuberantly sees the world through language—things exist as his words for them—and much of the exceptional beauty of the book lies in the unusual incidence of passages that, in the most surprising contexts, are so piercing in their poetic intensity. But the most remarkable feat of language in the book is Melville's ability to make us see that man is not a blank slate passively open to events, but a mind that constantly seeks meaning in everything it encounters. In Melville the Protestant habit of moralizing and the transcendental passion for symbolizing all things as examples of "higher laws" combined to make a mind that instinctively brought an inner significance to each episode. Everything in *Moby-Dick* is saturated in a mental atmosphere. Nothing happens for its own sake in this book, and in the midst of the chase, Ishmael can be seen meditating it, pulling things apart, drawing out its significant point.

But Ishmael is not just an intellectual observer; he is also very much in the story. He suffers; he is there. As his name indicates, he is an estranged and solitary man; his only friend is Queequeg, a despised heathen from the South Seas. Queequeg, a fellow "isolato" in the smug world of white middle-class Christians, is the only man who offers Ishmael friendship; thanks to Queequeg, "no longer my splintered heart and maddened hand were turned against the wolfish world. This soothing savage had redeemed it." Why does Ishmael feel so alone? There are background reasons, Melville's own: his father went bankrupt and then died in debt when Melville was still a boy. Melville-Ishmael went to sea —"And at first," he tells us, "this sort of thing is unpleasant enough.

It touches one's sense of honor, particularly if you come of an old established family in the land." But there is a deeper, a more universal reason for Ishmael's apartness, and it is one that will strangely make him kin to his daemonic captain, Ahab. For the burden of his thought, the essential cause of his estrangement, is that he cannot come to any conclusion about anything. He feels at home with ships and sailors because for him, too, one journey ends only to begin another; "and a second ended, only begins a third and so on, for ever and for aye. Such is the endlessness, yea, the intolerableness of all earthly effort."

Ishmael is not merely an orphan; he is an exile, searching alone in the wilderness, with a black man for his only friend. He suffers from doubt and uncertainty far more than he does from homelessness. Indeed, this agony of disbelief *is* his homelessness. For him nothing is ever finally settled and decided; he is man, or as we like to think, modern man, cut off from the certainty that was once his inner world. Ishmael no longer has any sure formal belief. All is in doubt, all is in eternal flux, like the sea. And so condemned, like "all his race from Adam down," to wander the seas of thought, far from Paradise, he now searches endlessly to put the whole broken story together, to find a meaning, to ascertain—where but in the ceaselessness of human thought?—"the hidden cause we seek." Ishmael does not perform any great actions, as Ahab does; he is the most insignificant member of the fo'c'sle and will get the smallest share of the take. But his inner world of thought is almost unbearably symbolic, for he must think, and think, and think, in order to prove to himself that there is a necessary connection between man and the world. He pictures his dilemma in everything he does on board the ship, but never so clearly as when he is shown looking at the sea, searching a meaning to existence from the inscrutable waters.

What Melville did through Ishmael, then, was to put man's distinctly modern feeling of "exile," of abandonment, directly at the center of his stage. For Ishmael there are no satisfactory conclusions to anything; no final philosophy is ever possible. All that man owns in this world, Ishmael would say, is his insatiable mind. This is why the book opens on a picture of the dreaming contemplativeness of mind itself: men tearing themselves loose from their jobs to stand "like silent sentinels all around the town . . . thousands of mortal men fixed in ocean reveries." Narcissus was bemused by that image which "we ourselves see in all rivers and oceans," and this, says Ishmael when he is most desperate, is all that man ever finds when he searches the waters—a reflection of himself. All is inconclusive, restless, an endless flow. And Melville's own style rises to its highest level not in the neo-Shakespearean speeches of Ahab, which are sometimes bombastic, but in those amazing prose flights on the whiteness of the whale and on the Pacific where Ishmael reproduces, in the rhythms of the prose itself, man's brooding interrogation of nature.

II

But Ishmael is a witness not only to his own thoughts, but also a witness to the actions of Captain Ahab. The book is not only a great skin of language stretched to fit the world of man's philosophic wandering; it is also a world of moral tyranny and violent action, in which the principal actor is Ahab. With the entry of Ahab a harsh new rhythm enters the book, and from now on two rhythms—one reflective, the other forceful—alternate to show us the world in which man's thinking and man's doing each follows its own law. Ishmael's thought consciously extends itself to get behind the world of appearances; he wants to see and to understand everything. Ahab's drive is to *prove*, not to discover; the world that tortures Ishmael by its horrid vacancy has tempted Ahab into thinking that he can make it over. He seeks to dominate nature, to impose and to inflict his will on the outside world—whether it be the crew that must jump to his orders or the great white whale that is essentially indifferent to him. As Ishmael is all rumination, so Ahab is all will. Both are thinkers, the difference being that Ishmael thinks as a bystander, has identified his own state with man's utter unimportance in nature. Ahab, by contrast, actively seeks the whale in order to assert man's supremacy over what swims before him as "the monomaniac incarnation" of a superior power:

"If man will strike, strike through the mask! How can the prisoner reach outside except by thrusting through the wall? To me, the white whale is that wall, shoved near to me. Sometimes I think there's naught beyond. But 'tis enough He tasks me; he heaps me; I see in him outrageous strength, with an inscrutable malice sinewing it. That inscrutable thing is chiefly what I hate; and be the white whale agent, or be the white whale principal, I will wreak that hate upon him. Talk not to me of blasphemy, man; I'd strike the sun if it insulted me. For could the sun do that, then could I do the other; since there is ever a sort of fair play herein, jealousy presiding over all creations. But not my master, man, is even that fair play. Who's over me? Truth hath no confines."

This is Ahab's quest—and Ahab's magnificence. For in this speech Ahab expresses more forcibly than Ishmael ever could, something of the impenitent anger against the universe that all of us can feel. Ahab may be a mad sea captain, a tyrant of the quarter deck who disturbs the crew's sleep as he stomps along on his ivory leg. But this Ahab does indeed speak for all men who, as Ishmael confesses in the frightening meditation on the whiteness of the whale, suspect that "though in many of its aspects this visible world seems formed in love, the invisible spheres were formed in fright." So man, watching the sea heaving around him, sees it as a mad steed that has lost its rider, and looking at his own image in the water, is tortured by the thought that man himself may be an accident, of no more importance in this vast oceanic emptiness than one of Ahab's rare tears dropped into the Pacific.

To the degree that we feel this futility in the face of a blind impersonal nature that "heeds us not," and storm madly, like Ahab, against the dread that there's "naught beyond"—to this extent all men may recognize Ahab's bitterness, his unrelentingness, his inability to rest in that uncertainty which, Freud has told us, modern man must learn to endure. Ahab figures in a symbolic fable; he is acting out thoughts which we all share. But Ahab, even more, is a hero; we cannot insist enough on that. Melville believed in the heroic and he specifically wanted to cast his hero on American lines—someone noble by nature, not by birth, who would have "not the dignity of kings and robes, but that abounding dignity which has no robed investiture." Ahab sinned against man and God, and like his namesake in the Old Testament, becomes a "wicked king." But Ahab is not just a fanatic who leads the whole crew to their destruction; he is a hero of thought who is trying, by terrible force, to reassert man's place in nature. And it is the struggle that Ahab incarnates that makes him so magnificent a *voice,* thundering in Shakespearean rhetoric, storming at the gates of the inhuman, silent world. Ahab is trying to give man, in one awful, final assertion that his will *does* mean something, a feeling of relatedness with his world.

Ahab's effort, then, is to reclaim something that man knows he has lost. Significantly, Ahab proves by the bitter struggle he has to wage that man is fighting in an unequal contest; by the end of the book Ahab abandons all his human ties and becomes a complete fanatic. But Melville has no doubt—nor should we!—that Ahab's quest is *humanly* understandable. And the quest itself supplies the book with its technical *raison d'être.* For it leads us through all the seas and around the whole world; it brings us past ships of every nation. Always it is Ahab's drive that makes up the *passion* of *Moby-Dick,* a passion that is revealed in the descriptive chapters on the whale, whale-fighting, whale-burning, on the whole gory and fascinating industrial process aboard ship that reduces the once proud whale to oil-brimming barrels in the hold. And this passion may be defined as a passion of longing, of hope, of striving: a passion that starts from the deepest loneliness that man can know. It is the great cry of man who feels himself exiled from his "birthright, the merry May-day gods of old," who looks for a new god "to enthrone . . . again in the now egotistical sky; in the now unhaunted hill." The cry is Ahab's— "Who's to doom, when the judge himself is dragged to the bar?"

Behind Ahab's cry is the fear that man's covenant with God has been broken, that there is no purpose to our existence. The *Pequod* is condemned by Ahab to sail up and down the world in search of—a symbol.

But this search, mad as it seems to Starbuck the first mate, who is a Christian, nevertheless represents Ahab's real humanity. For the ancient covenant is never quite broken so long as man still thirsts for it. And because Ahab, as Melville intended him to, represents the aristocracy of intellect in our democracy, because he seeks to transcend the limitations that good conventional men like Starbuck, philistine materialists like Stubb, and unthinking fools like Flask want to impose on everybody else, Ahab speaks for the humanity that belongs to man's imaginative vision of himself.

Yet with all this, we must not forget that Ahab's quest takes place, unceasingly, in a very practical world of whaling, as part of the barbaric and yet highly necessary struggle by man to support himself physically in nature. It is this that gives the book its primitive vitality, its burning authenticity. For *Moby-Dick,* it must be emphasized, is not simply a symbolic fable; nor, as we have already seen, can it possibly be construed as simply a "sea story." It is the story of agonizing thought in the midst of brutal action, of thought that questions every action, that annuls it from within, as it were—but that cannot, in this harsh world, relieve man of the fighting, skinning, burning, the back-breaking row to the whale, the flying harpoons, the rope that can take you off "voicelessly as Turkish mutes bowstring their victims." *Moby-Dick* is a representation of the passionate mind speaking, for its metaphysical concerns, out of the very midst of life. So, after the first lowering, Queequeg is shown sitting all night in a submerged boat, holding up a lantern like an "imbecile candle in the heart of that almighty forlornness . . . the sign and symbol of a man without hope, hopelessly holding up hope in the midst of despair." Melville insists that our thinking is *not* swallowed up by practical concerns, that man constantly searches for a reality equal to his inner life of thought—and it is his ability to show this in the midst of a brutal, dirty whaling voyage that makes *Moby-Dick* such an astonishing book. Just as Ahab is a hero, so *Moby-Dick* itself is a heroic book. What concerns Melville is not merely the heroism that gets expressed in physical action, but the heroism of thought itself as it rises above its seeming insignificance and proclaims, in the very teeth of a seemingly hostile and malevolent creation, that man's voice *is* heard for something against the watery waste and the deep, that man's thought has an echo in the universe.

III

This is the quest. But what makes *Moby-Dick* so fascinating, and in a sense even uncanny, is that the issue is always in doubt, and remains so to the end. Melville was right when he wrote to Hawthorne: "I have written a wicked book, and feel as spotless as the lamb." And people who want to construe *Moby-Dick* into a condemnation of mad, bad Ahab will always miss what Melville meant when he wrote of his book:

"It is not a piece of fine feminine Spitalfields silk—but it is of the horrible texture of a fabric that should be woven of ships' cables & hawsers. A Polar wind blows through it, & birds of prey hover over it." For in the struggle between man's effort to find meaning in nature, and the indifference of nature itself, which simply eludes him (nature here signifies the whole external show and force of animate life in a world suddenly emptied of God, one where an "intangible malignity" has reigned from the beginning), Melville often portrays the struggle from the side of nature itself. He sees the whale's view of things far more than he does Ahab's: and Moby-Dick's milk-white head, the tail feathers of the sea birds streaming from his back like pennons, are described with a rapture that is like the adoration of a god. Even in the most terrible scenes of the shark massacre, where the sharks bend around like bows to bite at their own entrails, or in the ceaseless motion of "my dear Pacific," the "Potters' fields of all four continents," one feels that Melville is transported by the naked reality of things, the great unending flow of the creation itself, where the great shroud of the sea rolls over the doomed ship "as it rolled five thousand years ago." Indeed, one feels in the end that it is only the necessity to keep one person alive as a witness to the story that saves Ishmael from the general ruin and wreck. In Melville's final vision of the whole, it is not fair but it is entirely *just* that the whale should destroy the ship, that man should be caught up on the beast. It is just in a cosmic sense, not in the sense that the prophet (Father Mapple) predicts the punishment of man's disobedience in the telling of Jonah's story from the beginning, where the point made is the classic reprimand of God to man when He speaks out of the whirlwind. What Melville does is to speak for the whirlwind, for the watery waste, for the sharks.

It is this that gives *Moby-Dick* its awful and crushing power. It is a unique gift. Goethe said that he wanted, as a writer, to know what it is like to be a woman. But Melville sometimes makes you feel that he knows, as a writer, what it is like to be the eyes of the rock, the magnitude of the whale, the scalding sea, the dreams that lie buried in the Pacific. It is all, of course, seen through human eyes—yet there is in Melville a cold, final, ferocious hopelessness, a kind of ecstatic masochism, that delights in punishing man, in heaping coals on his head, in drowning him. You see it in the scene of the whale running through the herd with a cutting spade in his body, cutting down his own; in the sharks eating at their own entrails and voiding from them in the same convulsion; in the terrible picture of Pip the cabin boy jumping out of the boat in fright and left on the Pacific to go crazy; in Tashtego falling into the "honey head" of the whale; in the ropes that suddenly whir up from the spindles and carry you off; in the final awesome picture of the whale butting its head against the *Pequod*. In all these scenes there is an ecstasy in horror, the horror of nature in itself, nature "pure," without God or man: the void.

It is symbolized by the whiteness of the whale, the whiteness that is not so much a color as the absence of color. "Is it that by its indefiniteness it shadows forth the heartless voids and immensities of the universe, and thus stabs us from behind with the thought of annihilation, when beholding the white depths of the milky way?" And it is this picture of existence as one where man has only a peep-hole on the mystery itself, that constitutes the most remarkable achievement of Melville's genius. For as in the meditation on the whiteness of the whale, it becomes an uncanny attempt to come to grips with nature as it might be conceived with man entirely left out; or, what amounts to the same thing, with man losing his humanity and being exclusively responsive to primitive and racial memories, to the trackless fathomless nothing that has been from the beginning to the very essence of a beginning that, in contradiction to all man's scriptures, had no divine history, no definite locus, but just *was*—with man slipped into the picture much later.

This view of reality, this ability to side with nature rather than with man, means an ability to love what has no animation, what is inhumanly still, what is not in search, as man himself is—a hero running against time and fighting against "reality." Here Melville puts, as it were, his ear to reality itself: to the rock rather than to the hero trying to get his sword out of the rock. He does it by constantly, and bitterly, and savagely, in fact, comparing man with the great thing he is trying to understand. Ahab may be a hero by trying to force himself on what is too much for him, but Melville has no doubt that man is puny and presumptuous and easily overwhelmed—in short, drowned—in the great storm of reality he tries to encompass.

This sense of scale lies behind the chapters on the natural history of the whale, and behind the constant impressing on our minds of the contrast between man and the whale—man getting into a small boat, man being overwhelmed by his own weapons. The greatest single metaphor in the book is that of bigness, and even when Melville laughs at himself for trying to hook this Leviathan with a pen—"Bring me a condor's quill! Bring me Vesuvius' crater for an inkstand!"—we know that he not merely feels exhilaration at attempting this mighty subject, but that he is also abashed, he feels grave; mighty waters are rolling around him. This compelling sense of magnitude, however, gets him to organize the book brilliantly, in a great flood of chapters—some of them very small, one or two only a paragraph long, in the descriptive method which is the great homage that he pays to his subject, and which so provides him with an inexhaustible delight in devoting himself to every conceivable detail about the whale. And, to go back to a theme mentioned earlier, it is this sense of a limitless subject that gives the style its peculiarly loping quality, as if it were constantly looking for connectives, since on the subject of the whale no single word or statement is enough. But these details tend, too, to heap up in such a staggering array as to combine into the awesomeness of a power against which Ahab's challenge is utterly vain, and against which his struggle to show his superiority over the ordinary processes of nature becomes blasphemous. The only thing left to man, Melville seems to tell us, is to take the span of this magnitude—to feel and to record the power of this mighty torrent, this burning fire.

And it is this, this poetic power, rather than any specifically human one, this power of transcription rather than of any alteration of life that will admit human beings into its tremendous scale, that makes up the greatness of the book—by giving us the measure of Melville's own relation to the nature that his hero so futilely attempts to master or defy. For though Melville often takes a grim and almost cruel pleasure in showing man tumbling over before the magnitude of the universe, and though much of the book is concerned, as in the sections on fighting and "cooking" the whale, with man's effort to get a grip on external nature, first through physical assault and then by scientific and industrial cunning, man finds his final relatedness to nature neither as a hero (Ahab) nor by heeding Father Mapple's old prophetic warning of man's proper subservience to God. Though all his attempted gains from nature fail him, and all goes down with the *Pequod*—all man's hopes of profit, of adjustment to orthodoxy (Starbuck), even of the wisdom that is in madness (Pip)—man, though forever alien to the world, an Ishmael, is somehow in tune with it, with its torrential rhythms, by dint of his art, by the directness with which his words grasp the world, by the splendor of his perceptions, by the lantern which he holds up "like a candle in the midst of the almighty forlornness." Man is not merely a waif in the world; he is an ear listening to the sea that almost drowns him; an imagination, a mind, that hears the sea in the shell, and darts behind all appearance to the beginning of things, and runs riot with the frightful force of the sea itself. There, in man's incredible and unresting mind, is the fantastic gift with which we enter into what is not our own, what is even against us—and for this, so amazingly, we can speak.

Melville and *Moby-Dick*

by *Richard Chase*

How Moby-Dick *Was Written*

The scope and tone of *Moby-Dick* appear to have changed while Melville was writing it. Just what the changes were, and what induced them, is the subject of much interesting scholarship. For our purposes, certain plausible speculations by George R. Stewart, in an essay called "The Two Moby-Dicks," will suffice.

With the exception of the fanciful *Mardi,* Melville's first five books had been based partly on personal experience. The first book, *Typee,* told a somewhat romanticized story of the author's actual sojourn in the Marquesas Islands after he deserted the whaling ship *Acushnet,* on which he had sailed some months previous. Mr. Stewart conjectures that in its original conception *Moby-Dick* was to be another of Melville's quasi-autobiographical travelogues, this time recounting his adventures on the *Acushnet* up to the time of his leaving the ship in the Marquesas. As he wrote, however, the story took on ever new possibilities for him, and these possibilities finally crystallized into a whole new conception of the book. Having already substantially completed the writing of the story as he first conceived it, however, the author did not start entirely afresh but included all or most of the original version, with varying degrees of revision, in the book as we now have it.

Thus we may suppose that Chapters 1-15, in which after various adventures Ishmael and Queequeg arrive in Nantucket, are substantially as they were in the original version. Chapters 16-22, concerning the preliminaries to sailing, belong to the original version, but with considerable rewriting. Chapters 23 to the end constitute the new version of the book, with the exception of certain passages which appear to have been salvaged and interpolated from the original version.

Something like this undoubtedly happened, and it accounts for certain inconsistencies in the book. For example, the fact that the *Pequod* appears to head for Cape Horn but actually, without sufficient reason for the change, rounds the Cape of Good Hope, that the *Pequod* is said sometimes to have a wheel and other times a whale-bone tiller, that Stubb is called both third and second mate (although Melville settles on the latter), and so on. More remarkable is the virtual disappearance of some of the characters who figure largely in the opening chapters. Queequeg, to whom we have been introduced in much detail, becomes merely one of the harpooners. Bulkington, although apparently destined for some heroic role, is dismissed with a poetic epitaph. Ishmael himself all but disappears as a character and as the observer becomes hardly more than the voice of the omniscient author. Ahab, perhaps originally conceived as one more portrait in Melville's gallery of tyrannical and irritable captains, becomes a great, doomed hero. The language itself, rather jocose and colloquial at first, becomes opulent with metaphor, simile, and oratorical flourishes.

What caused this flowering of Melville's genius cannot, of course, be known. But figuring prominently in the miracle must be his rereading of Shakespeare during the time he was working on the book. The influence of *Lear* and *Macbeth* is felt as one beholds Ahab and listens to his speeches and soliloquies. The language and metaphor of Shakespeare make themselves strongly felt in *Moby-Dick,* though not, we observe, in the earlier chapters. Probably it occurred to Melville, as he paused in the process of writing, that two factual narratives about whaling which he had read might be woven into his narrative—one concerning the ramming and sinking by a whale of the Nantucket ship *Essex,* another concerning a monstrous white whale called "Mocha Dick." It is probable too that he discovered that the legends, tall tales, and folklore of whaling could be more than embellishments to his narrative; they could be for him what other bodies of folklore had been for Homer, Virgil, or Camoëns (an author of whom Melville was fond)—the materials of an epic. Finally, one may suppose that partly under the influence of Hawthorne he saw that Ahab might be not only a quasi-Shakespearean hero, doomed by an inordinate pride or tragic ignorance, but also the protagonist in a kind of Puritan inner drama, a drama of the mind in its isolation and obsession. For if Ahab is akin to Shakespeare's heroes, he is more so to such Hawthorne characters as Chillingworth, the pattern of whose life also became, in Hawthorne's phrase, "a dark necessity."

The reason one is interested in the process by which *Moby-Dick* evolved from a travelogue to the complex book it is is that readers we often seem to share Melville's excitement as he and we make new discoveries—as we push farther into the unknown and find metaphors and formulations that make the unknown knowable. Melville thought of art as a process, as an emergent, ever creative, but never completed metaphor. Thus he makes his imaginary poet in *Mardi* triumphantly exclaim, in reference to the epic he has written, "I have created the creative!" In taking the view that a work of art is not a completed object but is an imperfect form which should be left only potentially complete, Melville is much closer to Whitman than to Hawthorne. And what he says about the technical whaling sections of *Moby-Dick* applies as well to the whole book.

> It was stated at the outset, that this system would not be here, and at once, perfected. You cannot but plainly see that I have kept my word. But I now leave my Cetological System standing thus unfinished, even as the great Cathedral of Cologne was left, with the crane still standing upon the top of the uncompleted tower. For small erections may be finished by their first architects; grand ones, true ones, ever leave the copestone to posterity. God keep me from ever completing anything. This whole book is but a draught—nay, but the draught of a draught. Oh, Time, Strength, Cash, and Patience!

Moby-Dick, like the cathedral with the crane on its tower, allows us to see—in fact insists that we shall see—some of the machinery by which it was built, some of the processes of construction. Two passages may be quoted in this connection. The first was presumably interpolated in Chapter 16 and sounds, as Mr. Stewart suggests, like something one might as soon expect to find in a novelist's notebook as in his novel. Melville seems almost to be arguing himself into believing that a tragic hero might be made out of a Nantucket whaleman, especially if he spoke in the Quaker manner:

> So that there are instances among [the Nantucketers] of men, who, named with Scripture names—a singularly common fashion on the island—and in childhood naturally imbibing the stately dramatic thee and thou of the Quaker idiom; still, from the audacious, daring, and boundless adventure of their subsequent lives, strangely blend with these unoutgrown peculiarities, a thousand bold dashes of character, not unworthy of a Scandinavian sea-king, or a poetical Pagan Roman. And when these things unite in a man of greatly superior natural force, with a globular brain and a ponderous heart; who has also by the stillness and seclusion of many long night-watches in the remotest waters, and beneath constellations never seen here at the north, been led to think untraditionally and independently; receiving all nature's sweet or savage impressions fresh from her own virgin voluntary and confiding breast, and thereby chiefly, but with some help from accidental advantages, to learn a bold and nervous lofty language—that man makes one in a whole nation's census—a mighty pageant creature, formed for noble tragedies. Nor will it at all detract from him, dramatically regarded, if either by birth or other circumstances, he have what seems a half wilful overruling morbidness at the bottom of his nature. For all men tragically great are made so through a certain morbidness. Be sure of this, O young ambition, all mortal greatness is but disease.

In this passage we join in the discovery of ideas that were to produce Ahab. In Chapter 14, "Nantucket," we participate in the process by which an epic emerges—namely, by the transmutation of the central facts about the life of a culture into poetry by means of the accretion of folklore, legend, and myth. The wavelike amplification and building-up, followed by the lyric subsidence at the end, is characteristic of Melville's imagination and is similar to the action of the book as a whole, as well as to various sections of it. One may be pardoned, then, for including here a long quotation:

Nantucket! Take out your map and look at it. See what a real corner of the world it occupies; how it stands there, away off shore, more lonely than the Eddystone lighthouse. Look at it—a mere hillock, and elbow of sand; all beach, without a background. There is more sand there than you would use in twenty years as a substitute for blotting paper. Some gamesome wights will tell you that they have to plant weeds there, they don't grow naturally; that they import Canada thistles; that they have to send beyond seas for a spile to stop a leak in an oil cask; that pieces of wood in Nantucket are carried about like bits of the true cross in Rome; that people there plant toadstools before their houses, to get under the shade in summer time; that one blade of grass makes an oasis, three blades in a day's walk a prairie; that they wear quicksand shoes, something like Laplander snowshoes; that they are so shut up, belted about, every way inclosed, surrounded, and made an utter island of by the ocean, that to their very chairs and tables small clams will sometimes be found adhering, as to the backs of sea turtles. But these extravaganzas only show that Nantucket is no Illinois.

Look now at the wondrous traditional story of how this island was settled by the red-men. Thus goes the legend. In olden times an eagle swooped down upon the New England coast, and carried off an infant Indian in his talons. With loud lament the parents saw their child borne out of sight over the wide waters. They resolved to follow in the same direction. Setting out in their canoes, after a perilous passage they discovered the island, and there thy found an empty ivory casket,—the poor little Indian's skeleton.

What wonder, then, that these Nantucketers, born on a beach, should take to the sea for a livelihood! They first caught crabs and quohogs in the sand; grown bolder, they waded out with nets for mackerel; more experienced, they pushed off in boats and captured cod; and at last, launching a navy of great ships on the sea, explored this watery world; put an incessant belt of circumnavigations round it; peeped in at Behring's Straits; and in all seasons and all oceans declared everlasting war with the mightiest animated mass that has survived the flood; most monstrous and most mountainous! That Himmalehan, salt-sea Mastodon, clothed with such portentousness of unconscious power, that his very panics are more to be dreaded than his most fearless and malicious assaults!

And thus have these naked Nantucketers, these sea hermits, issuing from their ant-hill in the sea, overrun and conquered the watery world like so many Alexanders; parcelling out among them the Atlantic, Pacific, and Indian oceans, as the three pirate powers did Poland. Let America add Mexico to Texas, and pile Cuba upon Canada; let the English overswarm all India, and hang out their blazing banner from the sun; two thirds of this terraqueous globe are the Nantucketer's. For the sea is his; he owns it, as Emperors own empires; other seamen having but a right of way through it.

Merchant ships are but extension bridges; armed ones but floating forts; even pirates and privateers, though following the sea as highwaymen the road, they but plunder other ships, other fragments of the land like themselves, without seeking to draw their living from the bottomless deep itself. The Nantucketer, he alone resides and riots on the sea; he alone, in Bible language, goes down to it in ships; to and fro ploughing it as his own special plantation. *There* is his home; *there* lies his business which a Noah's flood would not interrupt, though it overwhelmed all the millions in China. He lives on the sea, as prairie cocks in the prairie; he hides among the waves, he climbs them as chamois hunters climb the Alps. For years he knows not the land; so that when he comes to it at last, it smells like another world, more strangely than the moon would to an Earthman. With the landless gull, that at sunset folds her wings and is rocked to sleep between billows; so at nightfall, the Nantucketer, out of sight of land, furls his sails, and lays him to his rest, while under his very pillow rush herds of walruses and whales.

An Epic Romance

This term is perhaps the inevitable one for Melville's great book. But *Moby-Dick* is extremely impure art; it is a hybrid, one of the most audacious, surely, that have ever been conceived. As Melville himself exclaims at one point, "I try everything. I achieve what I can."

The partly romanticized travelogue-novel which the book was apparently first intended to be still contributes its considerable realism and wealth of detail to the whole. And of course those admonitory critics who are always telling us that *Moby-Dick* is just a good whaling yarn and should be discussed only as such seem at first to have their point. But the realistic sea-going novel as practiced by Melville and by Cooper, Smollett, Marryat, and Dana, whose example Melville followed, is not a particularly interesting form, exciting as it is to read. Although *Moby-Dick* contains many novelistic elements—of character, panorama, scene, and action—it has fewer that repay study than, for example, *The Scarlet Letter.* If we are to follow Melville's imagination, we have to go afield from the sea-novel, although we always come back to it as we read.

As was suggested earlier, in discussing allegory and symbol, *Moby-Dick* is in one sense a symbolist poem. It contains also strong melodramatic, if not fully tragic, elements. It is certainly in one sense a comic work. And some passages, such as appear in the inconceivably beautiful chapters called "The Funeral," "The Pacific," "The Dying Whale," and "The Symphony," are sheer lyric.

One does not detract from the book in saying that it has a "made-up" quality, that it is a good deal "put together," and is very much a piece of literary fabrication. In view of this one has trouble associating it quite so readily with the epic imagination of the Bronze Age and the Age of the Vikings as Newton Arvin does in his book on Melville (which is, however, at least through the chapter on *Moby-Dick,* much the best book).

As an epic, *Moby-Dick* follows in some ways the universal convention to which it belongs. It celebrates, that is, customs, techniques, occupations, ideals, and types of heroic humanity which are characteristic of the culture in which they appear. Given the culture Melville is expressing, what would we expect him to include in his epic? We must have heroes, nobility, and these will be the heroes of the American nineteenth century —hunters, exploiters, captains of industry (for Ahab *is* one of these, and the Pequod is a beautifully efficient factory for the production of whale oil). What skills and preoccupations will be stressed? Not the martial skills of the *Iliad,* nor the political and moral skills of the *Aeneid,* nor the theological and political prowess of *Paradise Lost,* but the techniques of subduing nature—and thus the descriptions, as loving and detailed as that of Achilles's shield in the *Iliad,* of the ship, the whale boats, and all their intricate apparatus. But although superficially resembling the *Odyssey, Moby-Dick* lacks, among other things, the rich observation of *ethos,* of ways of life, real and fabulous, which we find in Homer's poem. The *Odyssey* is extremely sophisticated about manners and morals and is actually more novelistic than *Moby-Dick.*

In a democratic epic such as *Moby-Dick* avowedly is we would expect a celebration of the ideals of equality and brotherhood, on the one hand, and individualism, on the other. The ideal masculine attachment here is not the hierarchic relation of Achilles and Patroclus, tender as that is, but the perfect fraternal equality of persons of different race. Thus Ishmael and Queequeg join the much discussed company of Natty Bumppo and Chingachgook, Huck Finn and Jim. The different ideal of individualism is expressed in the ready derring-do and self-respecting unconventionality of all the main figures. And Ahab becomes, as the "dark necessity" of the story sets in, a heightened example of independent man, as if Melville were out to test some of the extreme implications of the dominant Emersonian creed of self-reliance.

As is suggested by the passage about Nantucket, quoted above, the raw material for the great metaphors of Melville's epic is "American humor" —that is, the body of folk sayings, jokes, and tall tales that had formed by Melville's time a reservoir of legendary materials on which he could draw. The story of the white whale is of course in itself a very tall tale and, in the manner of the tale teller. Melville adduces a considerable number of fancies and rumors about Moby-Dick's almost supernatural powers. One finds frequent references to semilegendary early heros, like George Washington, Andrew Jackson, Franklin. The main characters, even Ahab, behave and speak sometimes like the humorous, boastful frontiersmen and canny, canting, mystical Yankee peddlers who figured in the oral legend and on the popular stage of Melville's time.

The native legends, which Melville was the first important writer to use with any fullness, are unusual in the history of the world by being predominantly humorous. The humor, as Constance Rourke has shown, oscillates rather wildly between extremes, being on the one hand boasting, oratorical, even megalomaniac and on the other meditative, soliloquizing, oddly indirect, covert, and sad. It is characteristically oral, even after being incorporated into so literary, so *written* a book as *Moby-Dick*. For Melville presents his story to us as if he felt the necessity of talking us, and himself, into accepting it. He does not accredit it by saying that the Muse told it to him. He assumes, rather, the guise of the salesman and the showman. In the very first chapter we find that whereas a hero of another epic might attribute his turn of fortune to Hera or Zeus, Ishmael regards himself as a sort of bit player in an extravaganza produced by "those stage managers, the Fates"—showmen who, as we may think more than once in reading *Moby-Dick*, resemble P. T. Barnum, rather than Zeus.

And, doubtless, my going on this whaling voyage formed part of the grand programme of Providence that was drawn up a long time ago. It came in as a sort of brief interlude and solo between more extensive performances. I take it that this part of the bill must have run something like this:

"*Grand Contested Election for the Presidency of the United States.*

"WHALING VOYAGE BY ONE ISHMAEL.
"*BLOODY BATTLE IN AFGHANISTAN.*"

Though I cannot tell why it was exactly that those stage managers, the Fates, put me down for this shabby part of a whaling voyage, when others were set down for magnificent parts in high tragedies, and short and easy parts in genteel comedies, and jolly parts in farces—though I cannot tell why this was exactly; yet, now I recall all the circumstances, I think I can see a little into the springs and motives which being cunningly presented to me under various disguises, induced me to set about performing the part I did, besides cajoling me into the delusion that it was a choice resulting from my own unbiased freewill and discriminating judgment.

The brash, vaunting tone of "American humor" is heard throughout *Moby-Dick*, as in the episode (to take but one example out of a hundred) in which Stubb bedevils and hoodwinks the master of the French ship Rosebud.

Yet the most beautiful pages in *Moby-Dick* are those in which the insistent, though often disembodied voice of Ishmael takes on the flowing, meditative tone of introspection and revery. Thus at the end of Chapter 35 we have Ishmael on the masthead. He is so engrossed in his own thoughts that he forgets to watch for whales, meriting the reproach that "Whales are scarce as hen's teeth whenever thou art up there." But then with an abrupt but not disconcerting change from this jocose beginning we follow Ishmael's flow of consciousness as he "takes the mystic ocean at his feet for the visible magic of that deep, blue, bottomless soul, pervading mankind and nature; and every strange, half-seen, beautiful thing that eludes him; every dimly-discovered, uprising fin of some undiscernible form, seems to him the embodiment of those elusive thoughts that only people the soul by continually flitting through it." Then nearly losing consciousness under the spell of the fantasy, he imagines himself in a moment of panic dropping with a shriek into the sea. And Melville winds up the chapter, as he often does, with a moral based on an elaborate analogy: "Heed it well, ye Pantheists!" "American humor," with its sense of violence and the precariousness of life, is aware of ranges of reality unsuspected by "pantheists"—or by the Emersonian transcendentalists Melville may have in mind when in describing the "mystic ocean" into which Ishmael gazes he makes it resemble the Oversoul.

To pursue the method suggested in Constance Rourke's *American Humor* (for that is what I have been doing in the above paragraphs) is to discover the legendary materials of Melville's epic of whaling. It gives us some insight into the origins of the great images, persons, and actions of the book. It is even a way of understanding some of the author's leading attitudes about life. It gives us, above all, the sense of the genial, the humane, and the creative. And if it does not show us all that is apprehended by what Ahab calls the "high perception," it does make us feel the natural, the aesthetic texture of life that appeals to the "low enjoying power." Perhaps only Mark Twain and Faulkner have known as well as Melville how to capture in their stories the variegated musings of the folk humor, and how to play these off against actions whose meaning is abstract and universal.

The Meaning of Moby-Dick

If we think of the dramatic action involving Ahab and the pursuit of the whale, isolating this in our minds from the almost encyclopedic context in which it occurs, we are conscious of a meaning, even of a didactic purpose. Just what the meaning is has been the subject of much speculation. Undoubtedly the first step towards understanding *Moby-Dick* is to observe what is really very obvious: it is a book about the alienation from life that results from an excessive or neurotic self-dependence. Melville has conceived of his moral fable in a way which makes *Moby-Dick* distinctly a book of its time and place and allies it intimately with the work of other American writers. As Newton Arvin demonstrates, there is some reason to think of Ahab as guilty of *hybris,* in the Greek sense, or of excessive pride, in the Christian sense; but there is more reason to think of him as guilty of or victimized by a distorted "self-reliance." An alternative to Ahab's suicidal course is proposed by the author. But since Mr. Arvin explains this in a way which seems generally to confirm the view of the American imagination as we are attempting to understand it in the present book, let us listen to him. Mr. Arvin begins by saying that "the alternative to Ahab's egotism" is not the Greek "ideal of 'nothing too much' " nor the Christian ideal of "a broken and contrite heart." Rather, he says,

> On one level it is an intuition that carries us beyond morality, in the usual sense, into the realm of cosmic piety; on the usual ethical level, however, it is a strong intuition of human solidarity as a priceless good. Behind Melville's expression of this, one is conscious of the gravity and the tenderness of religious feeling, if not of religious belief; it came to him in part from the Christian tradition in which he had been nurtured. The form it took in him, however, is no longer specifically Christian; as with Hawthorne and Whitman, it was the natural recoil of a sensitive imagination, enriched by the humanities of romantic idealism, against the ruinous individualism of the age. It is Melville's version of Hawthorne's "magnetic chain of humanity," of Whitman's "manly attachment": so far, it is an essentially humanistic and secular principle.

The only caveat that needs to be added to these words is that the "intuition of human solidarity as a priceless good" is stronger in Melville and Whitman than in Hawthorne and that for all of them "human solidarity" means not a settled social order but a more or less unstable idyllic relationship, a personal and ideal sharing of the human fate among people temporarily brought together by chance or by a common purpose. The intuition of solidarity tends to come to American writers only when the solidarity is precarious and doomed by the passing of time or by the mere anarchic instinct of the individual. And so the American novel is full of idealized momentary associations—Natty Bumppo and his companions, Hawthorne's Blithedalers, Ishmael, Queequeg and the crew of the *Pequod,* Huck Finn and Nigger Jim on their raft, or—that classic example of the instability and mixed motives that characterize united action among Americans—the Bundren family in Faulkner's *As I Lay Dying.* Even such relatively stable social orders as that of the Bostonians described in James's *The Europeans* or that of the New Yorkers in Edith Wharton's *Age of Innocence* have to regroup themselves and suffer a good deal of agony in order to put up a united front against the foreigner who, in each novel, threatens invasion.

But to take up Mr. Arvin's argument again, one notes, in carrying it a step further, that the moral action of *Moby-Dick* is not strictly tragic or Christian. It is an action conceived as taking place in a universe of extreme contradictions. There is death and there is life. Death—spiritual, emotional, physical—is the price of self-reliance when it is pushed to the point of solipsism, where the world has no existence apart from the all-sufficient self. Life is to be clung to, if only precariously and for the moment, by natural piety and the ability to share with others the common vicissitudes of the human situation. These are the clear alternatives.

What must be remembered is that this is a melodramatic view of things.

Strictly speaking, both Greek and Christian tragedy offer an ideal of catharsis or redemption—forms of harmonious life that come about *through* death. It is this life through death that Ishmael seems to have been given in the Epilogue, when he alone is saved by the coffin-lifebuoy. But is this really a catharsis, a redemption, a rebirth? The momentary sense of harmony and joy is all too easily dispelled by the chilly gloom, the final despair, of the last words. "On the second day, a sail drew near, nearer, and picked me up at last. It was the devious-cruising Rachel, that in her retracing search after her missing children, only found another orphan."

For Melville there is little promise of renewal and reward after suffering. There is no transcendent ground where the painful contradictions of the human dilemma are reconciled. There is no life *through* death. There is only life *and* death, and for any individual a momentary choice between them. What moves Melville most powerfully is the horror that is the violent result of making the wrong choice. He is moved too by the comic aspect of the spectacle, the absurdity of such a creature as man, endowed with desires and an imagination so various, complex, and procreative yet so much the prisoner of the cruel contradictions with which, in his very being, he is inexorably involved. Finally, he is moved by the blissful, idyllic, erotic attachment to life and to one's ideal comrades, which is the only promise of happiness.

Solipsism, hypnotic self-regard, imprisonment within the self—these themes have absorbed American novelists. The Concord transcendentalism, of which Melville was very much aware and whose sensibility he in many ways shared, was a philosophy—or rather an ethical poetry—of the self. The idea of the image reflected in the mirror or in the water appeals as strongly to Melville as to Hawthorne, and like Hawthorne he uses this literary convention to point up the dangers of an exaggerated self-regard, rather than, as Whitman and Emerson loved to do, to suggest the vital possibilities of the self. At the very beginning of *Moby-Dick* we are shown "crowds of water-gazers" who are "posted like silent sentinels" around the shores of Manhattan and are "fixed in ocean reveries." And then, says Melville, amplifying his effect with his usual semi-humorous parody of learning, there is the still deeper "meaning of that story of Narcissus, who because he could not grasp the tormenting, mild image he saw in the fountain, plunged into it and was drowned. But that same image, we ourselves see in all rivers and oceans. It is the image of the ungraspable phantom of life; and this is the key to it all."

This last statement is tantalizing and although it sounds a little offhand, like a too facile way to end a paragraph, it also sounds and *is* important. For the book is to offer the alternative of Narcissus. One may, like Ahab, look into the water, or into the profound and ultimately unknowable abyss of nature, and see only one's own image or an ungraspable phantom, a white whale which is only a projection of self. Or, like Ishmael or

Starbuck, one may see one's own image but in a context of life and reality which is *not* one's self. To be Ahab is to be unable to resist the hypnotic attraction of the self with its impulse to envelop and control the universe. To be Ishmael is to be able at the last minute to resist the plunge from the masthead into the sea one has with rapt fascination been gazing at, to assert at the critical moment the difference between the self and the not-self. To be Starbuck is to understand what the white whale might mean to a man like Ahab but to insist "with the stubbornness of life" that the whale is merely "a dumb brute" to seek vengeance on which is "blasphemous" and "madness."

Chapter 99, "The Doubloon," tells us much about the meaning of *Moby-Dick*. The doubloon is a gold coin Ahab has nailed to the main mast. It is to be won by whoever first sights the white whale. Ishmael describes the coin in detail (if indeed Ishmael can be called the narrator at this point; he is always ostensibly the narrator but in much of the latter part of the novel he is not *felt* as such). The coin is from Ecuador. "So this bright coin came from a country planted in the middle of the world, and beneath the great equator, and named after it; and it had been cast midway up the Andes, in the unwaning climate that knows no autumn." In the ambiguous symbolism of the coin, involving three mountains crowned respectively with a flame, a tower, and a crowing cock, we see "the keystone sun entering the equinoctial point at Libra" (the Scales). Without worrying over the rather labored symbolism, we note that for author-Ishmael the coin represents the equator, the dividing line in a dualistic world. From the point of view of the equator, there are in human destiny two grand alternatives: the self-absorption which leads to isolation, madness, and suicide, or the imperfect but more or less objective perceptions of the world which allow one to cling to life. All this is shown in the procession of the main figures of the drama as each in turn meditates momentarily on the coin.

Ahab soliloquizes thus:

> the firm tower, that is Ahab: the volcano, that is Ahab; the courageous, the undaunted, and victorious fowl, that, too, is Ahab; all are Ahab; and this round gold is but the image of the rounder globe, which, like a magician's glass, to each and every man in turn but mirrors back his own mysterious self.

The others respond to the symbolism of the coin in their different ways, but each is free of Ahab's imprisonment. Starbuck sees the symbolism of the ordinary pious Christian life. Stubb is reminded of his *carpe diem* philosophy, his jolly acceptance of life and death. Flask, even less imaginative, sees simply a gold coin that, as he pauses to calculate, would buy nine hundred and sixty cigars. The Manxman, a primitive soothsayer, sees merely a vague doom. Fedallah, the Parsee harpooner Ahab has smuggled aboard, sees the fire worshiped in his religion. Pip, rather reminiscent of King Lear's fool, expresses with a theological despair, one may think, the impossibility of seeing anything, the impossibility of knowledge. To him it is not only Ahab who is imprisoned within the self; it is in the nature of man to seek but not to find, to look but not to see. Thus he mutters: "I look, you look, he looks; we look, ye look, they look." Little Pip is Melville's Christian caveat. As we are told in "The Castaway" (Chapter 93), Pip "saw God's foot upon the treadle of the loom, and spoke it; and therefore his shipmates called him mad. So man's insanity is heaven's sense. . . ." Heaven's sense may be glimpsed by visionaries, Melville concedes, but it cannot be brought to bear on such actions as are reported in *Moby-Dick*.

As a symbol the whale is endlessly suggestive of meanings. It is as significant and manifold as Nature herself, and, of course, that is the point. Like nature the whale is paradoxically benign and malevolent, nourishing and destructive. It is massive, brutal, monolithic, but at the same time protean, erotically beautiful, infinitely variable. It appears to be unpredictable and mindless; yet it is controlled by certain laws. The chapter on "The Whiteness of the Whale" is a *tour de force* of learning and ingenuity such as Melville liked to get off. It remains, however, rather inert, and like some of the excessively extended chapters on cetology, or the interpolated story of the Town-Ho, it forces us to step outside the action of the book in order to take in a sort of sideshow at a moment when we are all for getting on with the main event. Still the idea of the whale's whiteness is indispensable. Whiteness is the paradoxical color, the color that involves all the contradictions Melville attributes to nature. It signifies death and corruption as readily as virginal purity, innocence, and youth. It has the advantage of being, from one point of view, the color that contains all colors, whereas from another point of view, it suggests a *tabula rasa* which may be imaginatively endowed with significance according to the desire or obsession of him who beholds it. It also readily suggests the sense of the uncanny or the preternatural out of which mythic and religious ideas are formed.

As Melville writes:

> Is it that by its indefiniteness it shadows forth the heartless voids and immensities of the universe, and thus stabs us from behind with the thought of annihilation, when beholding the white depths of the milky way? Or is it, that as in essence whiteness is not so much a color as the visible absence of color, and at the same time the concrete of all colors; is it for these reasons that there is such a dumb blankness, full of meaning, in a wide landscape of snows—a colorless, all-color of atheism from which we shrink?

These rhetorical questions help us to understand what Melville has in mind. Yet the most memorable passages about the whiteness of the whale are in other chapters where Melville the unsurpassable poet lays aside the rather awkward philosophizings that encumber portions of his book. The essential voice of Melville is to be heard in the half humorous, subtly erotic lyric tone which is peculiar to *Moby-Dick:*

> A gentle joyousness—a mighty mildness of repose in swiftness, invested the gliding whale. Not the white bull Jupiter swimming away with ravished Europa clinging to his graceful horns; his lovely, leering eyes sideways intent upon the maid; with smooth bewitching fleetness, rippling straight for the nuptial bower in Crete; not Jove, not that great majesty Supreme! did surpass the glorified White Whale as he so divinely swam.

But we should not think Melville a very great poet if he had not written passages like the following (from "The Funeral," Chapter 69):

> The vast tackles have now done their duty. The peeled white body of the beheaded whale flashes like a marble sepulchre; though changed in hue, it has not perceptibly lost anything in bulk. It is still colossal. Slowly it floats more and more away, the water round it torn and splashed by the insatiate sharks, and the air above vexed with rapacious flights of screaming fowls, whose beaks are like so many insulting poniards in the whale. The vast white headless phantom floats further and further from the ship, and every rod that it so floats, what seem square roods of sharks and cubic roods of fowls, augment the murderous din. For hours and hours from the almost stationary ship that hideous sight is seen. Beneath the unclouded and mild azure sky, upon the fair face of the pleasant sea, wafted by the joyous breezes, that great mass of death floats on and on, till lost in infinite perspectives.

The point of these remarks on "the meaning of *Moby-Dick*" will have been missed unless it is seen that they attribute a less manifold meaning to the book than is sometimes attributed to it. The symbols are manifold and suggestive; the epic scope is opulent; the rhetoric is full and various; the incidental actions and metaphors are richly absorbing. The meaning is profound. But at the same time it is narrow. The issues, as opposed to the states of mind and feeling they generate, are all simplified; they are abstracted and compressed to a degree incompatible with the broader reach, the more comprehensive concreted significance of greater poems like *King Lear, The Divine Comedy,* or *The Iliad.* These poems bring to the given facts of human destiny a universal tragic conception of their meaning. Melville's mind, no less profound in its intuitive sense of life, is nevertheless comparatively narrow and abstract. In this as in its incomparable discoveries of language, its appropriation of new subject matters, and its opening out of new aesthetic experience, *Moby-Dick* is at once the most startling and the most characteristic product of the American imagination.

"In Nomine Diaboli"

by Henry A. Murray

Next to the seizures and shapings of creative thought—the thing it-self—no comparable experience is more thrilling than being witched, illumined, and transfigured by the magic of another's art. This is a trance from which one returns refreshed and quickened, and bubbling with un-envious praise of the exciting cause, much as Melville bubbled after his first reading of Hawthorne's *Mosses*. In describing *his* experience Melville chose a phrase so apt—"the shock of recognition"—that in the Thirties Edmund Wilson took it as the irresistibly perfect title for his anthology of literary appreciations. Acknowledging a shock of recognition and pay-ing homage to the delivering genius is singularly exhilarating, even today —or especially today—when every waxing enthusiasm must confront an outgoing tide of culture.

In our time, the capacities for wonder and reverence, for generous judgments and trustful affirmations, have largely given way, though not without cause surely, to their antitheses, the humors of a waning ethos: disillusionment, cynicism, disgust, and gnawing envy. These states have bred in us the inclination to dissect the subtlest orders of man's wit with ever sharper instruments of depreciation, to pour all values, the best con-founded by the worst, into one mocking-pot, to sneer "realistically," and, as we say today, to "assassinate" character. These same humors have dis-posed writers to spend immortal talent in snickering exhibitions of vul-garity and spiritual emptiness, or in making delicate picture-puzzles out of the butt-ends of life.

In the face of these current trends and tempers, I, coming out of years of brimming gratefulness for the gift of *Moby-Dick,* would like to praise Herman Melville worthily, not to bury him in a winding sheet of scien-tific terminology. But the odds are not favorable to my ambition. A com-mitment of thirty years to analytic modes of thought and concepts lethal to emotion has built such habits in me that were I to be waked in the night by a cry of "Help!" I fear I would respond in the lingo of psychol-

" 'In Nomine Diaboli.' " From *The New England Quarterly*, XXIV, 435-452 (December 1951). Copyright 1951 by *The New England Quarterly*. Reprinted by permission of the editors of *The New England Quarterly*.

ogy. I am suffering from one of the commonest ailments of our age—trained disability.

The habit of a psychologist is to break down the structure ot each personality he studies into elements, and so in a few strokes to bring to earth whatever merit that structure, as a structure, may possess. Furthermore, for reasons I need not mention here, the technical terms for the majority of these elements have derogatory connotations. Consequently, it is difficult to open one's professional mouth without disparaging a fellow-being. Were an analyst to be confronted by that much heralded but still missing specimen of the human race—the normal man—he would be struck dumb, for once, through lack of appropriate ideas.

If I am able to surmount to some extent any impediments of this origin, you may attribute my good fortune to a providential circumstance. In the procession of my experiences *Moby-Dick* anteceded psychology; that is, I was swept by Melville's gale and shaken by his appalling sea dragon before I had acquired the all-leveling academic oil that is poured on brewed-up waters, and before I possessed the weapons and tools of science—the conceptual lance, harpoons, cutting irons, and whatnots—which might have reduced the "grand hooded phantom" to mere blubber. Lacking these defenses I was whelmed. Instead of my changing this book, this book changed me.

To me, *Moby-Dick* was Beethoven's *Eroica* in words: first of all, a masterly orchestration of harmonic and melodic language, of resonating images and thoughts in varied meters. Equally compelling were the spacious sea-setting of the story; the cast of characters and their prodigious common target; the sorrow, the fury, and the terror, together with all those frequent touches, those subtle interminglings of unexampled humor, quizzical, and, in the American way, extravagant; and finally the fated closure, the crown and tragic consummation of the immense yet firmly welded whole. But still more extraordinary and portentous were the penetration and scope, the sheer audacity of the author's imagination. Here was a man who did not fly away with his surprising fantasies to some unbelievable dreamland, pale or florid, shunning the stubborn objects and gritty facts, the prosaic routines and practicalities of everyday existence. Here was a man, who, on the contrary, chose these very things as vessels for his procreative powers—the whale as a naturalist, a Hunter or a Cuvier, would perceive him, the business of killing whales, the whaleship running as an oil factory, stowing-down—in fact, every mechanism and technique, each tool and gadget, that was integral to the moneyminded industry of whaling. Here was a man who could describe the appearance, the concrete matter-of-factness, and the utility of each one of these natural objects, implements, and tools with the fidelity of a scientist, and while doing this, explore it as a conceivable repository of some aspect of the human drama; then, by an imaginative tour de force, deliver a vital essence, some humorous or profound idea, coalescing with its embodiment. But still more. Differing from the symbolists of our time, here was a man who offered us essences and meanings which did not level or depreciate the objects of his contemplation. On the contrary, this loving man exalted all creatures—the mariners, renegades, and castaways on board the *Pequod*—by ascribing to them "high qualities, though dark" and weaving round them "tragic graces." Here, in short, was a man with the myth-making powers of a Blake, a hive of significant associations, who was capable of reuniting what science had put asunder—pure perception and relevant emotion—and doing it in an exultant way that was acceptable to skepticism.

Not at first, but later, I perceived the crucial difference between Melville's dramatic animations of nature and those of primitive religion-makers; both were spontaneous and uncalculated projections, but Melville's were in harmony, for the most part, with scientific knowledge, because they had been recognized as projections, checked, and modified. Here, then, was a man who might redeem us from the virtue of an incredible subjective belief, on the one side, and from the virtue of a deadly objective rationality, on the other.

For these and other reasons the reading of *Moby-Dick*—coming before psychology—left a stupendous imprint, too vivid to be dimmed by the long series of relentless analytical operations to which I subsequently subjected it. Today, after twenty-five years of such experiments, *The Whale* is still *the* whale, more magnificent, if anything, than before.

Before coming to grips with the "mystery" of *Moby-Dick* I should mention another providential circumstance to which all psychologists are, or should be, forever grateful—and literary critics too, since without it no complete understanding of books like *Moby-Dick* would be possible today. Ahead of us were two greatly gifted pioneers, Freud and Jung, who, with others, explored the manifold vagaries of unconscious mental processes and left for our inheritance their finely written works. The discoveries of these adventurers advantaged me in a special way: they gave, I thought, support to one of Santayana's early convictions, that in the human being imagination is more fundamental than perception. Anyhow, adopting this position, some of us psychologists have been devoting ourselves to the study of dreams, fantasies, creative productions, and projections—all of which are primarily and essentially emotional and dramatic, such stuff as myths are made of. Thus, by chance or otherwise, this branch of the tree of psychology is growing in the direction of Herman Melville.

To be explicit: psychologists have been recognizing in the dream figures and fantasy figures of today's children and adolescents more and more family likenesses of the heroes and heroines of primitive myths, legends, and fables—figures, in other words, who are engaged in comparable heroic strivings and conflicts and are experiencing comparable heroic triumphs and fatalities. Our ancestors, yielding to an inherent propensity of the mind, projected the more relevant of these figures into objects of their environment, into sun, moon, and stars, into the unknown deeps of the sea and of the earth, and into the boundless void of heaven; and they worshiped the most potent of these projected images, whether animal or human, as superbeings, gods, or goddesses. On any clear night one can see scores of the more luminous of such divinities parading up and down the firmament. For example, in fall and winter, one looks with admiration on that resplendent hero Perseus and above him the chained beauty Andromeda, whom he saved from a devouring monster, ferocious as Moby-Dick. Now, what psychologists have been learning by degrees is that Perseus is in the unconscious mind of every man and Andromeda in every woman—not, let me hasten to say, as an inherited fixed image, but as a potential set of dispositions which may be constellated in the personality by the occurrence of a certain kind of situation. Herman Melville arrived at this conclusion in his own way a hundred years ago, sooner and, I believe, with more genuine comprehension than any other writer.

An explanation of all this in scientific terms would require all the space permitted me and more. Suffice it to say here that the psychologists who are studying the elementary myth-makings of the mind are dealing with the germy sources of poetry and drama, the fecundities out of which great literature is fashioned. Furthermore, in attempting to formulate and classify these multifarious productions of the imagination, the psychologist uses modes of analysis and synthesis very similar to those that Aristotle used in setting forth the dynamics of Greek tragedy. In these and other trends I find much encouragement for the view that a rapprochement of psychology and literary criticism is in progress, and that it will prove fruitful to both callings. As an ideal meeting ground I would propose Melville's world of "wondrous depths."

To this Columbus of the mind, the great archetypal figures of myth, drama, and epic were not pieces of intellectual Dresden china, heirlooms of a classical education, ornamental bric-a-brac to be put here and there for the pleasure of genteel readers. Many of the more significant of these constellations were inwardly experienced by Melville, one after the other, as each was given vent to blossom and assert itself. Thus we are offered a spectacle of spiritual development through passionate identifications. Only by proceeding in this way could Melville have learned on his pulses what it was to be a Narcissus, Orestes, Oedipus, Ishmael, Apollo, Lucifer. "Like a frigate," he said, "I am full with a thousand souls."

This brings me to the problem of interpreting *Moby-Dick*. Some writers have said that there is nothing to interpret: it is a plain sea story marred here and there by irrelevant ruminations. But I shall not cite the abundant proof for the now generally accepted proposition that in *Moby-Dick* Melville "meant" something—something, I should add, which he considered "terrifically true" but which, in the world's judgment, was so harmful "that it were all but madness for any good man, in his own proper character, to utter or even hint of." What seems decisive here is the passage in Melville's celebrated letter to Hawthorne: "A sense of unspeakable security is in me this moment, on account of your having understood the book." From this we can conclude that there *are* meanings to be understood in *Moby-Dick,* and also—may we say for our own encouragement?—that Melville's ghost will feel secure forever if modern critics can find them and, since Hawthorne remained silent, set them forth in print. Here it might be well to remind ourselves of a crucial statement which follows the just quoted passage from Melville's letter: "I have written a wicked book." The implication is clear: all interpretations which fail to show that *Moby-Dick* is, in some sense, wicked have missed the author's avowed intention.

A few critics have scouted all attempts to fish Melville's own meaning out of *The Whale,* on the ground that an interpretation of a work of art so vast and so complex is bound to be composed in large measure of projections from the mind of the interpreter. It must be granted that preposterous projections often do occur in the course of such an effort. But these are not inevitable. Self-knowledge and discipline may reduce projections to a minimum. Anyhow, in the case of *Moby-Dick,* the facts do not sustain the proposition that a critic can see nothing in this book but his own reflected image. The interpretations which have been published over the last thirty years exhibit an unmistakable trend toward consensus in respect to the drama as a whole as well as to many of its subordinate parts. Moreover, so far as I can judge, the critics who, with hints from their predecessors, applied their intuitions most recently to the exegesis of *The Whale* can be said to have arrived, if taken together, at Melville's essential meaning. Since one or another of these authors has deftly said what I clumsily thought, my prejudices are strongly in favor of their conclusions, and I am whole-hearted in applauding them—Newton Arvin's most especially—despite their having left me with nothing fresh to say. Since this is how things stand, my version of the main theme of *Moby-Dick* can be presented in a briefer form, and limited to two hypotheses.

The first of them is this: Captain Ahab is an embodiment of that fallen angel or demi-god who in Christendom was variously named Lucifer, Devil, Adversary, Satan. The Church Fathers would have called Captain Ahab "Antichrist" because he was not Satan himself, but a human creature possessed of all Satan's pride and energy, "summing up within himself," as Irenaeus said, "the apostasy of the devil."

That it was Melville's intention to beget Ahab in Satan's image can hardly be doubted. He told Hawthorne that his book had been broiled in hell-fire and secretly baptized not in the name of God but in the name of the Devil. He named his tragic hero after the Old Testament ruler who "did more to provoke the Lord God of Israel to anger than all the Kings of Israel that were before him." King Ahab's accuser, the prophet Elijah, is also resurrected to play his original role, though very briefly, in Melville's testament. We are told that Captain Ahab is an "ungodly, god-like" man who is spiritually outside Christendom. He is a well of blasphemy and defiance, of scorn and mockery for the gods—"cricket-players and pugilists" in his eyes. Rumor has it that he once spat in the holy goblet on the altar of the Catholic Church at Santa. "I never saw him kneel," says Stubb. He is associated in the text with scores of references to the Devil. He is an "anaconda of an old man." His self-assertive sadism is the linked antithesis of the masochistic submission preached by Father Mapple.

Captain Ahab-Lucifer is also related to a sun-god, like Christ, but in reverse. Instead of being light leaping out of darkness, he is "darkness leaping out of light." The *Pequod* sails on Christmas Day. *This* new year's sun will be the god of Wrath rather than the god of Love. Ahab does not emerge from his subterranean abode until his ship is "rolling through the bright Quito spring" (Eastertide, symbolically, when the all-fertilizing sun-god is resurrected). The frenzied ceremony in which Ahab's followers are sworn to the pursuit of the White Whale—"Commend the murderous chalices!"—is suggestive of the Black Mass; the lurid operations at the tryworks is a scene out of Hell.

There is some evidence that Melville was rereading *Paradise Lost* in the summer of 1850, shortly after, let us guess, he got the idea of transforming the captain of his whale-ship into the first of all cardinal sinners who fell by pride. Anyhow, Melville's Satan is the spitting image of Milton's hero, but portrayed with deeper and subtler psychological insight, and placed where he belongs, in the heart of an enraged man.

Melville may have been persuaded by Goethe's Mephistopheles, or even by some of Hawthorne's bloodless abstracts of humanity, to add Fedallah to his cast of characters. Evidently he wanted to make certain that no reader would fail to recognize that Ahab had been possessed by, or had sold his soul to the Devil. Personally, I think Fedallah's role is superfluous, and I regret that Melville made room for him and his unbelievable boat-crew on the ship *Pequod*. Still, he is not wholly without interest. He represents the cool, heartless, cunning, calculating, intellectual Devil of the medieval myth-makers, in contrast to the stricken, passionate, indignant, and often eloquent rebel angel of *Paradise Lost,* whose role is played by Ahab.

The Arabic name "Fedallah" suggests "dev(il) Allah," that is, the Mohammedans' god as he appeared in the mind's eye of a Crusader. But we are told that Fedallah is a Parsee—a Persian fire-worshiper, or Zoroastrian, who lives in India. Thus, Ahab, named after the Semitic apostate who was converted to the orgiastic cult of Baal, or Bel, originally a Babylonian fertility god, has formed a compact with a Zoroastrian whose name reminds us of still another Oriental religion. In addition, Captain Ahab's whaleboat is manned by a crew of unregenerated infidels, as defined by orthodox Christianity; and each of his three harpooners, Queequeg,

Tashtego, and Daggoo, is a member of a race which believed in other gods than the one god of the Hebraic-Christian Bible.

Speaking roughly, it might be said that Captain Ahab, incarnation of the Adversary and master of the ship *Pequod* (named after the aggressive Indian tribe that was exterminated by the Puritans of New England), has summoned the various religions of the East to combat the one dominant religion of the West. Or, in other terms, that he and his followers, Starbuck excepted, represent the horde of primitive drives, values, beliefs, and practices which the Hebraic-Christian religionists rejected and excluded, and by threats, punishments, and inquisitions forced into the unconscious mind of Western man.

Stated in psychological concepts, Ahab is captain of the culturally repressed dispositions of human nature, that part of personality which psychoanalysts have termed the "Id." If this is true, his opponent, the White Whale, can be none other than the internal institution which is responsible for these repressions, namely the Freudian Superego. This, then, is my second hypothesis; Moby Dick is a veritable spouting, breaching, sounding whale, a whale who, because of his whiteness, his mighty bulk and beauty, and because of one instinctive act that happened to dismember his assailant, has received the projection of Captain Ahab's Presbyterian conscience, and so may be said to embody the Old Testament Calvinistic conception of an affrighting Deity and his strict commandments, the derivative puritan ethic of nineteenth-century America and the society that defended this ethic. Also, and most specifically, he symbolizes the zealous parents whose righteous sermonizings and corrections drove the prohibitions in so hard that a serious young man could hardly reach outside the barrier, except possibly far away among some tolerant, gracious Polynesian peoples. The emphasis should be placed on that unconscious (and hence inscrutable) wall of inhibition which imprisoned the puritan's thrusting passions. "How can the prisoner reach outside," cries Ahab, "except by thrusting through the wall? To me, the white whale is that wall, shoved near to me . . . I see in him outrageous strength, with an inscrutable malice sinewing it." As a symbol of a sounding, breaching, white-dark, unconquerable New England conscience what could be better than a sounding, breaching, white-dark, unconquerable sperm whale?

Who is the psychoanalyst who could resist the immediate inference that the imago of the mother as well as the imago of the father is contained in the Whale? In the present case there happens to be a host of biographical facts and written passages which support this proposition. Luckily, I need not review them, because Mr. Arvin and others have come to the same conclusion. I shall confine myself to one reference. It exhibits Melville's keen and sympathetic insight into the cultural determinants of his mother's prohibiting dispositions. In *Pierre*, it is the "high-up, and towering and all-forbidding . . . edifice of his mother's immense pride

. . . her pride of birth . . . her pride of purity," that is the "wall shoved near," the wall that stands between the hero and the realization of his heart's resolve. But instead of expending the fury of frustration upon his mother, he directs it at Fate, or, more specifically, at his mother's God and the society that shaped her. For he sees "that not his mother has made his mother; but the Infinite Haughtiness had first fashioned her; and then the haughty world had further molded her; nor had a haughty Ritual omitted to finish her."

Given this penetrating apprehension, we are in a position to say that Melville's target in *Moby-Dick* was the upper-middle class culture of his time. It was *this* culture which was defended with righteous indignation by what he was apt to call "the world" or "the public," and Melville had very little respect for "the world" or "the public." The "public," or men operating as a social system, was something quite distinct from "the people." In *White-Jacket* he wrote: "The public and the people! . . . let us hate the one, and cleave to the other." "The public is a monster," says Lemsford. Still earlier Melville had said: "I fight against the armed and crested lies of Mardi (the world)." "Mardi is a monster whose eyes are fixed in its head, like a whale." Many other writers have used similar imagery. Sir Thomas Browne referred to the multitude as "that numerous piece of monstrosity." Keats spoke of "the dragon world." But closest of all was Hobbes: "By art is created that great Leviathan, called a commonwealth or state." It is in the laws of this Leviathan, Hobbes made clear, that the sources of right and wrong reside. To summarize: the giant mass of Melville's whale is the same as Melville's man-of-war world, the *Neversink,* in *White-Jacket,* which in turn is an epitome of Melville's Mardi. The Whale's white forehead and hump should be reserved for the world's heavenly King.

That God is incarnate in the Whale has been perceived by Geoffrey Stone, and, as far as I know, by every other Catholic critic of Melville's work, as well as by several Protestant critics. In fact, Richard Chase has marshaled so fair a portion of the large bulk of evidence on this point that any more from me would be superfluous. Of course, what Ahab projects into the Whale is not the image of a loving Father, but the God of the Old Dispensation, the God who brought Jeremiah into darkness, hedged him about, and made his path crooked; the God adopted by the fire-and-brimstone Puritans, who said: "With fury poured out I will rule over you." "The sword without and the terror within, shall destroy both the young man and the virgin." "I will also send the teeth of beasts upon them." "I will heap mischiefs upon them." "To me belongeth vengeance and recompense."

Since the society's vision of deity, and the society's morality, and the parents and ministers who implant these conceptions, are represented in a fully socialized personality by an establishment that is called the Superego—conscience as Freud defined it—and since Ahab has been proclaimed the "Captain of the Id," the simplest psychological formula for Melville's dramatic epic is this: an insurgent Id in mortal conflict with an oppressive cultural Superego. Starbuck, the first mate, stands for the rational realistic Ego, which is overpowered by the fanatical compulsiveness of the Id and dispossessed of its normal regulating functions.

If this is approximately correct, it appears that while writing his greatest work Melville abandoned his detached position in the Ego from time to time, hailed "the realm of shades," as his hero Taji had, and, through the mediumship of Ahab, "burst his hot heart's shell" upon the sacrosanct Almighty and the sacrosanct sentiments of Christendom. Since in the world's judgment, in 1851, nothing could be more reproachable than this, it would be unjust, if not treacherous, of us to reason *Moby-Dick* into some comforting morality play for which no boldness was required. This would be depriving Melville of the ground he gained for self-respect by having dared to abide by his own subjective truth and write a "wicked book," the kind of book that Pierre's publishers, Steel, Flint, and Asbestos, would have called "a blasphemous rhapsody filched from the vile Atheists, Lucian and Voltaire."

Some may wonder how it was that Melville, a fundamentally good, affectionate, noble, idealistic, and reverential man, should have felt impelled to write a wicked book. Why did he aggress so furiously against Western orthodoxy, as furiously as Byron and Shelley, or any Satanic writer who preceded him, as furiously as Nietzsche or the most radical of his successors in our day?

In *Civilization and Its Discontents* Freud, out of the ripeness of his full experience, wrote that when one finds deepseated aggression—and by this he meant aggression of the sort that Melville voiced—one can safely attribute it to the frustration of Eros. In my opinion this generalization does not hold for all men of all cultures of all times, but the probability of its being valid is extremely high in the case of an earnest, moralistic, nineteenth-century American, a Presbyterian to boot, whose anger is born of suffering—especially if this man spent an impressionable year of his life in Polynesia and returned to marry the very proper little daughter of the chief justice of Massachusetts, and if, in addition, he is a profoundly creative man in whose androgynic personality masculine and feminine components are integrally blended.

If it were concerned with *Moby-Dick,* the book, rather than with its author, I would call *this* my third hypothesis: Ahab-Melville's aggression was directed against the object that once harmed Eros with apparent malice and was still thwarting it with presentiments of further retaliations. The correctness of this inference is indicated by the nature of the injury—a symbolic emasculation—that excited Ahab's ire. Initially, this threatening object was, in all likelihood, the father; later, possibly, the mother. But, as Melville plainly saw, both his parents had been fashioned by the Hebraic-Christian, American Calvinistic tradition, the tradition which conceived of a deity in whose eyes Eros was depravity. It was the first Biblical myth-makers who dismissed from heaven and from earth the Great Goddess of the Oriental and primitive religions, and so rejected the feminine principle as a spiritual force. Ahab, protagonist of those rejected religions, in addressing heaven's fire and lightning, what he calls "the personified impersonal," cries: "but thou art my fiery father; my sweet mother I know not. Oh, cruel! What hast thou done with her?" He calls this god a foundling, a "hermit immemorial," who does not know his own origin. Again, it was the Hebraic authors, sustained later by the Church Fathers, who propagated the legend that a woman was the cause of Adam's exile from Paradise, and that the original sin was concupiscence. Melville says that Ahab, spokesman of all exiled princes, "piled upon the whale's white hump the sum of all the general rage and hate felt by his whole race from Adam down." Remember also that it was the lure of Jezebel that drew King Ahab of Israel outside the orthodoxy of his religion and persuaded him to worship the Phoenician Astarte, goddess of love and fruitful increase. "Jezebel" was the worst tongue-lash a puritan could give a woman. She was sex, and sex was Sin, spelled with a capital. It was the church periodicals of Melville's day that denounced *Typee,* called the author a sensualist, and influenced the publishers to delete suggestive passages from the second edition. It was this long heritage of aversion and animosity, so accentuated in this country, which banned sex relations as a topic of discourse and condemned divorce as an unpardonable offense. All this has been changed, for better and for worse, by the moral revolutionaries of our own time who, feeling as Melville felt but finding the currents of sentiment less strongly opposite, spoke out, and with their wit, indignation, and logic, reinforced by the findings of psychoanalysis, disgraced the stern-faced idols of their forebears. One result is this: today an incompatible marriage is not a prison-house, as it was for Melville, "with wall shoved near."

In *Pierre* Melville confessed his own faith when he said that Eros is god of all, and Love "the loftiest religion on this earth." To the romantic Pierre the image of Isabel was "a silent and tyrannical call, challenging him in his deepest moral being, and summoning Truth, Love, Pity, Conscience to the stand." Here he seems to have had in mind the redeeming and inspiriting Eros of courtly love, a heresy which the medieval church had done its utmost to stamp out. *This,* he felt convinced, was *his* "path to God," although in the way of it he saw with horror the implacable conscience and worldly valuations of his revered mother.

If this line of reasoning is as close as I think it is to the known facts, then Melville, in the person of Ahab, assailed Calvinism in the Whale because it blocked the advance of a conscience beneficent to evolutionary love. And so, weighed in the scales of its creator, *Moby-Dick* is not a wicked book but a *good* book, and after finishing it Melville had full reason to feel, as he confessed, "spotless as the lamb."

But then, seen from another point, *Moby-Dick* might be judged a wicked book, not because its hero condemns an entrenched tradition, but because he is completely committed to destruction. Although Captain Ahab manifests the basic stubborn virtues of the arch-protestant and the rugged individualist carried to their limits, *this* god-defier is no Prometheus, since all thought of benefiting humanity is foreign to him. His purpose is not to make the Pacific safe for whaling, nor, when blasting at the moral order, does he have in mind a more heartening vision for the future. The religion of Eros which might once have been the secret determinant of Ahab's undertaking is never mentioned. At one critical point in *Pierre* the hero-author, favored by a flash of light, exclaims, "I will gospelize the world anew"; but he never does. Out of light comes darkness: the temper of Pierre's book is no different from the temper of *Moby-Dick.* The truth is that Ahab is motivated by his private need to avenge a private insult. His governing philosophy is that of nihilism, the doctrine that the existing system must be shattered. Nihilism springs up when the imagination fails to provide the redeeming solution of an unbearable dilemma, when "the creative response," as Toynbee would say, is not forthcoming, and a man reacts out of a hot heart—"to the dogs with the head"—and swings to an instinct, "the same that prompts even a worm to turn under the heel." This is what White-Jacket did when arraigned at the mast, and what Pierre did when fortune deserted him, and what Billy Budd did when confronted by his accuser. "Nature has not implanted any power in man," said Melville,

> that was not meant to be exercised at times, though too often our powers have been abused. The privilege, inborn, and inalienable, that every man has, of dying himself and inflicting death upon another, was not given to us without a purpose. These are the last resources of an insulted and unendurable existence.

If we grant that Ahab is a wicked man, what does this prove? It proves that *Moby-Dick* is a *good* book, a parable in epic form, because Melville makes a great spectacle of Ahab's wickedness and shows through the course of the narrative how such wickedness will drive a man on iron rails to an appointed nemesis. Melville adhered to the classic formula for tragedies. He could feel "spotless as the lamb," because he had seen to it that the huge threat to the social system immanent in Ahab's two cardinal defects—egotistic self-inflation and unleashed wrath—was, at the end, fatefully exterminated, "and the great shroud of the sea rolled on as it rolled five thousand years ago." The reader has had his catharsis, equilibrium has been restored, sanity is vindicated.

This is true, but is it the whole truth? In point of fact, while writing *Moby-Dick* did Melville maintain aesthetic distance, keeping his own feelings in abeyance? Do we not hear Ahab saying things that the later

Pierre will say and that Melville says less vehemently in his own person? Does not the author show marked partiality for the "mighty pageant creature" of his invention, put in *his* mouth the finest, boldest language? Also, have not many interpreters been so influenced by the abused Ahab that they saw nothing in his opponent but the source of all malicious agencies, the very Devil? As Lewis Mumford has said so eloquently, Ahab is at heart a noble being whose tragic wrong is that of battling against evil with "power instead of love," and so becoming "the image of the thing he hates." With this impression imbedded in our minds, how can we come out with any moral except this: evil wins. We admit that Ahab's wickedness has been canceled. But what survives? It is the much more formidable, compacted wickedness of the group that survives, the world that is "saturated and soaking with lies," and its man-of-war God, who is hardly more admirable than a primitive totem beast, some oral-aggressive, child-devouring Cronos of the sea. Is this an idea that a man of good will can rest with?

Rest with? Certainly not. Melville's clear intention was to bring not rest, but *unrest* to intrepid minds. All gentle people were warned away from his book "on risk of a lumbago or sciatica." "A polar wind blows through it," he announced. He had not written to soothe, but to kindle, to make men leap from their seats, as Whitman would say, and fight for their lives. Was it the poet's function to buttress the battlements of complacency, to give comfort to the enemy? There is little doubt about the nature of the enemy in Melville's day. It was the dominant ideology, that peculiar compound of puritanism and materialism, of rationalism and commercialism, of shallow, blatant optimism and technology, which proved so crushing to creative evolutions in religion, art, and life. In such circumstances every "true poet," as Blake said, "is of the Devil's party," whether he knows it or not. Surveying the last hundred and fifty years, how many exceptions to this statement can we find? Melville, anyhow, knew that *he* belonged to the party, and while writing *Moby-Dick* so gloried in his membership that he baptized his work *In Nomine Diaboli.* It was precisely under these auspices that he created his solitary masterpiece, a construction of the same high order as the Constitution of the United States and the scientific treatises of Willard Gibbs, though huge and wild and unruly as the Grand Canyon. And it is for this marvel chiefly that he resides in our hearts now among the greatest in "that small but high-hushed world" of bestowing geniuses.

The drama is finished. What of its author?

Moby-Dick may be taken as a comment on the strategic crisis of Melville's allegorical life. In portraying the consequences of Ahab's last suicidal lunge, the hero's umbilical fixation to the Whale and his death by strangling, the author signalized not only his permanent attachment to the imago of the mother, but the submission he had foreseen to the binding power of the parental conscience, the Superego of middle-class America. Measured against the standards of *his* day, then, Melville must be accounted a *good* man.

But does this entitle him to a place on the side of the angels? He abdicated to the conscience he condemned, and his ship *Pequod*, in sinking, carried down with it the conscience he aspired to, represented by the sky-hawk, the bird of heaven. With his ideal drowned, life from then on was load, and time stood still. All he had denied to love he gave, throughout a martyrdom of forty years, to death.

But "hark ye yet again—the little lower layer." Melville's capitulation in the face of overwhelming odds was limited to the sphere of action. His embattled soul refused surrender and lived on, breathing back defiance, disputing "to the last gasp" of his "earthquake life" the sovereignty of that inscrutable authority in him. As he wrote in *Pierre,* unless the enthusiast "can find the talismanic secret, to reconcile this world with his own soul, then there is no peace for him, no slightest truce for him in this life." Years later we find him holding the same ground. "Terrible is earth" was his conclusion, but despite all, "no retreat through me." By this stand he bequeathed to us the unsolved problem of the talismanic secret.

Only at the very last, instinct spent, earthquake over, did he fall back to a position close to Christian resignation. In his Being, was not this man "a wonder, a grandeur, and a woe"?

The Craft of Herman Melville:
A Putative Statement

by R. P. Blackmur

This essay proposes to approach Herman Melville altogether gingerly and from behind the safe bulwark of his assured position—whatever that is—in American literature,—whatever *that* may be. The tacit assumption will be all along that Melville is a sufficiently great writer in a sufficiently interesting literature to make the sidelong look, the biased comment, and even a little boring-from-within, each valuable in itself, if perhaps only as characterizing an inadequate response on the part of one reader. We need, of course, a preliminary assertion to get us under way; and the last thing we want is anything in the direction of reducing Melville's greatness to subhuman terms. What we want is an ssertion that, pursued, will elucidate one aspect of the work actually performed, irrespective of its greatness.

If we assert that Melville was an imaginative artist in the realm of fiction, then it is legitimate to think of him as he was concerned with the craft of fiction in his two most interesting works, *Moby-Dick* and *Pierre*. As a further limitation, let us think of the craft principally under two heads: dramatic form with its inspiriting conventions, and the treatment of language itself as a medium. Other matters may come in by the way, and further matters may suggest themselves in conclusion; but the mode of discovery will be everywhere at bottom in the consideration of the tools by which Melville himself secured his effects: the tools of craft.

It is of preliminary interest that Melville never influenced the direction of the art of fiction, though in *Pierre* he evidenced the direction, and it is astonishing, when you consider the magnitude of his sensibility, that he never affected the modes of apprehension, the sensibilities, of even the ablest of his admirers. He added nothing to the novel as a form, and his work nowhere showed conspicuous mastery of the formal devices of fiction which he used. Unlike most great writers of fiction, he left nothing to those who followed him except the general stimulus of high and devoted purpose and the occasional particular spur of an image or a rhythm. It is not that he is inimitable but that there was nothing formally organized enough in his work to imitate or modify or perfect. It is easy enough to say on this score that Melville was a sport, and unique, and perhaps that is the right thing to say; but it would be more useful if we were able to say that Melville's lack of influence at least partly arose from a series of technical defects in persuasive craft—from an inefficient relation between the writer and the formal elements of his medium. None of us would want to recommend his wares along the lines of Melville's strategy. To adumbrate such a statement is a part of this essay's purpose.

Of secondary, but deeply contributory interest is the fact that though a young man still as writers go, Melville wrote nothing of major significance in the forty years he lived after writing *Pierre*. (I mean that only a lesser case could be made out for *The Confidence-Man* and *Billy Budd* than for *Pierre*, not that the later books were uninteresting; they could not fail of interest as forced through Melville's sensibility.) It was not that his mind rotted or that insight faltered. It was not, I think, that the poor reception of *Pierre*, nor the long aggravation of his private life, dried his desire as a novelist. It was, I think, partly bad luck—the luck of the age, if you like—though it was no worse than Dante's luck and not so bad as Villon's, as Melville himself knew; and it was partly that his work discovered for itself, if we may say so, and in the very process of writing, that it was not meant to be fiction. Melville was only a story teller betimes, for illustrative or apologetic or evangelical purposes, and when the *writing* of *Pierre* proved that the material of illustration had been exhausted in *Moby-Dick*—which is one way of noting the breakdown of *Pierre* as a story—there was no longer any need to tell a story. His means determined, as they always do, not the ends in view, but the ends achieved; and Melville had never predominantly relied upon the means of the novelist, had never attempted to use more than the overt form of the novel, until he attempted to compose *Pierre*.

What is really interesting, and what this essay intends to make most use of in this corner, is the light that *Pierre*, technically considered as a novel, casts upon the means, quite different from the means of fiction, which Melville actually employed both in *Moby-Dick* and *Pierre* itself. For these books with their great effects, if they were not written out of the means of the novelist, were written out of great means of some other mode or modes of the imagination. It will most likely appear that there is an operative connection between Melville's lack of influence upon following writers and his forty years of comparative silence; and it is, again, a connection, as moral as may be, that can best be seen as a technical consideration. Similarly, the problem of the inarticulateness of *Hamlet* is better accounted for technically than philosophically. We shall see, or try to see, what modes determined what ends—but always provisionally within the modes of the rational imagination.

There is, again on this train, a dubious kind of consideration which in the very doubtfulness of its nature exerts its great attraction. In our literature we are accustomed to the question precisely because it gets itself asked at every turn. It is a coroner's question: what devilish thing did his age do to Melville? What malevolence was there in the current of American life that struck from the heights of possibility writer after writer, even those most satisfied with the American scene?—for the Longfellows, the Whittiers, the Holmeses were as fatally struck as Hawthorne and Melville and Mark Twain. But does an age act? Is not an age itself a long action, an unfolding, a display, a history, with limits set by the discernment and capacity of the observer, never by Clio herself? And is not every age an enemy of every artist it cannot directly use, an enemy not out of antipathy but of inner necessity? An age moves; it is momentum felt. An artist expresses an arrested version of movement, expresses it at the level of actuality. But this is pushing consequence intolerably. We are all enemies of our age the moment we begin to tamper with it, whether we arrest it to take its picture, hasten it toward its end in the guise of leadership, or just consciously live in it our own lives. Consciousness is the agent, not the age.

It is the whole consciousness, not its mere miniscule conscience, that makes us cowards. Hence in all large doings we are adept at removing compassion from our experience by at once inserting it in the formula of a dead convention; and so are often enabled to skip consciousness, along with conscience, altogether. How otherwise could we attend the Christian service of Holy Communion, quite aside from the matter of faith and for the "poetry" in it merely, without terror and dismay and the conviction of inadequacy. How could we attend *King Lear* on the stage if we did not commonly channelize our attention upon the obscuring details of the performance, letting the actual play work in us, if at all, unawares? This is precisely what the artist cannot substantially do if his work is to live; and this is precisely what society compels him to seem to do if his work is to succeed in the open—that is, be widely persuasive upon the consciousness of the great audience most artists aim at. Upon his skill and luck in performing this equivocal act depends all that part of an artist's achievement which rests on a firm relation with his age.

Here we have a crux in the deliberately maintained, willfully heightened consciousness of the artist. It is the crux in which we see that the conceptual faculty of consciousness is honesty if we can manage it, but that the executive faculty of consciousness must be hypocrisy. I do not wish to strain or seem far-fetched, but I believe this to be a technical matter in so far as we think of the arts—whatever it may be in religion **or** politics, which are not always condemned to actuality but can often play free havoc with the ideal. What it comes to in practice is that the artist must dramatize his theme, his vision, his observation, his "mere" story, in terms of existing conventions however adverse those conventions may seem to his intentions, or however hollow or vain they ring when struck. The deadest convention was meant for life—to take its place; and if by putting life into it the artist does not always change it for the better, he at least shows it for what it is. Instinctive artists commonly resort to the nearest conventions susceptible of dramas. Consider the Negro spirituals or the anonymous architecture of the twelfth century. Highly individualized artists have done the same. There is Dante who mastered the conventions of Thomistic Christianity to represent the actuality— far from Thomistic—of fourteenth century Italy; and there is Henry James who resorted to the "social" conventions so well that many people for long believed he was taken in by them, when his predominant concern was to dramatize the actual good and evil of his time in terms of the conventions through which he most saw good and evil operating.

The point here is, for us, that Melville either refused or was unable to resort to the available conventions of his time as if they were real; he either preferred or was compelled to resort to most of the conventions he used for dramatic purposes not only as if they were unreal but also as if they were artificial. Artificial they surely were to the kind of philosopher Melville was—though they would not have seemed unreal to Montaigne or Plato; but to the dramatist of any description they would have glowed with the possibility of every reality. As for Melville's case we have his own words, put in extremity, for his attitude toward all conventions of the mind.

> For the more and the more that he wrote, and the deeper and deeper that he dived, Pierre saw the everlasting elusiveness of Truth; the universal lurking insincerity of even the greatest and purest written thoughts. Like knavish cards, the leaves of all great books were covertly packed. He was but packing one set the more; and that a very poor and jaded set and pack indeed.

Here we see the ineptitude, for the artist, of moral preoccupation with what ought to be as compared with the equally moral obsession with what is. As thought, we can leave Melville's text alone, and insist merely that as an artist Melville misunderstood the import of his own words. The "universal lurking insincerity" he spoke of, is just the most fascinating aspect of the face of dramatic truth; and the conviction of it should liberate the artist's honesty among his material generally, as the preposterous fables of *Lear, Othello,* and the *Merchant of Venice* particularly liberated the profound honesty of Shakespeare, or as the *smallness* of life in Emma Bovary's town liberated Flaubert's honesty. Melville apparently felt that his insight condemned him to a species of dishonesty. Feeling the necessity—feeling the condemned state as unreprievable—he proceeded to employ conventions of character and form in which he obviously and almost avowedly did not believe. Had he been a convicted and not a condemned novelist he would have felt his insight of insincerity on the same level that he felt the convention in the following lines, in which he never detected the insincerity at all.

> It is a thing most sorrowful, nay shocking, to expose the fall of valor in the soul. Men may seem detestable as joint stock-companies and nations; knaves, fools, and murderers there may be; men may have mean and meagre faces; ing creature, that over any ignominious blemish in him all his fellows should but man, in the ideal, is so noble and so sparkling, such a grand and glow- run to throw their costliest robes. That immaculate manliness we feel within ourselves, so far within us, that it remains intact though all the outer character seem gone; bleeds with the keenest anguish at the undraped spectacle of a valor-ruined man. Nor can pity itself, at such a shameful sight, completely stifle her upbraidings against the permitting stars.

At his best—his best as a novelist of character and aspiration—this sentiment controlled Melville's perception of dramatic fate. Had he felt the immaculate manliness as Henry James, say, felt his perception of the Sacred Fount, as a germinal, copulative, and plastic principle in every human relation; and also as the very prod and forward stress toward form, then his sentiment would not only have opened up inexhaustible subject matter, but would also have required of him that in his execution every resource, every trick, every mediate insincerity, either of craft or of social pattern, be used for the utmost there was in them. That would have been to work on the representative, the dramatic level. What he did, as we shall see more particularly below, was to work on the putative level. His work constantly *said* what it was doing or going to do, and then, as a rule, stopped short.

As it happens, Melville's is not a putative smallness but a putative immensity, and he puts it with such eloquence that the mere statement produces a lasting tone in the general atmosphere. He was without knowing it in the habit of succumbing to the greatest insincerity of all, the intoxicating insincerity of cadence and rhythm and apt image, or, to put it on another plane, the insincerity of surrendering to the force of a single insight, which sometimes amounts to a kind of self-violation. Who can measure for example the effect of the preparatory statements about Ahab upon our actual reception of him when he appears? For instance, in Chapter XVI there is a paragraph about the greatness of some whaling men rising from a combination of Quaker blood and the perils of the sea. "Nor will it at all detract from him, dramatically regarded, if either by birth or other circumstances, he have what seems a half wilful, overruling morbidness at the bottom of his nature. For all men tragically great are made so through a certain morbidness. Be sure of this, O young ambition, all mortal greatness is but disease." . . . This is but one of the many preparatory, almost minatory statements that Melville made about Ahab.

Many directly named him; many more, like this one, were purely indirect and putative in character. Ahab is not mentioned, but the reader
who remembers the passage will know that it was he who was meant all
the same; and if the reader does remember, it may well occur to him
that Melville meant his sentences about greatness and disease to spread
throughout the novel. They were planted of a purpose, whether by
instinct or intention, to prefigure in the general atmosphere the specific
nature of the burden Ahab wore.

The interesting thing is that Melville preferred to make his statement,
in which one version of the whole theme of the book is expressed, not
only baldly in isolation, but out of place and rootlessly; which is how the
reader will ultimately remember it. It worked, indeed; but it worked outside the story. A dramatist would have been compelled to find the sentiment of these sentences in a situation, an action, and they could have been
used only as the situation called for them and the action carried them
along; and a novelist when he can should follow the example of the
dramatist. Melville, as we have said, preferred the nondramatic mode. To
put it sharply, he did not write of characters in action; he employed
the shells of stock characters, heightened or resounding only by the
eloquence of the author's voice, to witness, illustrate, decorate, and often
as it happened to impede and stultify an idea in motion. This is, if you
like, the mode of allegory—the highest form of the putative imagination,
in which things are *said* but need not be *shown* to be other than they
seem, and thus hardly require to *be* much of anything. But successful
allegory—*La Vita Nuova* and *Pilgrim's Progress*—requires the preliminary possession of a complete and stable body of belief appropriate
to the theme in hand. Melville was not so equipped; neither was Hawthorne; neither was anyone in nineteenth century America or since. That
is why Melville's allegorical devices and patterns had to act *as if* they
were agents in a novel; and that is why we are compelled to judge Melville
at his most allegorical yet formally as a novelist.

Perhaps the point needs laboring. Many critics—many students of
Melville—have done a good deal to make an allegorical interpretation of
Moby-Dick, and I am sure they are right and accurate in the form of what
they say. Melville certainly had allegorical intentions. My argument—
again it is technical—is that the elaboration of these intentions was
among the causes that prevented him from the achievement of enacting
composition and the creation of viable characters. He mistook allegory
in *Moby-Dick* as a sufficient enlivening agent for the form of the novel.
Actually it was a chief defective element which, due to the peculiarly confused, inconsistent, and incomplete state of belief he was in, he could
not possibly have used to good advantage. In the craft of writing, in any
form of expression, artificial allegory, like willed mysticism (of which
Melville showed a trace), is a direct and easy mode only in that it puts so
much in by intention as to leave nearly everything out in execution.

Bad allegory, even to the allegorist, comes very soon to seem not worth doing; which is why charades and political parties break down. Melville's allegory in *Moby-Dick* broke down again and again and with each resumption got more and more verbal, and more and more at the mercy of the encroaching event it was meant to transcend. It was an element in the putative mode in which, lofty as it was, Melville himself could not long deeply believe.

We have so far been concerned mostly with what Melville did not do as a practitioner in the novel and with certain possible causes which, technically, prevented him from doing what he wanted to do. Let us now examine particular instances of what he did do under the two heads first mentioned: dramatic form with its inspiriting conventions, and the treatment of language itself as medium. If anything so far said has made its point it will be in the degree that it certifies and illuminates what follows—in the degree, that is, that it makes it seem natural and just and necessary to find so much fault in a genius so great.

The dramatic form of a novel is what holds it together, makes it move, gives it a center and establishes a direction; and it includes the agency of perception, the consciousness set up in the book upon which or through which, the story is registered. Dramatic form cannot in practice be wholly isolated from other formal elements; form is the way things go together in their medium—and the medium itself, here language, may properly be considered the major element of form; but we may think of different ways in which things go together in a given work, and strangely, the labor of abstraction and violation will seem to deepen our intimacy with the substance of the work and, more valuable, to heighten our sense of how that substance is controlled. The sense of control is perhaps the highest form of apprehension; it is understanding without immersion.

The question we have here to ask then is how did Melville go about controlling his two novels, *Moby-Dick* and *Pierre?* The general, strictly true, and mainly irrelevant answer would be: haphazardly—that is, through an attitude which varied from the arrogance of extreme carelessness to the humility of complete attention. It is not that he attended only to what seriously interested him, for he was as careless of what he thought important as of what he thought trivial, but that apparently he had no sure rule as to what required management and what would take care of itself. His rule was vagary, where consequential necessities did not determine otherwise. And even there, Melville's eye was not good; he did not always see that if you took one series of steps your choice of further directions was narrowed, and that you could not step in two directions at once without risk of crippling yourself. It is perhaps his intellectual consistency, which he felt putatively omniform, that made him incorrigibly inconsistent in the technical quarter. For example, in *Moby-Dick*, after setting up a single consciousness to get inside of, he shifted from that consciousness at will without sense of inconsistency, and therefore, which is the important thing, without making any effort to warrant the shifts and make them credible. Ignorance could not have excused him, because he had the example of Hawthorne, who was adept at shifting his compositional centers without disturbing his gravity, plumb in front of him. Not ignorance, but ineptitude and failure to discriminate. For the contrary example, I can think of only three occasions of importance in *Pierre*, if we except the digressions of the author himself in his own voice, where the consciousness of the hero is not left the presumed sole register of the story. Of these occasions, two are unnecessary to the story, and the third, where in the very end the perceiving center is turned over to the turnkey in the prison, funks its job. Yet in *Pierre* the theme cried out, one would think, for as many and as well chosen centers of consciousness as possible, all to be focussed on Pierre himself, the distraught and ambiguous, otherwise not measurable: the principle being that the abnormal can only be seen as viable, as really moving in response to the normal world, if seen through normal eyes.

Meanwhile we have approached a little nearer the composition of the two novels. Melville was right, granting the theme of *Moby-Dick*, in choosing Ishmael the novice, to represent a story in which he had only a presumed and minor but omnipresent part; he was only wrong where he breached his choice without covering up. Ishmael, not otherwise ever named, is as mysterious as Ahab, but he is credible because he tells us not what he is but what he sees and what he sees other people see. The mere interposition of a participating consciousness between the story and its readers, once it has been made logical by tying the consciousness to the story, is a prime device of composition: it limits, compacts, and therefore controls what can be told and how. The only error Melville made is that he failed to distinguish between what Ishmael saw and what the author saw on his own account. If an author is to use digressions, which are confusing but legitimate by tradition, he ought to follow Fielding and put them in inter-chapters, and especially where the narrative is technically in the first person. Otherwise, as with Ishmael, the narrator will seem to know too much at a given time for the story's good; it will tend to tell itself all at once, and the necessary modicum of stupidity in the operative consciousness will be blighted by excess intelligence. As Ahab said to the carpenter who handed him a lantern: "Thrusted light is worse than presented pistols." Ishmael of course is Melville's alter ego, which explains why so much is imputed to him, but does not condone the excess.

On the whole the mode of Ishmael is a success exactly where the mode of Pierre (another alter ego of Melville) is wrong. Ishmael is looking on, and able to see; Pierre is in the center of his predicament, and lost in the action. Ishmael represents speech; Pierre represents rhetoric. Ishmael reports the abnormal, driven and demonic Ahab, either through his own normal sensibility or through the reported sensibilities of the mates and crew. Pierre is seen principally without the intervening glass and focus of any sensibility whatever—so that he falls apart into a mere voice whenever he speaks, whereas the voice of Ahab, equally eloquent and rhetorical past belief, rings true in ears that have actually heard it.

It should be noted, curiously, that Ishmael is the only character in the book not "characterized" by Melvile; he is merely situated in the center, explained a little, and let speak his part of recording angel. The curiosity is that all the other characters except Ahab and Queequeg near the beginning (the night at the inn), although given set characterizations as they appear, are far less viable and are far less *present* in the book than Ishmael. The reason may be that the other characters are only pulled out at intervals and are usually given stock jobs to do, set speeches to make, whereas Ishmael, sacking his creative memory, is occupied all the time. Which suggests two or three things: that character requires the sense of continuous action to show continuously, that the mates and crew were not *in* the book substantially but that their real use was to divide up the representation of the image of Ahab. There is nothing illegitimate about such characters, but to be successful and maintain interest they must be given enough to do to seem everywhere natural, and never obviously used, as here, *only* to make the wheels go round. One suspects, therefore, that Ahab comes out a great figure more because of the eloquence of the author's putative conception of him, and Ishmael's feeling for him, than from any representational aids on the part of the crew. The result is a great figure, not a great character. Ahab is as solitary in the book as he was in his cabin.

Pierre was in his way as compositionally isolated as Ahab; he was so situated, and so equipped as a consciousness, that he recorded his own isolation to the point of solipsism. If Pierre was real, as he was asserted to be, then nothing else properly in the novel was real except in terms of his perception or through the direct and unwarrantable intervention of the author. That is the risk attached to making the protagonist record the action in which he participates to the exclusion of other agents and while the action is going on. Melville instinctively tried to get round the difficulty by resorting to a series of dramatic scenes in which Pierre was chief interlocutor. The device was the right one—or one of the right ones—but it failed to work for a number of reasons, of which the chief was that Melville had no talent for making his dramatic scenes objective except by aid of external and unrelated force—as in *Moby-Dick* he was able to resort to the ordinary exigencies of life on a whaling ship. In *Pierre* the White Whale was entirely in the protagonist's own inadequate perception of it; and the real weight of the book—what it was really about: tragedy by unconsidered virtue—was left for the author's digressions and soliloquies to carry as it could; which is to say that the book had no compositional center at all.

Something of the same sort may also be true of *Moby-Dick*. Is it not possible to say that Ishmael, the narrator, provides only a false center?

Is it not true that a great part of the story's theme escapes him, is not recorded through his sensibility, either alone or in connection with others?
Then the real center would lie where? It would lie variously, I think, in
the suspense attached to the character of Ahab and the half imputed,
half demonstrated peril of the White Whale—the cold, live evil that is
momently present. If we think of the book in that way, we may say that
its compositional form is a long, constantly interrupted but as constantly
maintained suspense, using as nexi or transitions the recurring verbal signs
of Melville's allegory, Ahab's character, and the business of whaling. The
business of whaling, including both the essays on anatomy and those on
butchery, takes the most space and provides the most interest. All the
reader has to do is to *feel* whaling as interest and he will recognize it as
a compositional device mounting to the force of drama. Indeed we speak
of the drama of whaling, or of cotton, or of gold without substantial injustice to the language; and I cannot for the life of me see why the drama
of whaling should not be as efficient an agent of interest, if well felt, as
the drama of who fired the second shot; and with Melville there is the
additional advantage that the business of whaling points to the everlasting assassin instead of the casual and no doubt remorseful murderer.
Interest is the thing of prime importance as any artist and any audience
will tell you. If it takes up time and prepares for life, it does not matter
how it is secured and does not fatally matter if it is overdone or vulgar
in its appeal as it is in *Moby-Dick*.

But is the real interest in the whaling or in the firing of the shot? Is
it not always partly in the presentation, the feeling of detail and design,
and partly in the image toward which the design points? Melville was
lucky in *Omoo* and *Typee,* to a less degree in *Mardi* and *White-Jacket,*
and most of all in *Moby-Dick;* he was lucky or it was his genius that he
had material in perfect factual control with which to take up time and
point toward an image—in *Moby-Dick* a profound and obsessive image
of life. As it happened, it was in each case the material of a special and
vanishing experience, dramatic enough in its own right to require very
little fictionizing—very little actualizing—to exert the invaluable hold
of natural interest over the average reader. If to interest, you add eloquence, you have all the essentials of the great novel below the first order.
Many readers will be deceived and think the provision greater than it is.
I have discovered a number of readers who on being asked reported en-
joyment of a great story in a book of which Henry James would have said
that it told no story to speak of; which indeed it does not.

In *Pierre* we are in a different box; a box quite empty of special material of objective interest to do for compositional strength otherwise lacking. There is no sea, or ship, or whale, or unique tradition of behavior, no
unusual daily life—most precious of all—to give atmosphere, and weight
and movement to carry the book toward the image of its chosen end.
Melville was required to depend more than ever before upon the actual

technique of the craft, and nothing much else, to make the book hang together. What is most illuminating is most pitiful. The glaring weaknesses of *Pierre* show up the hidden weaknesses of *Moby-Dick,* and each set of weaknesses shows the other as essential—at least in the critical context in which we here provisionally place both books.

That one novel may criticize another is a commonplace when we think of different authors, as when we say that the novels of Henry James form a criticism of the novels of Flaubert and Turgenev, or that, in a way, the *Comédie Humaine* is a critique of the Waverly Novels. I think it is equally true that a consideration of the failures of a single author will often form the severest criticism of his successes, and a consideration of his successes may relatively improve our estimation of his failures. A great author is of one substance and often of one theme, and the relation between his various creations is bound to be reciprocal, even mutual; each is the other in a different form. So with *Pierre* and *Moby-Dick.* If we wish to take up thinking of the two novels together in this way—which is the purpose of this essay—the alert consciousness will be struck with the repetition of the vices of *Pierre* in *Moby-Dick,* or struck the other way round with the fact that the tragedy of *Pierre* fails to come off as well as *Moby-Dick* only because the later book lacked the demonstrable extraneous interest of whaling. The efforts at plot in the two books are as lame; narrative runs as often offside. Dramatic motive on the subordinate level is as weakly put; Starbuck's tentative rebellion against Ahab and the threatened revenge of Glendinning Stanly and Frederick Tarton upon Pierre are equally unconvincing. The dialogue is as by turns limp and stiff and flowery in one book as the other. The delineations of character are almost interchangeable examples of wooden caricature. And so on. More important, the force and nobility of conception, the profundity of theme, were as great in either book—not from the dramatic execution but in spite of it, in the simple strength of the putative statement, and in the digressions Melville made from the drama in front of him, which he could not manage, into apologues or sermons, which he superbly could.

The strength of the putative statement is only simple when thought of abstractly and as appealing to the intellect—to the putative element in appreciation: if we read lyric poetry solely for the schematic paraphrase we make of it in popular discussion, or as if, in contemplating war, we thought only of political causes or in terms of the quartermaster's technique alone. What we want is to see what is the source of putative strength and how deeply its appeal is asserted; and in that pursuit we shall find ourselves instantly, I think, in the realm of language itself. Words, and their intimate arrangements, must be the ultimate as well as the immediate source of every effect in the written or spoken arts. Words bring meaning to birth and themselves contained the meaning as an imminent possibility before the pangs of junction. To the individual artist the use of words is an adventure in discovery; the imagination is heuristic among the words it manipulates. The reality you labor desperately or luckily to put into your words—and you may put it in consciously like Coleridge or by instinct as in the great ballads or from piety and passion like the translators of the Bible—you will actually have found there, deeply ready and innately formed to give objective being and specific idiom to what you knew and did not know that you knew. The excitement is past belief; as we know from the many myths of heavenly inspiration. And the routine of discovery is past teaching and past prediction; as we know from the vast reaches of writing, precious and viable to their authors, wholly without the conviction of being. Yet the adventure into the reality of words has a technique after the fact in the sense that we can distinguish its successful versions from those that failed, can measure provisionally the kinds and intensities of reality secured and attempted, and can even roughly guess at the conditions of convention and belief necessary for its emergence.

Melville is an excellent example for such an assay. We have only to relate the conception of the reality of language just adumbrated to the notion of the putative statement to see whence the strength of the latter comes; and we have only to relate the conception of language to its modifying context of conventions in order to understand the successes and at least excuse the many shortcomings and overleapings of Melville's attempts at the paramount and indefeasible reality that great words show. For Melville habitually used words greatly.

Let us take first an example not at all putative and with as little supporting context of convention as possible: an example of words composed entirely of feelings and the statement of sensuous facts, plus of course the usual situating and correlative elements which are the real syntax of imaginative language.

> To a landsman, no whale, nor any sign of a herring, would have been visible at that moment; nothing but a troubled bit of greenish white water, and thin scattered puffs of vapor hovering over it, and suffusingly blowing off to leeward, like the confused scud from white rolling billows. The air around suddenly vibrated and tingled, as it were, like the air over intensely heated plates of iron. Beneath this atmospheric waving and curling, and partially beneath a thin layer of water, also, the whales were swimming. Seen in advance of all the other indications, the puffs of vapor they spouted, seemed their forerunning couriers and detached flying outriders.

This is the bottom level of good writing, whether in prose or verse; and a style which was able to maintain the qualities of accurate objective feeling which it exemplifies at other levels and for other purposes could not help being a great style. The words have feelers of their own, and the author contributes nothing to the emotion they call forth except the final phrasing, which adds nothing but finish to the paragraph. It is an example of words doing their own work; and let no one think it is not imaginative work, or does not come to an emotion, because the mode is that of close description, and neither directly expressive nor enacting. Let us compare it, with achieved emotion in mind, with a deliberately "emotional" description taken from the chapter called Enceladus in *Pierre*.

Cunningly masked hitherto, by the green tapestry of the interlacing leaves, a terrific towering palisade of dark mossy massiness confronted you; and, trickling with unevaporable moisture, distilled upon you from its beetling brow slow thunder-showers of water-drops, chill as the last dews of death. . . . All round and round, the grim scarred rocks rallied and re-rallied themselves; shot up, protruded, stretched, swelled, and eagerly reached forth; on every side bristling radiated with hideous repellingness. . . . 'Mid this spectacle of wide and wanton spoil, insular noises of falling rocks would boomingly explode upon the silence and fright all the echoes, which ran shrieking in and out among the caves, as wailing women and children in some assaulted town.

This is, if I may insist on the term, putative description. It asserts itself to be description and passes for description until it is looked into, when you see that it is primarily the *assertion* of an emotional relation to landscape, and through effects of which landscape is incapable. Its force depends on the looseness, vagueness, and tumultuousness of the motion of the words. As a matter of fact the words are so chosen and arranged that they cannot contribute any material of emotion beyond that which may be contained in a stock exclamation. The primary point of our comparison is that the second passage dilutes and wastes an emotion assumed to have existed prior to its expression, whereas the first passage built up and united the elements of an emotion which exists only and actually in the words employed. The first passage discovers its meaning in words, the second never reached the condition of meaning. The first passage reminds you of Gerard Hopkins, the second of Ann Radcliffe; a contrast which brings up the secondary point of our comparison.

The spirit of the gothic novel ran frothily through the popular literature of America in the first half of the nineteenth century, ending possibly with its own travesty in *The Black Crook*. Melville, faced with the bad necessity, as it must have seemed to him, of popularizing the material of *Pierre* and *Moby-Dick*, adopted outright the gothic convention of language with all its archaisms and rhetorical inflations. The effect in the two books was similar in fact though not quite the same in effect. Some of the soliloquies in *Moby-Dick* seem more like tantrums than poetry, but they were the tantrums of a great imagination fed with mastered material. In *Pierre*, without any fund of nourishing material, the dialogues, soliloquies, and meditations got lost in the flatulence of words.

Now, the gothic convention is not susceptible of reality in itself, as we see in Beckford and Peacock and Brontë—perhaps in Poe and occasionally in Hawthorne—but it requires on the part of the author unconditional assent to it as a convention. This assent Melville could not give; he used it, so far as I can see, as a solemn fraud and hoped for the best. In *Moby-Dick* the fraud passed preliminary muster because the lofty "unreal" terror that rode the *Pequod* made it seem at least plausible, even in its greatest extravagance, as a vehicle of response. And there is the further defense, often made, that the worst excesses of language and sentiment are excusable because of the poetry they are supposed to hold. To which the answer is that the poetry would have been better without the excess; when Melville dropped the mode and wrote in a language comparable to the passage first quoted above, as in Ahab's last soliloquy, better poetry was actually produced. But no one, so far as I know, unless it be Foster Damon who writes *con amore* of anything both American and gothic, has defended the excesses of *Pierre,* of which the passage quoted above is a tame example.

It may be said in passing that what is often called the Elizabethan influence in Melville's prose might more accurately be called the gothic influence heightened by the greatness of Melville's intentions. If I may have the notation for what it is worth, I suspect that in "the three boats swung over the sea like three samphire baskets over high cliffs," while the samphire baskets undoubtedly came from *King Lear,* still they had got well spattered with gothic mire on the long journey. Again, the sister-brother crux in *Pierre,* while it may be found in John Ford, has a very different reality of expression from that in Ford's verse.

> The menacings in thy eyes are dear delights to me; I grow up with thy own glorious stature; and in thee, my brother, I see God's indignant ambassador to me, saying—Up, up, Isabel, and take no terms from the common world, but do thou make terms to it, and grind thy fierce rights out of it! Thy catching nobleness unsexes me, my brother; and now I know that in her most exalted moment, then woman no more feels the twin-born softness of her breasts, but feels chain-armour palpitating there!

These lines, spoken by Isabel in response to similar declarations on the part of Pierre on the occasion of their second conversation, could not have been matched in Ford, but they could be matched a hundred times in the popular gothics. As for the minor effects of Elizabethan influence, where it has been said, by Mumford among others, that Melville's prose is Websterian—and perhaps it sometimes is—yet it far more often supplies us with Marlovian tropes. For every phrase such as "the cheeks of his soul collapsed in him," there are a dozen on the tone of the following: "With a frigate's anchors for my bridle-bits and fasces of harpoons for spurs, would I could mount that whale and leap the topmast skies . . . !" This is the Marlowe of *Tamerlane,* and the unregenerate Marlowe letting himself go, not the Marlowe remodeled and compacted of *Faustus* and *The Jew*. Occasionally there is such a triumphant meeting of rhetoric and insight as the passage which contains the famous phrases: "To trail the genealogies of these high mortal miseries, carries us at last among the sourceless primogenitures of the gods"—a passage more mindful of the *Urn Burial* than of anything in *The Duchess of Malfi,* but which is mindful most of Melville himself.

If it was the gothic excess that gave occasional opportunity for magnificent flashes, we should be grateful to it that much: it is at least a delight by the way; but it far more often produced passages like the speech of Isabel, which are perhaps collector's items, but not delights. Besides, what is most and finally illuminating, when Melville really had something to say, and was not making a novel, he resorted to another mode, which was perhaps the major expressive mode of his day, the mode of the liberal Emersonian sermon, the moral apologue on the broad Christian basis. There Melville's natural aptitude lay; when he preaches he is released, and only then, of all weak specifications. That the sermon was to say the best of it an artificial mode in fiction mattered nothing, and emphasizes the fact that Melville was only a novelist betimes. He made only the loosest efforts to tie his sermons into his novels, and was quite content if he could see that his novels illustrated his sermons and was reasonably content if they did not; or so the books would show. He preached without scruple, and with full authority, because he felt in full command of the mode he used: he believed in its convention of structure and its deeper convention of its relation to society with all his heart. Father Mapple's sermon on Jonah and Plotinus Phinlimmon's lecture—it is really a sermon—on Chronometricals and Horologicals are the two sustained examples of self-complete form in his work. The doctrine might not have appealed to Channing or Parker, but the form, the execution, the litheness and vigor and verve, the homely aptnesses, the startling comparison, the lucidity of presentation of hard insights, the dramatic and pictorial quality of the illustrations, and above all the richness of impact and the weighted speed of the words, would have appealed as near perfection.

The curiosity—and Melville looked at is all curiosity—that needs emphasis here is that the vices of his style either disappeared or transpired only as virtues when he shifted his mode to the sermon, and his without any addition of insight or eloquence, but simply, I believe, because he had found a mode which suited the bent of his themes, which allowed the putative statement to reach its full glory without further backing, which made room for rhetoric and demanded digression, and which did not trouble him, so great was his faith in it, with its universal lurking insincerity. Consider the following lines, which form the counter sermon to Phinlimmon's lecture in *Pierre*.

All profound things, and emotions of things are preceded and attended by Silence. What a silence is that with which the pale bride precedes the responsive *I will*, to the priest's solemn question, *Wilt thou have this man for thy husband?* In silence, too, the wedded hands are clasped. Yea, in silence the child Christ was born into the world. Silence is the general consecration of the universe. Silence is the invisible laying on of the Divine Pontiff's hands upon the world. Silence is at once the most harmless and the most awful thing in all nature. It speaks of the Reserved Forces of Fate. Silence is the only Voice of our God.

Nor is this so august Silence confined to things simply touching or grand. Like the air, Silence permeates all things, and produces its magical power, as well during that peculiar mood which prevails at a solitary traveller's first setting forth on a journey, as at the unimaginable time when before the world was, Silence brooded on the face of the waters.

The author of these paragraphs was at home in his words and com-pletely mastered by them; and he had reached in that language, what Pierre never reached, the "sense of uncapitulatable security, which is only the possession of the furthest advanced and profoundest souls."

In our present context there seems little more to say. The consideration of Melville as a novelist should have shown, at least in the superficial aspects which this brief essay has been able to touch, that it was precisely the practice of that craft that put his books, and himself, at a loss, and left him silent, stultified, and before the great face of possibility, im-potent for forty years of mature life. I trust that it will have been shown as at least plausible that Melville suffered the exorbitant penalty of his great failure, not as a result of the injuries inflicted upon him by his age, but because of his radical inability to master a technique—that of the novel—radically foreign to his sensibility. The accidents of his career, the worse accidents of his needs, brought him to a wrong choice. Yet had he made a right choice, the accident of his state of beliefs might well have silenced him altogether. Judging by the reception of his two serious books, he would have been anathema as a preacher and unpublishable as an essayist. We should be grateful for his ill luck in only a lesser sense than we are for Dante's, or we should have lost the only great imagination in the middle period of the American nineteenth century: a putative state-ment to which all readers must assent.

Melville and the Democratic Experience

by Marius Bewley

I

Democracy is based on a belief in the perfectibility of man. At heart democracy is always optimistic. But the very idea of perfectibility, of progression in specific directions which are indicated by the requirements of man's social nature and the political goals he sets for himself, introduces the idea of an ordered universe. Perfectibility and progress are intelligible concepts only in relation to certain objective norms and goals which, at least for practical purposes, are taken as absolutes. Behind the belief in social and political improvement, in perfectibility, there lies, at any rate by implication, a working idea of good and evil. The historical democrat is traditionally reluctant to face the issue when couched in theological terms, and perhaps this reluctance shows his wisdom, for a God who works through democratic machinery afflicts his followers with many cruel paradoxes. This was one of the discoveries it was the lot of the Adams family to make. Brooks Adams in his remarkable introduction to his brother's volume, *The Degradation of the Democratic Dogma*, describes the anguish of his grandfather, John Quincy Adams, when he was forced to recognize, through the events of history, the double-dealing character of a God conceived in democratic terms:

> Mr. Adams as a scientific man was a precursor of the later Darwinians who have preached the doctrine of human perfectibility, a doctrine in which the modern world has believed and still professes to believe. Granting that there is a benign and omnipotent Creator of the world, who watches over the fate of men, Adams' sincere conviction was that such a being thinks according to certain fixed laws; that these laws may be discovered by human intelligence and when discovered may be adapted to human uses. And if so discovered, adapted, and practiced they must lead man certainly to an approach to perfection, and more especially to the elimination of war and slavery. The theory was pleasing, and since the time of Mr. Adams it has

been generally accepted as the foundation of American education and the cornerstone of democracy. But mark how far it led Mr. Adams astray in 1828, and how at last it broke his heart. Eli Whitney's cotton gin was certainly one of the most famous and successful of the applications of science to a supremely bountiful gift of God, in making American cotton serviceable and cheap to the whole human race. But it propagated slavery, it turned the fair state of Virginia into an enormous slave-breeding farm, whence forty-thousand blacks were annually exported to the South, and thus inexorably induced the Civil War; so with the public lands which Mr. Adams would willingly have given his life to save for his contemporaries and their posterity. Railroads and canals raised the price of these lands by making them accessible. And this is what Mr. Adams saw in the House of Representatives in 1838, and this is his comment on the humanizing effect of applied science. It was the triumph of Benton and Jackson, of the very essence of evil, over him. "The thirst of a tiger for blood is the fittest emblem of the rapacity with which the members of all new states fly at the public lands. The constituents upon whom they depend are all settlers, or tame and careless spectators of the pillage. They are themselves enormous speculators and land-jobbers. It were a vain attempt to resist them here." This was written on June 12, 1838, and thus had the bargain of Benton with the planters been consummated by means of applied science. Such bargains were to have been anticipated and would have been taken as a matter of course by an ordinary political huckster, but Mr. Adams, though after his defeat in 1828 he did practically, as he states here, give up the contest, because he had ceased to believe that God supported him, never could nor ever did reconcile himself to the destiny which this betrayal by God entailed on the world.[1]

Although the terms in which the problem is presented here are so different, a moment's reflection will persuade one that the kind of theological doubt engendered in John Quincy Adams by his contemplation of the democratic process is similar to the doubts that were to torment Melville. At bottom, it is an inability to keep the terms of good and evil distinct from each other; and it comes about because the democrat in the beginning making a close identification between God and democratic society, later carries this spurious identification over to the defects and failures of democracy. When the human perfectibility that God seemed to promise when he crowned the great American experiment with brotherhood from sea to shining sea conspicuously fails to develop, the disillusioned democrat proceeds from his earlier faith—which itself had been tainted with materialism—either to cynicism or hatred, and God is cast in the role of the great betrayer. That this was not quite the fate of John Quincy Adams was merely a matter of his great personal integrity; but the general proposition helps to explain why Americans have often found it easy to reject the idea of Original Sin one day, and to express the utmost

[1] *The Degradation of the Democratic Dogma* (New York, 1919), pp. 30-2.

hatred of creation the next. Democracy tends to make it a case of all or nothing.

Democracy, as I said, demands an ordered universe in which good and evil are distinguishable; but at the same time it makes it extremely difficult to tell them apart. Cooper, Hawthorne, and James avoided this dilemma by approaching it on a pragmatic level. . . . in discussing Leather stocking's symbolic significance I [have] remarked that "the ability to distinguish good from evil is the ultimate note of Natty Bumppo's character" and that Cooper refers to this faculty as "the choicest—perhaps the rarest—gift of nature." Cooper himself was an Anglican, and particularly during the latter part of his life he was interested in theological problems. *The Sea Lions* (1849), for example, in addition to being an adventure story laid among the Antarctic wastes, is also a tract on Trinitarianism. Cooper's temperament naturally gravitated towards a hieratic theology corresponding to his sense of status and class. Although Natty is no churchman, the security of his moral distinctions, as well as a hagiographic quality with which Cooper has invested him, point to a distinctly theological bent in his creator's character—and one that has nothing to do with New England Calvinism. But with Cooper, theology seems to have social or class roots. He reserves his intensities most often for such questions as whether or not the Littlepage family pew in the parish church is to be permitted to retain its distinguishing canopy, symbol of aristocratic status. It is with a good deal of reluctance that Cooper allows it to be removed. Cooper, in short, is concerned with religion in almost the same way that he is concerned with the American political and social tensions.

It is obvious that these tensions on the political, economic, and social levels have made it easier for Cooper to deal with the problem of good and evil in his fiction. By equating good with that side of the conflict on other levels that he favors, and evil with the opposite side, Cooper really cancelled the metaphysical aspects of the problem. The metaphysical ordering of the universe proceeds directly from his ordering on the lower levels rather than vice versa. And in different ways this is also true of Hawthorne and James. For Hawthorne, evil springs from an incorrect relation with the "inner sphere" of reality, both in oneself and in others. But the integrity of one's relation to this area of reality is guaranteed only by maintaining the most delicate adjustments with society, which are themselves dependent on the way one resolves the political and social tensions of American experience. The metaphysical ordering of James's universe is more difficult to analyze, but it appears to have been fundamentally pragmatic. One constructed a universe of good or evil from the truth or falseness of one's perceptions and relationships, and that moral universe was finally validated or rejected by the *process* of events.[2] It is

[2] I have discussed this in *The Complex Fate*, pp. 79-113 and 145-9.

easy to see how, in all three cases, the problems naturally raised by the
rift in American experience would ultimately issue in certain moral
positions that implied a metaphysic, and a certain predictable grouping
of good and evil. If we except Calvinism which, as an active theology,
had already given way before the growing popularity of Transcendentalism at the time Hawthorne began to write, America inherited no
great theological system with which to order experience. To some extent,
the structural tensions we have considered here were a substitute. They
raised certain recurrent and fundamental questions, and the questions
themselves moulded the answers. We should not be surprised, then, to
find certain basic elements in common among Cooper, Hawthorne, and
James, when they come to treat such a problem as that of good and evil,
since they frequently arrive at their conclusions by way of certain common
questions. Making allowances always for the Christian orthodoxy in
Cooper which his Anglicanism dictated, we find that all three are primarily interested in good and evil as it affects men living in society and
as it enriches or degrades their relations with other human beings. The
problem of eternal sanctions never really bothers any of them very much.
But Melville's concern was metaphysically more pure.

Apart from his actual works we do not know very much about the state
of Melville's mind, and in attributing to him a profound disillusionment
with American democracy I am looking ahead to that appalling picture
of the American mind and heart he has given us in *The Confidence-Man*.
It is in this book that his despair, though so much more ferocious and
intense than John Quincy Adams's, takes on certain characteristics of the
elder man's disillusionment. Melville was not a political writer in the
sense that Cooper was, but the profound disillusionment that fills his
later books strikes one as being, partly at least, political in character.
The rift in American experience, which Cooper, Hawthorne, and James
dealt with pragmatically, was approached more directly by Melville, who,
undercutting these proximate tensions, struck at the metaphysical heart
of the dilemma. Yet, paradoxically, what finally confronted him was not a
polarity between good and evil, corresponding to the polarity of the
others' tensions, but a tragic confusion in which good and evil were
indistinguishable. As for the elder Adams, so for Melville—the very
texture of the American universe revealed the way it had been betrayed
by God. Democracy existed only in ruthless competition, and God, who
alone might have redeemed it, was unequal to the task: that, if anything,
seems to be the meaning of the final chapter of *The Confidence-Man*.

But before that stage had been reached, Melville made a tremendous
effort, in *Moby-Dick*, to introduce order into his moral universe, and to
establish a polarity between good and evil without which he could not
give form either to his experience or to his art. In terms of this one book
he succeeded magnificently; but in *Pierre* and *The Confidence-Man* the
distinction he had made in his great masterpiece could not be sustained,

and a pursuit of the knowledge of good and evil was replaced by a suffocating sense of the ambiguity which he formally and cynically seemed to formulate and preach as the ultimate knowable moral truth. In other words, moral action (which is to say, *human* action) became an impossibility. With no metaphysical poles of good and evil, and no dialectical pattern on the pragmatic levels of life to guide them, Melville's heroes became incapable of development or progression. They became the passive victims of their situation in life, trapped in the endless unfolding of moral ambiguities whose total significance was to drain all possible meaning from life. Reality which is conceived as endlessly ambiguous, never coming to rest in any certainty, is the negation of form. Because it is everything, it can be determined as nothing specifically. Such a reality cannot be interpreted as an action in that sense in which we predicated it of Cooper. It is, at most, a commotion that must sooner or later collapse into stasis through sheer exhaustion. I shall speak of this phase of Melville, later, but first I wish to discuss *Moby-Dick* from that point of view I have already suggested—as his single but heroic attempt to distinguish good from evil: his single attempt, that is, if we disregard *Billy Budd,* which seems to me, at best, a very partial recovery after the collapse following *Moby-Dick,* and a rather uninteresting recovery at that.

II

The magnitude and complexity of *Moby-Dick* is discouraging. There is so much to say that if one were to say all, even of the little oneself has to say, emphasis would be lost and accent blurred. Read, one after the other, what any three or four critics say of *Moby-Dick:* take, for example, Richard Chase, Newton Arvin, William Sedgwick, Lewis Mumford, and Lawrance Thompson—the result is painfully indigestible, both in the mind and in the emotional response one brings to Melville, which is not to say anything to the discredit of these critics. Where the possibilities of exegesis are so vast, the result must inevitably be a loss of salience. I begin in this fashion, not only by way of apology for resorting to an exegetical approach myself, but in particular to mark out the limits of my interest in the following discussion, which will be concerned *only* with Melville's attempt to distingush between good and evil, and to establish that polarity in a universe in which it seemed to him in radical danger of dissolving.

In a recent book on Melville, *Melville's Quarrel with God,* Mr. Lawrance Thompson has undertaken to cast Melville in the role of Godhater. His position will provide a convenient foil for presenting its opposite. In *Moby-Dick* Melville is not attacking God; he is attempting to rescue the idea of the good, to push back from his darkening consciousness that instinctive reaction of the disillusioned American: hatred of creation itself. A large part of Mr. Thompson's argument is based on

Melville's intense dislike of the Dutch Reformed Church in which he grew up, and a good many of the insults against Christianity that Mr. Thompson uncovers are delivered at the level of the Calvinism preached by that bleak institution. The trouble with using Melville's attitude to that form of Calvinism as a touchstone by which to gauge his attitude to religion generally is simply that one is compelled to simplify disastrously.

Early in his discussion of *Moby-Dick* Mr. Thompson takes up the question of Ahab's name, which derives from the wicked King of Israel in the First Book of Kings. This is a crucial problem in any interpretation of *Moby-Dick*, for it helps us guard against that romantic exaltation of Ahab which has resulted in missing Melville's point. A just appreciation of Melville's reasons for choosing this name, among all others, for his monomaniac captain, will reveal a great deal about his creative intentions. Mr. Thompson, in conformity with his general argument, sees in Melville's choice an instance of his habit of beguiling Christian readers:

> But there is one other correlation, far more interesting, between these two Ahabs. Each of them is seduced to his death by a prophet, and Captain Ahab's misleading prophet is Fedallah. . . . Consider, however, the hint in First Kings as to how it happened that King Ahab was similarly victimized: "I saw the Lord sitting on his throne, and all the host of heaven standing by him, on his right hand and the left. And the Lord said, Who shall persuade Ahab, that he may go up and fall at Ramoth-gilead? . . . And there came forth a spirit, and stood before the Lord, and said, I will persuade him. And the Lord said unto him, Wherewith? And he said, I will go forth, and I will be a lying spirit in the mouth of all his prophets. And the Lord said, Thou shalt persuade him, and prevail also: go forth and do so."
>
> For Melville's anti-Christian purposes, that passage lends itself nicely to a correlated series of insinuations that God is a malicious double-crosser, a deceiver, who is not above employing a "lying spirit" . . . to lead a man to his death. . . .[3]

Mr. Thompson's reading of the twenty-second chapter of First Kings is so unusual that one's best alternative, in commenting on it, is to digress for several paragraphs in the role of Biblical commentator. The meaning of *Moby-Dick* is, I think, in deep accord with a somewhat less "sinister" reading of the scriptural chapter.

It may be recalled that as the chapter opens, King Jehosophat has arrived from Judah on a social visit to King Ahab of Israel. During an early conversation, Ahab raises the question of Ramoth-gilead, formerly a tributary city of his in the north, but for some time since, by the power of possession, in the hands of the King of Syria. Ahab wants it back, and persuades Jehosophat to assist him in a military expedition. Being more devout than Ahab, Jehosophat insists that the prophets be officially consulted to insure that Jehovah's blessing rest on the undertak-

[3] Lawrance Thompson, *Melville's Quarrel with God* (Princeton, 1952, p. 153.)

ing. So at Jehosophat's insistence, Ahab summoned four hundred prophets
—that is to say, four hundred of the clergy of the Established Church—
to appear and prophesy before them in a public place. Two thrones were
erected, and at the appointed time the two Kings in full royal regalia
took their places. The four hundred prophets, passing before them,
prophesied great success for their arms. One of them went so far as to wear
iron horns to suggest the way in which Ahab would crush his enemies. It
is perfectly clear from the chapter as a whole that they were not unaware
of the private expediency of their tack. In fact, ever since their day the
clergies of most countries have not found it difficult to prophesy glory for
the arms of their temporal sovereigns. But apparently Jehosophat was
not deceived, for turning to King Ahab, he asked: "Is there not here a
prophet of the Lord besides, that we might enquire of him?" Why, yes:
Ahab admitted that there was, but he never had anything agreeable to
say. But Jehosophat would not be put off, and so Ahab had to send a
messenger to summon the prophet Micaiah. But it is clear that he in-
structed his messenger to have a private talk with Micaiah, for coming
before him the messenger said: "Behold now, the words of the prophets
declare good unto the King with one mouth; let thy word, I pray thee,
be like the word of one of them, and speak that which is good." It was,
as who should say, an order; and as an obedient subject of his temporal
ruler, Micaiah obeyed. But Ahab understood well enough the way in
which he had sealed the lips of his prophet. It is intriguing to speculate
what compulsive drive led him to blurt out at the crucial moment, just
when Micaiah had prophesied good as the King had commanded him to
do through the messenger: "How many times shall I adjure thee that thou
tell me nothing but that which is true in the name of the Lord?" Nothing
could be clearer than that this is an implicit confession that he hadn't
believed the lying four hundred prophets in the first place, being so aware
of the way he had projected his royal will into their servility. Being thus
adjured to speak, not in the name of his King but of his God, Micaiah
prophesied the defeat of Ahab's army, and his death. Ahab's response to
this, apart from putting Micaiah into prison, was to turn to Jehosophat
and enquire: Didn't I tell you he would only speak evil about me? It is
the perfect picture of a man who will not admit a truth that he knows
to be true. It is, then, at this point, before being led away to jail for
having prophesied truly, that Micaiah turns to Ahab and speaks that
passage about the "lying spirit" and the four hundred prophets leading
Ahab to destruction—the passage that leads Mr. Thompson to speak of
God as a malicious double-crosser, at least for the purposes of his critical
argument. It is a little difficult to see how Mr. Thompson's reading can
be accepted as plausible at any level of interpretation. Mr. Thompson has
radically criticized the immaturity of meaning with which Melville invested Captain Ahab. Actually, Melville was as aware of the moral limitations of Ahab as Mr. Thompson, and a proof of it is that he chose the

name Ahab for very different reasons than those Mr. Thompson attributes
to him.

What, in fact, did Melville see in the Biblical King? So far from being
a victim, King Ahab is one of the most petulant self-asserters among
Israel's rulers. His God-defiance never really got above the level of a
foot-stamping "I won't!" Ahab didn't have a great will, but he had a
leech-like will. Once he had fastened it to a purpose it was a little difficult
to disengage it. With a blue-print of his own destruction in his hand he
deliberately followed it to the last line and letter. He is one of the most
remarkable delineations of a perverse will in sacred or profane literature,
and what we see is not a Titan but a weakling. Melville's Ahab is certainly not a weakling in the usual sense—but then the King was never
more typical than when he insisted on going to war with the knowledge
that he would be killed, and much of his army also. This, I think, was
what influenced Melville in First Kings, chapter twenty-two. The flaw
in the King and the Captain is identical.

But Melville might, conceivably, have found other congenial elements
in the Biblical passage. The persons in the chapter are operating under
two distinct ideas of God. There is the true God of Micaiah, and the
false God of the prophets—yet he is ostensibly the same. Actually, the
verses which Mr. Thompson quotes with such dark designs, so far from
representing God as a malicious double-crosser and deceiver, are a divine
satire on the time-serving prophets, and if one wishes to believe that Melville connected them in his imagination with the clergy of the Dutch
Reformed Church (though Mr. Thompson doesn't make this point) I see
no objection to doing so. It at any rate suggests what ample scope Melville
might have found in First Kings for ecclesiastical satire and censure without the necessity of shaking his fist in God's face, or proclaiming that the
universe was essentially evil.

Another scriptural correspondence, also made in the interests of a God-
hating Melville, seems equally unfortunate—at least in the way Mr.
Thompson interprets it, for the correspondence itself is undeniable. Melville, according to this argument, hated God because God is the creator of
evil as well as good, and Mr. Thompson argues that the White Whale is
essentially a symbol of evil to Melville, though not an abstract, but a very
specific, theological kind of evil that corrupts the universe. One of the
great chapters of *Moby-Dick* is the one in which Starbuck's whaling boat
harpoons an old bull whale, crippled and enfeebled by age. The chapter
is moving because of the powerfully evoked pity—a pity that exists at a
much higher level of the imagination than one of A.S.P.C.A. decency.
The scriptural correspondence of which I spoke a moment ago is the
one which Mr. Thompson draws between the imagery of this chapter,
describing the sufferings of the harpooned old whale, and the forty-first
chapter of Job, in which Jehovah describes the impregnable attributes of
Leviathan, thereby, as it were, taunting the afflicted man. According to Mr.

Thompson, Melville's chapter is built up of concealed sarcasms at God's expense—a case of taunting the Taunter, dismembering the Dismemberer. The correspondence is there, but this reading of it promotes a sad falling off in Melville. Prefiguring the sufferings of Christ, the Psalmist cried: "They have pierced my hands and feet, they have numbered all my bones." This seems a better commentary on those chapters in *Moby-Dick* in which we are presented with lengthy commentaries on the dismembering of the whales than the charge that Melville is insulting God thereby. Read from this point of view, we have in the image of the suffering Leviathan not only an image of the suffering God, but simultaneously the agonized whale, as a magnificent image of created nature, reveals the awful wrack in that creation which men themselves cause.

If the image of Leviathan can, at one level, be interpreted as the image of the suffering God, we would expect to find in the record of his afflictions some allusions to Christ. And I think we do. I would cite as a single instance at this point the passage which Mr. Thompson quotes as an example of Melville's concealed jibing against God—a passage which describes a harpooned whale attached by lines to three whaling-boats from the *Pequod:*

> Seems it credible that by three such thin threads the great Leviathan was suspended like the big weight to an eight day clock. Suspended? and to what? To three bits of board. Is this the creature of whom it was once so triumphantly said—"Canst thou fill his skin with barbed irons? or his head with fish-spears? The sword of him that layeth at him cannot hold, the spear, the dart, nor the habergeon: he esteemeth iron as straw; the arrow cannot make him flee; darts are counted as stubble; he laugheth at the shaking of a spear!" This the creature? this he? Oh! that unfulfilments should follow the prophets. For with the strength of a thousand thighs in his tail, Leviathan had run his head under the mountains of the sea, to hide him from the *Pequod*'s fishspears.

As one returns to this chapter with the whole of *Moby-Dick* in mind, I think it not unreasonable to see something reminiscent of the three arms of the cross from which Christ hung in those three bits of wood from which Leviathan is suspended. "Oh! that unfulfilments should follow the prophets!" It seems probable to me that this is a rhetorical exclamation calling attention to the fact that the old prophecies have indeed been fulfilled. The tormented Leviathan, running his head under the mountains of the sea, recalls Psalm 69, which is commonly accepted as prefiguring the sufferings of Christ and the malice of his persecutors:

> Save me, O God; for the waters are come in unto my soul.
> I sink in deep mire, where there is no standing: I am come into deep waters, where the floods overflow me.
> I am weary of my crying: my throat is dried: mine eyes fail while I wait for my God. . . .

Deliver me out of the mire, and let me not sink: let me be delivered from
them that hate me and out of the deep waters.
Let not the waterflood overflow me, neither let the deep swallow me up,
and let not the pit shut her mouth upon me.

The connection is at least not as tenuous as some Mr. Thompson
proposes. And one might, to sustain the spirit of the counter-argument,
surmise that since Christ was pierced by a spear, and since the Fish was
an early symbol of Christ, it is possible that Melville's reference to the
Pequod's fish-spears is, most deeply, at the expense of Ahab and his crew
rather than at the expense of God. I am trying here to point to the
function that this idea of the suffering Leviathan performs in the novel.
It is a symbol in which Melville was not only able to express his growing
horror of evil in the universe, but his positive affirmation of an in-
destructible good. It is a deeply tragic symbol redeemed by a yet profounder religious intuition.

D. H. Lawrence in an early essay on Melville said that probably
Melville himself did not know what the White Whale meant.[4] But
Lawrence did not mean that the White Whale was a vague symbol that
could mean everything or nothing. He only meant that what it actively
realized in itself—realized with the complexity and mystery of a living
thing—was incapable of being neatly itemized or systematized. The White
Whale is Melville's profoundest intuition into the nature of creation,
and it is an intuition in which God and nature are simultaneously present
and commenting on each other.

The evil of the world filled Melville with horror, and there is little
doubt that because of that horror a Manichean element colours his
sensibility. Many critics before Mr. Thompson have seen in the White
Whale a symbol of God, and some of them have viewed that God as
predominantly an evil one. And yet it seems to me that Melville makes
some clear distinctions which, if not necessarily pointing towards a rig-
orously orthodox Christian God, exonerate the White Whale from that
burden of malignancy that Ahab's own perverse will has projected into
his image. I would point particularly to Chapter LIX entitled "Squid."
It is one of the most imaginatively terrifying chapters in the novel, and
also one of the most beautifully written. On a beautiful blue morning
"when the slippered waves whispered together as they softly ran on"—
just such a morning as would banish any thought of evil from the mind
—the crew of the *Pequod* is given a vision of pure evil, and at first they
mistake it for the White Whale. From his lookout post on the mainmast,
Daggoo, the harpooner, sights a huge rolling mass of white in the sea
ahead, and cries out to those below, "The White Whale, the White
Whale!"

[4] D. H. Lawrence, *Studies in Classic American Literature* (London, 1937) (Pocket
Edition), 145.

Instantly four boats and their crews are lowered in pursuit, but as they approach the floating mass it is not Moby-Dick they see:

> Soon it went down, and while, with oars suspended, we were waiting its reappearance, lo! in the same spot where it sank, once more it slowly rose. Almost forgetting for the moment all thoughts of Moby-Dick, we now gazed at the most wondrous phenomenon which the secret seas have hitherto revealed to mankind. A vast pulpy mass, furlongs in length and breadth, of a glancing cream colour, lay floating on the water, innumerable long arms radiating from its centre, and curling and twisting like a nest of anacondas, as if blindly to catch at any hapless object within reach. No perceptible face or front did it have; no conceivable token of either sensation or instinct; but undulated there on the billows, an unearthly, formless, chance-like apparition of life.

In Zoroastrianism, with which Melville, to some extent at least, was familiar, the world is divided between a good and an evil principle, and they are twin brothers. In the end the good will triumph, but their conflict is for the length of time. The giant Squid was surely meant by Melville for his symbol of evil. It is, one would expect, evil in a Manichean rather than in a Christian sense, but the Squid's horrid anaconda arms invoke the Christian serpent; and they also give an added meaning to a later reference to Captain Ahab as an anaconda of an old man— for he also has blindly caught at the hapless members of his crew, and carried them down to destruction. But what is most significant is the resemblance of this symbol of evil, when viewed at a little distance, to the White Whale. They are, as one might say, twin brothers. They resemble each other most in their whiteness and their facelessness, and both of these attributes signify the inscrutability of the divided yet impenetrable universe in which it is so difficult to distinguish good from evil. And as between the twin brothers of Zoroastrianism, so between the White Whale and the White Squid there is eternal enmity:

> . . . the spermaceti whale obtains his food in unknown zones below the surface; and only by inference is it that anyone can tell of what, precisely, that food consists. At times, when closely pursued, he will disgorge what are supposed to be the detached arms of the squid; some of them thus exhibited exceeding twenty and thirty feet in length. They fancy that the monster to which these arms belonged ordinarily clings by them to the bed of the ocean; and that the sperm whale, unlike other species, is supplied with teeth in order to attack it.

One of the most striking threads of imagery in *Moby-Dick* is the 'feeding' imagery. What is fed upon becomes assimilated into the body of the feeder, and this idea sounds throughout *Moby-Dick* as a deep and ominous note of resonance. In an oddly subterranean way it keeps the perception bubbling that, through all this mutual devouring, good and evil become inextricably confused with each other, assimilated into each other's being until it is impossible to distinguish between them. In its vulture or sharkish aspect, which reflects Melville's shocked recoil from the world he saw, it comes to a head in the devastating chapter called "Shark Massacre," in which the sharks

> . . . viciously snapped, not only at each other's disbowelments, but like flexible bows, bent around and bit their own, till those entrails seemed swallowed over and over again by the same mouth, to be oppositely voided by the gaping wound.

It is almost like *Maldoror*; but Melville, in the great orgy of cannibalism and inter-feeding that goes on throughout the novel, is searching for some sacramental essence of good that persists through all devourings.

Significant from this point of view is the opening sentence of Chapter LXV where the second mate, Stubb, has had the cook prepare a whale steak for him:

> That mortal man should feed upon the creature that feeds his lamp, and, like Stubb, eat him by his own light, as you may say; this seems so outlandish a thing that one must needs go a little into the history and philosophy of it.

If the White Whale is a symbol of God, Melville's recurrent references to the light that is derived from his broken body are certainly important, and the metaphysical image of Stubb eating the whale by its own light is a sarcasm, not at God's expense, but at the expense of a hypocritical and savage world that, like the false four hundred prophets of King Ahab, uses the light of God for its own profit while lacerating the body of truth. The meaning of this image is enriched in what follows, for as Stubb eats the whale steak in his cabin, a ravenous shoal of sharks devour the body of the murdered whale that is tied to the side of the *Pequod*. When Stubb forces the old negro cook to preach a sermon to the sharks to quiet them down, before he goes onto the deck Stubb says to him: " 'Here, take this lantern,' snatching one from the sideboard: 'now, then, go and preach to them.' " So the old cook preaches over the ship's side to the sharks by the light of the whale they are devouring. No doubt it is an indictment of the perversions of Christianity in the world. But it is Christianity *in the world*; and it is the light of God, one might say by way of gloss, that reveals the horrors.

So far I may have seemed inconclusive in assuming, in opposition to Mr. Thompson's position, that the image of Leviathan is the symbol of a *good* God, although I have already given a number of reasons for taking such an attitude. The greatest chapter in *Moby-Dick* is Chapter LXXXVII, "The Grand Armada." It is even more important than the chapter on the White Squid for determining what Leviathan meant for Melville. As the voyage of the *Pequod* approaches its end, the ship sails through the straits of Sunda into the China seas, and it is confronted there by an immense aggregation of sperm whales, by what seemed thousands and thousands of them. The look-out first becomes aware of them as a great semicircle of spouting jets, "a continuous chain . . . up playing and sparkling in the noon-day air," and embracing one half of the level horizon. The *Pequod* sets off in pursuit, and the crew soon realizes that the crescent has come full circle, and that they are entirely surrounded by a vast circle of spouting jets—by what, as the chapter progresses, one feels might be called a heavenly host of whales. Three boats are lowered. The one in which Ishmael has his place fastens its harpoon in a whale which, plunging forward, heads into the heart of the great herd, drawing the boat behind it. There is something mystically portentous in the entry of Ishmael's whaling boat into the quiet center of the circling whales:

> . . . at last the jerking harpoon drew out, and the towing whale sideways vanished; then, with the tapering force of his parting momentum, we glided between two whales into the innermost heart of the shoal, as if from some mountain torrent we had slid into a serene valley lake. Here the storms in the roaring glens between the outermost whales, were heard but not felt. In this central expanse the sea presented a smooth satin-like surface. . . . Yes, we were now in that enchanted calm which they say lurks in the heart of every commotion. And still in the outer distance we beheld the tumults of the outer concentric circles, and saw successive pods of whales, eight or ten in each, swiftly going round and round, like multiplied spans of horses in a ring; and so closely shoulder to shoulder that a Titanic circus rider might easily have over-arched the middle ones, and so have gone round on their backs. . . .
>
> Now, inconclusive of the occasional wide intervals between the revolving outer circles, and inconclusive of the spaces between the various pods in any one of those circles, the entire area at this juncture, embraced by the wide multitude, must have contained at least two or three square miles. At any rate . . . spoutings might be discovered from our low boat that seemed playing up almost from the rim of the horizon.

It seems obvious to me that the source (though probably the unconscious source) of this vision of circling whales is Canto XXVIII of the *Paradiso*. We know that Melville's mind was filled with *The Divine Comedy* when he began writing *Pierre* almost immediately after finishing *Moby-Dick*, and at least from 1848, when Melville bought a copy of Cary's Dante, allusions are frequent.[5] The passage in question from *Moby-Dick* seems to me to be indubitably such an allusion. In Canto XXVIII, it will be recalled, Dante, turning from Beatrice, beholds a point of intensest

---

[5] Giovanni Giovanini has remarked in "Melville's *Pierre* and Dante's *Inferno*" (*PMLA*, March, 1949, p. 70) that "Melville, like many of his contemporaries, apparently did not extend his reading of Dante beyond the *Inferno*." But the reason for such a surmise is merely that no allusions to the *Purgatorio* and *Paradiso* have been recognized.

light around which spin the nine concentric circles of the angelic intelli-
gences—great wheels of fire which, as they revolve, shoot forth sparkles.
Visually, the circles of whales present a startlingly similar image to the
imagination as their water-spouts catch the light of the sun in great concentric rings that are enclosed by the horizon only. The visual similarity is
enhanced by the water imagery in which Dante describes the revolving
angelic orders. Thus, he compares them to the luminous ring of vapor
that sometimes surrounds the moon; and, again, he compares the reach of
the circles with the rainbow's arc.

Beatrice, explaining to Dante the center of intense light about which
the concentric circles eternally revolve, says: "From that point doth hang
heaven and all nature." Now the question is, what did the *Pequod*'s
whaling boat, when it broke through the living circles into the enchanted
calm, find there? It is here that Melville's writing achieved a beauty that
he never surpassed, or equalled:

> But far beneath this wondrous world upon the surface, another and still
> stranger world met our eyes as we gazed over the side. For, suspended in
> those watery vaults, floated the forms of the nursing mothers of the whales,
> and those that by their enormous girth seemed shortly to become mothers.
> The lake, as I have hinted, was to a considerable depth exceedingly trans-
> parent; and as human infants while suckling will calmly and fixedly gaze
> away from the breast, as if leading two different lives at the time; and while
> yet drawing mortal nourishment, be still spiritually feeding on some un-
> earthly reminiscence;—even so did the young of these whales seem looking
> up towards us, as if we were but a bit of Gulf-weed in their new-born sight.
> Floating on their sides, the mothers also seemed quietly eyeing us. One of
> these little infants that from certain queer tokens seemed hardly a day old,
> might have measured some fourteen feet in length and some six feet in girth.
> He was a little frisky; though as yet his body seemed scarce yet recovered
> from that irksome position it had so lately occupied in the maternal reticule;
> where, tail to head, and all ready for the final spring, the unborn whale lies
> bent like a Tartar's bow. The delicate side-fins, and the palms of his flukes
> still freshly retained the plaited crumpled appearance of a baby's ears newly
> arrived from foreign parts.

What we have here is a vision of the world in its primal innocence, an
image of the life principle presented in an intuition so profound that it
seems a part of God's being. The whale mother and her beautiful infant,
still attached by the umbilical cord, is an image as tender and reverent,
essentially as religious, as a Della Robbia Madonna and Child. The sheer
loveliness of that "enchanted calm" into which the whaling boat intrudes
is such that, leaning over its side and looking down into the transparent
depths wherein is reflected one of the most astonishing images of the
purity and mystery of life ever conceived by an artist—the sheer loveliness
of it is such that we almost say with Beatrice: From this point hangs
heaven and all nature.

Leviathan is not the tyrant, and Melville would leave us in no doubt. Into this paradisal context Melville, with the effect of almost unbearable shock, unexpectedly reintroduces his savage "feeding" imagery. Describing the breasts of the nursing whales he says: "When by chance these precious parts in a nursing whale are cut by the hunter's lance, the mother's pouring milk and blood rivallingly discolour the sea for rods. The milk is very sweet and rich; it has been tasted by man; it might do well with strawberries." It is not only that the twin images of the milk and blood, churned together in the sea, open into terrible perspectives for the imagination that dwells on them—there is also a kind of horrible-sweet facetiousness in the tone, and suddenly one realizes why the mediaeval mysteries presented Herod as a comic figure. Melville is here operating at that depth and height of the imagination.

In what I have just said of the influence of Dante I have had no intention of suggesting that Melville is trying to use Leviathan as a kind of symbol for the Beatific Vision—but the emotional impact of Dante's Canto on Melville clearly seems to be an important element in the wonderful achievement represented by "The Grand Armada." And the significance of this for determining what Leviathan meant for Melville when he wrote *Moby-Dick* can hardly, I think, be exaggerated. The image of God that Leviathan symbolizes is an image, certainly not beyond, but *outside* a *specific* theology. It represents a religious intuition of life itself in some of its most basic and positive affirmations. At the same time, it is essentially a tragic intuition, and Leviathan is a suffering God. If the image is not Christian, it is filled with Christian overtones, and they lend Leviathan a large part of his evocativeness. It is hardly too much to say that if we have seen Leviathan dismembered and his bones numbered by his enemies, we see him rise again after three days in Moby-Dick's final victory over the *Pequod* at the end of the third day's chase.

Captain Ahab is the focus of attention in the novel, and as the symbolic embodiment of the representative nineteenth century American the fate that overtakes him is an indication of Melville's own reaction to the American world of his day. There is no need here to argue this representative quality in Ahab. Nearly all critics are agreed on it.[6] But perhaps it is worthwhile remarking that in nothing is Ahab more representative (I use "representative," of course, in this context not to indicate the average but the paradigmatic) than in the transition he illustrates between the American democratic acceptance of creation, and hatred of that creation. Ahab is sometimes mistakenly identified with Melville's view-

---

[6] For example, H. B. Parkes, *The American People* (London, 1949), p. 202: "In Melville's Ahab the drive of the American will is carried to its furthermost limits"; Richard Chase, *Herman Melville* (New York, 1949), p. 101: "Ahab is the epic transmutation of the American free enterpriser"; Newton Arvin, *Herman Melville* (New York, 1950), p. 176: "He is modern man, and particularly American man, in his role as 'free' and 'independent' individual. . . ."

point in the novel, and, indeed, to some extent he represents a part of Melville's mind; and a much larger part if we consider the Melville of a year or so later. But it is Ishmael with whom we must identify Melville's viewpoint in the end; and this identification is essential if we are to discover a positive and coherent form in *Moby-Dick*.

Leviathan, I have argued, represents the *good* in Melville's universe, but through Ahab's and Ishmael's eyes we are given two different visions of him. Thus, the ambiguity that, in *Pierre*, will be rooted in the nature of reality itself, is, in *Moby-Dick*, restricted to the point of view. But beyond that point of view we sense a universe of objective values in which moral action and direction are still possibilities, though difficult to achieve. That Ishmael *does* achieve them constitutes the formal justification of the novel. Ishmael's solitary survival at the end of the novel is, in a sense, the validation of his vision; and it represents Melville's momentary triumph in having introduced an element of moral order into his universe, in having re-established, in the face of his growing doubts, the polarity of good and evil. I wish to consider here, as briefly as I may, the meaning of Ishmael's point of view, as opposed to Ahab's which usually gets most of the attention. For it is through Ishmael that Melville makes his positive affirmation.

The experiences in which Ishmael participates on the *Pequod* are, in a sense, his. They constitute a kind of passion play for him from which he is almost literally resurrected in the Epilogue into new life.[7] The opening paragraph indicates the problem that faces Ishmael, and to which the action of the novel brings a cosmic solution:

> Whenever I find myself growing grim about the mouth; whenever it is a damp drizzly November in my soul; whenever I find myself involuntarily pausing before coffin warehouses, and bringing up the rear of every funeral I meet; and especially whenever my hypos get such an upper hand of me, that it requires a strong moral principle to prevent me from deliberately stepping into the street, and methodically knocking people's hats off—then, I account it high time to get to sea as soon as I can.

Though so casually expressed, Ishmael's malaise as described here represents the essence of that despair, though then greatly exaggerated, which overtook Melville in *Pierre* and *The Confidence-Man*. But in *Moby-Dick* there will be, as the opening paragraph indicates, no submission to it, but a vigorous resistance. The sea is the source of life in the world, and it is to the sea that Ishmael returns whenever he feels symptoms of this depression. Ishmael, then, hardly less than Ahab may be said to do, sets out on the voyage on a quest, but it is a different quest from Ahab's. It is a quest for spiritual health, a desire to enter into a new and deeper

---

[7] The role of Ishmael and the positive values represented by Queequeg have recently received excellent treatment in *Ishmael* by James Baird (Baltimore, 1956).

harmony with creation. Ishmael accepts the mystery of creation—particularly as embodied in Leviathan—which Ahab does not. Ishmael's attitude towards Moby-Dick is one of respectful reverence and wonder, and although from time to time during the course of the *Pequod*'s voyage Ishmael comes under the influence of Ahab's intellectual domination, such occasions are momentary.

From the very beginning, Moby-Dick is not a symbol of evil to Ishmael, but a magnificent symbol of creation itself. Creation is not a pasteboard mask for Ishmael, to be broken through in some excess of spiritual pride, as it was for Ahab, whose attempt to penetrate visible creation, not through love but hatred, could only end in a material vision. The measure of Ishmael's contrast in this respect is given in the following passage. Ishmael is paying a visit to the whaling chapel in New Bedford:

> "Methinks that in looking at things spiritual, we are too much like oysters observing the sun through water, and thinking that thick water the thinnest air. In fact, take my body who will, take it, I say, it is not me. And therefore three cheers for Nantucket; and come a stove boat and stove my body when they will, for stave my soul Jove himself cannot."

We are sometimes inclined to lose sight of the elementary fact that the whole complex movement of *Moby-Dick* originates in Ahab's inability to resign himself, after Ishmael's fashion as indicated here, to the loss of a leg. Ahab is guilty of that most democratic of sins—of denying hierarchy between the body and soul, eternal and temporal values. He can proceed from a severed limb to a condemned and guilty universe with the greatest of ease. We are back at John Quincy Adams once again, who discovered in Eli Whitney's cotton gin God's great betrayal of the world. Essentially, democracy is the denial of degree, and, by implication, of limit also. But the very principle of form is boundary and limitation. Thus, the democratic aspiration that would deny the hieratic element in creation ends in a monstrous negation. It is the very essence of formlessness.

The degrees of knowledge are the most important of all for they most directly reflect the degrees of order and value in the spiritual world. It is an important element in Ahab's comprehensive significance that, in Chapter CXVIII, "The Quadrant," he symbolically destroys the instrument of knowledge by which he should determine his location—his place in creation, as it were:

> Then gazing at his quadrant, and handling, one after the other, its numerous cabalistical contrivances, he pondered again, and muttered: "Foolish toy! babies' plaything of haughty Admirals, and Commodores, and Captains; the world brags of thee, of thy cunning and might; but what after all canst thou do, but tell the poor, pitiful point, where thou thyself happenst to be on this wide planet, and the hand that holds thee: no! not a jot more!"

The manner in which the official hierarchy of the navy is merged here with the ordered knowledge for which the quadrant stands, is worth noting. The importance of this chapter is generally recognized; but there is still reason to insist that it is not science as such that Ahab is rejecting here. Rather, it is the idea of degree. It is precisely Ahab's *place* in the universe which he does not wish, indeed refuses, to know. And it is only his *place* that the quadrant can tell, his place with reference to the sun. Thus, the paradox of the democratic dogma that refuses to recognize anything above it exists in its being forced back on the degrees below: "Curse thee, thou quadrant! . . . no longer will I guide my earthly way by thee; the level ship's compass, and the level dead-reckoning, by log and by line; *these* shall conduct me, and show me my place on the sea." Once the ordered framework that controlled and directed the political version of John Adams, Cooper, and even of Jefferson, is rejected, we are confronted by a breed of nineteenth century Titans whose offspring is ultimately degraded to the "common man" of the twentieth century.

Ahab's attitude is the antithesis of life because it represents a rejection of creation. The analysis of this attitude forms the main substance of the novel, but its great formal achievement exists in the beautiful way that Melville placed the action in an evaluative perspective so that its final effect is one of positive affirmation. He achieved this in two ways. First, he built up the symbol of Leviathan, layer on layer, so that it became one of the most magnificent images in the language of the positive aspects of creation. Leviathan, especially in his greatest role of the White Whale, is the affirmation of all that Ahab denies. The impact of this recognition on the imagination is the greater because, if Melville leads one towards it irresistibly, we yet make the discovery in the midst of all the gargantuaι suffering of the whaling ground. We learn the triumph of life that tłe White Whale represents only because we come to it through such seas of death. This is the most deeply Christian note that Melville ever strikes.

Secondly, Melville achieved the evaluative perspective for the action of *Moby-Dick* through his use of Ishmael, and particularly by means of his "resurrection" in the Epilogue. Ishmael, as I said, enrolls in the crew because he himself wishes to recover spiritual health. The long voyage that is finally brought to its disastrous termination in the China Seas, to repeat an earlier remark, is a kind of long drawn out passion play for Ishmael, ending in his symbolical "resurrection," from which he returns to life, as we may surmise, cured of that spiritual malady from which we see him suffering in the first chapter of the book.

The relevant portions of the novel which deal with this symbolic resurrection are Chapter CX, and the Epilogue. It will be recalled that Ishmael's cannibal friend Queequeg is for a time so grievously afflicted with fever during the course of the voyage that his life is despaired of. As he seems to be dying, the ship's carpenter is asked to construct a coffin for him. But after the coffin is built, Queequeg recovers. The coffin itself has been strongly constructed, and Queequeg decides to use it for a sea chest, in his leisure moments covering the lid of it with a fancy design:

> With a wild whimsiness, he now used his coffin for a sea-chest; and emptying into it his canvas bag of clothes, set them in order there. Many spare hours he spent, in carving the lid with all manner of grotesque figures and drawings; and it seemed that hereby he was striving, in his rude way, to copy parts of the twisted tattooing on his body. And this tattooing had been a work of a departed prophet and seer of his island, who, by those hieroglyphic marks, had written out on his body a complete theory of the heavens and the earth, and a mystical treatise on the art of attaining truth; so that Queequeg in his own proper person was a riddle to unfold; a wondrous work in one volume; but whose mysteries not even himself could read, though his own live heart beat against them; and these mysteries were therefore destined in the end to moulder away with the living parchment whereon they were inscribed, and so be unsolved to the last.

Somewhat later in the novel it is discovered that the lifebuoys on the *Pequod,* which are sealed casks, have been warped by the sun so as to be useless. It occurs to Queequeg that his coffin might, if the lid were sealed on, substitute admirably for the ruined buoys, and so the coffin takes its place on the ship as a life-preserver. No more is heard of it until the Epilogue. After the *Pequod* has been rammed by Moby-Dick and has disappeared under the sea, Ishmael is saved by its means, and in such a manner as to make it almost appear, when he is picked up by the *Rachel,* as if he had been resurrected from his own coffin. And the coffin itself is a very special one. It belonged to his friend Queequeg, one of the noblest savages in literature—a primitive prince whose whole way of life is based, not on enmity to nature, as with Ahab, but on harmony with nature. And we know from Queequeg's whole life, as Melville gives it to us, that he represents a kind of instinctive charity and adjustment to the world that is the antithesis of Ahab's madness. To recapture the full flavor of Queequeg's moral implications, we have to go back to Chapter X:

> As I sat there in that lonely room; the fire burning low, in that mild stage when, after its first intensity has warmed the air, it then only glows to be looked at; the evening shades and phantoms gathering round the casements, and peering in upon us silent, solitary twain; the storm booming without in solemn swells; I began to be sensible of strange feelings. I felt a melting in me. No more my splintered heart and maddened hand were turned against the wolfish world. This soothing savage had redeemed it. There he sat, his very indifference speaking a nature in which there lurked no civilized hypocrisies, and bland deceits. Wild he was; a very sight of sights to see; yet I began to feel myself mysteriously drawn towards him.

What we have noticed particularly about Ishmael's survival is that it happens, in fact, virtually through Queequeg's agency. By virtue of the carving on the lid which duplicates the tattooing on Queequeg's body, the coffin stands in proxy for the savage himself. And we should remember what the design represented: ". . . a complete theory of the heavens and the earth, and a mystical treatise on the art of attaining truth." Although not obtrusive, this symbolism is nevertheless straightforward and clear. Ahab himself represents hatred of creation—an extremity of madness, symptoms of which Ishmael had begun to show when he took to the sea for a cure. He is saved, or cured, by an acceptance of nature, of the earth and the heavens. This is what the hieroglyphics on Queequeg's coffin lid symbolize, and Ishmael's physical survival by its means stands also for his spiritual recovery.

Moby-Dick is, then, Melville's great attempt to create order in a universe in which a breakdown of the polarity between good and evil is threatened. This threat comes from Ahab, whose hatred of creation is the symptom, or perhaps the consequence, of that democratic disillusionment with the universe I have spoken of—that resentment of the spirit's betrayal of matter, and of God's betrayal of the world. In so far as Melville's own thought is to be equated with any particular person's, it is with Ishmael's. Ishmael represents Melville's resistance against the temptation to follow Ahab which was so powerful for him; he represents Melville's hold on the world of reality and of nature. But as Melville plunged almost immediately into the writing of *Pierre* when he had finished *Moby-Dick,* the sanity and grace that had shaped the earlier of the two books was to vanish for good.

III

I have discussed *Moby-Dick* at some length because it represents a high point of form in the American novel. The structural tensions that Cooper, Hawthorne, and James employed were elevated here to a metaphysical level, and the struggle between good and evil not only became the form of the action, but the very terms themselves were newly carved out of the ambiguous element of the American experience by the creative fiat of the artist. But they were still grounded in an objective moral framework as it has been traditionally understood in the western world. Alexander Cowie perhaps phrased it as well as any when he wrote: "Melville was a sceptic but not by any means an atheist. Like many who question orthodoxy, he did so in order to prepare a place in which to build a faith for himself. Ironically, he was castigated for blasphemy when he was in search for spiritual security." [8] But he proved incapable of sustaining the

---

[8] Alexander Cowie, *The Rise of the American Novel* (American Book Company), p. 398.

elaborately achieved form of *Moby-Dick* in his later work. Mr. Henry A. Murray in his "Introduction" to *Pierre* suggests persuasive reasons for this:

> Wearied and exasperated by the relentless underlying conflict and confounded by the constant inversions of value from positive to negative and negative to positive, the man may finally arrive at a state of virtual paralysis with no capacity for decision, one effect of which is the constant apprehension that everything is almost equally meaningless and worthless—"all objects are seen in a dubious, uncertain, and refracting light . . . the most immemorially admitted maxims of men begin to slide and fluctuate, and finally become wholly inverted." By pursuing the trail of thought so far, an explorer "entirely loses the directing compass of his mind; for arrived at the Pole, to whose barrenness only it points, there, the needle indifferently respects all points of the compass alike." This state of feeling accounts for most of the remaining ambiguities, as well as for the pervasive moral of the book, which is that there is *no* moral; it is impossible for a man to reconcile this world with his own soul, and impossible to make a clean decision for one or for the other; there is evil in the good and good in the evil, gloom in the light and light in the gloom; a step beyond this bitter knowledge carries one to the indifferent thought that good and evil are but "shadows cast from nothing," the mind of man. "It is all a dream—we dream that we dreamed that we dream." [9]

I only wish to glance at *Pierre* . . . here sufficiently to indicate the relaxation of form, the general impression of motionlessness, that occurred after *Moby-Dick*. I am not speaking of conventional, externally imposed form here. From this point of view *Pierre* is more conventional than anything Melville had written so far. Referring to *Pierre*, Arvin writes:

> Nor was he more fortunate in the form he was attempting than in his manner. He had evolved a great and highly idiosyncratic form in *Moby-Dick* —as, in *Redburn* and *White-Jacket* he had moved toward it—and now, as if he were not a master but a disciple and a tyro, he put aside all that he had learned in doing this, denied himself all his most personal resources, and undertook to express himself in a hybrid form that had come to him, quite mistakenly, from a hodge-podge of models. [10]

To revert to a definition of form I used in Chapter IV, form is an action, and action is "the intensified motion of life in which the moral and spiritual faculties of men are no less engaged than their physical selves." The passage from Mr. Murray quoted above ends with a sentence from *Pierre*, and to understand what was happening in Melville, we can

[9] *Pierre*, edited by Henry A. Murray (New York, 1949).
[10] Newton Arvin, *Herman Melville* (New York, 1950), p. 227.

do nothing better than quote the context from which that sentence is taken. It occurs at the close of Book XIX:

> "Thou, Pierre, speakest of Virtue and Vice; life-secluded Isabel knows neither the one nor the other, but by hearsay. What are they in their real selves, Pierre? Tell me first what is Virtue:—begin!"
>
> "If on that point the gods are dumb, shall a pigmy speak? Ask the air!"
>
> "Then Virtue is nothing."
>
> "Not that!"
>
> "Then Vice?"
>
> "Look: a nothing is the substance, it casts one shadow one way, and another the other way; and these two shadows cast from one nothing; these, seems to me, are Virtue and Vice."
>
> "Then why torment thyself so, dearest Pierre?"
>
> "It is the law."
>
> "What?"
>
> "That a nothing should torment a nothing; for I am a nothing. It is all a dream—we dream that we dreamed we dream."

It is clear that all Melville had achieved in *Moby-Dick* is lost here. The polarity he had been at such pains to establish in his masterpiece— a polarity within the field of which moral action could occur without the danger of stasis setting in—gives way before a poisoned ambiguity that undermines the very foundation of reality itself. Pierre is engulfed by a nihilism which, as it proves the destructive element for him, is also the negation of form in the novel in so far as form is defined as the intensified motion of life:

> The old mummy lies buried in cloth on cloth; it takes time to unwrap this Egyptian king. Yet now, forsooth, because Pierre began to see through the first superficiality of the world, he fondly weens he has come to the unlayered substance. But, far as any geologist has yet gone down into the world, it is found to consist of nothing but surface stratified on surface. To its axis, the world being nothing but superinduced superficies. By vast pains we mine into the pyramid; by horrible gropings we come to the central room; with joy we espy the sarcophagus; but we lift the lid—and no body is there!—appallingly vacant as vast is the soul of man!

In such a passage we see the terrifying degree to which reality is drained from appearances. There has always been a tendency for the American to separate appearance and reality. I have discussed this tendency at some length, as it occurs in the works of Henry James, in *The Complex Fate*. But James employed this ambiguity as a positive principle of form, whereas in *Pierre* it is a principle of dissolution. It carries all before it, and the result is catastrophic. The role of the mind in moulding the appearances of reality was fully exhibited in *Moby-Dick* through the conflicting visions of Ahab and Ishmael; but Melville masterfully suggested there the objective existence of a reality beyond appearances. If Ishmael's vision corresponds to reality more nearly than Ahab's, it is a *correspondence*, and not a creation. Leviathan is, in the last word, the validation of Ishmael's vision of creation; that is to say, the whale is not, as Mr. Feidelson might argue, a symbol of a symbol—a complex image that reverberates with ultimate hollowness. It represents reality itself, suggestively constructed on the material plane through the long sequence of cetological chapters and issuing at last, for the imagination, as a principle of metaphysical order in the universe. But in *Pierre*, the mind does not correspond to, it *creates*, its reality, and we are left with almost no sense of an extramental world of things to corroborate the images formed in the mind. Mr. Feidelson's appreciation of the symbolic process, as described in his *Symbolism and American Literature*, can work admirably with second-rate examples of art, and it is only fair to add here that his analysis of *Pierre* (pp. 186-207) is brilliant. He shows, for example, how even the most physical facts and relationships of Pierre's life are, for him at least, not grounded in any objective reality, that he is incapable of distinguishing between the external and the internal, and that for him "the fiction is the thought and the fact" (p. 192). The dream-like movement that this induces, and the insufficiently grounded relations between the characters, defeat the physical action of *Pierre* almost as surely as the moral action is defeated by the pervading ambiguity that cancels all positive directions and motives. Viewed detachedly, this state of moral nihilism could become a successful subject for art. In his great short story, "Bartleby the Scrivener," Melville raised a somewhat similar condition of existence to a level of superb achievement. But, however much Bartleby may represent certain aspects of Melville's own plight and personality,[11] he yet avoided the kind of identification with Bartleby that he succumbed to in *Pierre*. In the story, we have a sense of an objective world with which Bartleby stands in tragic relation; but in *Pierre* the world itself is the tragic emanation of Melville's mind as it comes to a paralyzingly personal focus in Pierre's consciousness. All that is significant in reality is a mood, a cast of mind:

> Say what some poets will, Nature is not so much her own eversweet interpreter, as the mere supplier of that cunning alphabet, whereby selecting and combining as he pleases, each man reads his own peculiar lesson according to his own peculiar mind and mood.

As we know, Melville had never been much concerned at any level with that practical dialectic out of which Cooper, Hawthorne, and James

[11] See, for example, Leo Marx's "Melville's Parable of the Walls," *The Sewanee Review* (Autumn, 1953), pp. 602-27.

evolved the form of their fiction; which is to reaffirm once more that he had little interest in European as opposed to American experience, or in the interplay between them. What we are left with, in the absence of this dialectic, after the struggle with good and evil has subsided, is the terrible emptiness and solitude of the American sensibility, forced back upon itself in utter isolation, with no theology or faith, no sense of intimacy with the European past and present to impart significance to its own dissenting forms, and with a growing distrust of its own democratic credo. As Melville's work grows increasingly sombre, one is reminded of a passage from Santayana's *Reason in Common Sense*.

> An earnestness which is out of proportion to any knowledge or love of real things, which is therefore dark and inward, and thinks itself deeper than the earth's foundations—such an earnestness, until culture turns it into intelligent interests, will naturally breed a new mythology. It will try to place some world of Afrites and shadowy giants behind the constellations, which it finds too distinct or constant to be its companions or supporters; and it will assign itself vague or infinite tasks, for which it is doubtless better equipped than for those the earth now sets before it. . . . All will be a tossing servitude and illiberal mist, where the parts will have no final values and the whole no pertinent direction.[12]

The intellectual seriousness of the several novelists we have been concerned with in the main body of this book is a different thing from the disproportionate earnestness of which Santayana is speaking. The dialectical questions raised by the rift in American experience turned their creative drive towards intelligent interests that shaped the form of the novels they wrote. With them, we remain in a lightened air that is free of obscurantist ambiguities. Boundary or limit is essential to intelligibility and form. This is the lesson that the Old World had to teach the New above all others; and it was through their sense of the European experience that Cooper, Hawthorne, and James avoided that provincial formlessness that overtook Melville after *Moby-Dick*. In *Pierre* Melville wrote:

> Deep, Deep, and still deep and deeper must we go, if we would find out the heart of a man; descending into which is as descending a spiral stair in a shaft, without any end, and where the endlessness is only concealed by the spiralness of the stair and the blackness of the shaft.

It is usual to speak of this as illustrating Melville's interest in the unconscious. Perhaps it does; but the image itself suggests even more powerfully Melville's retreat from the real world. The task that he proposes here with so much earnestness is both vague and infinite in

[12] *The Philosophy of Santayana*, edited by Irwin Edman (New York, 1936), pp. 55-6.

Santayana's sense, and pursued to the end which the image itself proposes—or, to be more accurate, pursued through its endlessness and indetermination—would terminate in a negation of consciousness itself, an attempt to stretch a measurable meaning to infinity, and to escape the limits of the rational and the real. But one can escape from them only into nothingness. . . .

"Benito Cereno"

by Richard Harter Fogle

With the revival of Melville, "Benito Cereno" was placed very high. To Edward O'Brien it was "the noblest short story in American literature,"[1] to John Freeman, "a flaming instance of the author's pure genius."[2] In the opinion of Carl Van Doren, "it equals the best of Conrad in the weight of its drama and the skill of its unfolding."[3] These are judgments of the 1920's; fuller criticism was delayed until the Forties. The two full analyses of "Benito Cereno," by Rosalie Feltenstein and by Stanley T. Williams, agree with the earlier verdict; both are tributes to Melville's artistry. Miss Feltenstein demonstrates "the architectural skill with which the story is constructed," declaring that "there is not one careless, useless, weak, or redundant touch in the whole tale."[4] Professor Williams goes as far, or farther: "Only now are we beginning to realize the perfection of its form and the subtleties of its insights. It is even defensible to prefer 'Benito Cereno' to *Moby-Dick* and *Billy Budd*."[5]

On the other hand, two of Melville's best critics have raised important objections. Although F. O. Matthiessen found the story "one of Melville's most sensitively poised pieces of writing,"[6] he could not accept its symbolism, which "was unfortunate in raising unanswered questions."[7] Still more recently, Newton Arvin has rejected "Benito" completely. Its materials are unassimilated, its symbolism labored, its diction trite, its climax thrown away, its meaning trivial and obvious. It is, in short, vastly overrated.[8]

---

[1] "The Fifteen Finest Short Stories," *Forum*, Vol. LXXIX (1928), 909.
[2] *Herman Melville* (New York, 1926), 61.
[3] "A Note of Confession," *Nation*, Vol. CXXVII (December 5, 1928), 622.
[4] "Melville's 'Benito Cereno,'" *American Literature*, Vol. XIX (November, 1947), 246.
[5] "'Follow Your Leader':—Melville's 'Benito Cereno,'" *Virginia Quarterly Review*, Vol. XXIII (Winter, 1947), 61.
[6] *American Renaissance*, 373.
[7] *Ibid.*, 508.
[8] *Herman Melville*, 238-40.

How can one explain this wide divergence in intelligent opinions? The answer is the difficulty of the problems which the story raises. Melville drew it directly from a source, Captain Delano's *Voyages,*[9] and there is room for argument about his use of his source. He stays close enough to make "Benito Cereno" unusually detailed and documentary in its treatment of fact, and it is unquestionably slow-moving. Much of its concluding part is taken up with a court deposition, almost literally transcribed, so that it would be reasonable to judge with Arvin that the material has not been worked up into art. The work is too long for a short story and too short for a novel. Finally, the themes and the meaning of "Benito Cereno" are complex, and their proper relationships and ultimate unity are matters not easily settled.

In August, 1799, the American sealer *Bachelor's Delight,* commanded by Captain Amasa Delano, is lying in the harbor of an uninhabited island off the coast of Chili. On the second day of her stay she sights an approaching ship, which appears to be in difficulties. The good-natured Delano decides to board the stranger to steer her to anchorage and give whatever assistance is necessary. Viewed more closely, she proves to be the *San Dominick,* a huge old Spanish merchantman carrying a cargo of Negro slaves.

Aboard the *San Dominick* Delano finds a strange situation. Battered by storms off Cape Horn, long delayed by calms and contrary winds, she has lost by gales, fever, and scurvy the majority of her crew, all her passengers, and many of the slaves. The whites, however, seem to have suffered disproportionately. After this long ordeal, and with almost no officers, there is naturally little discipline left aboard the *San Dominick.* The black slaves swarm about the deck unhindered, and all is noisy confusion. Two particulars especially strike Delano's eye. Four elderly Negroes are so stationed above the crowd on deck as to hint that they exercise some power of control. On the poop sit six Ashantis, busied at polishing the rusty hatchets which are stacked about them. More casually, Delano notices that the ship's figurehead is covered as if for repairs.

Benito Cereno, captain of the *San Dominick,* is a young Spanish gentleman. He is dressed with singular and rather inappropriate richness but is sickly and bowed down by his misfortunes. His conduct is so strange that it suggests madness. Cereno is closely attended by a Negro servant, Babo, with whose fidelity Delano is greatly impressed.

Delano stays on board the *San Dominick* from early morning till six o'clock at night, when she is finally brought to anchor. The interval is caused by a prevailing calm, with contrary currents and tides. During this tedious period Delano is gradually oppressed by some mystery in the situation, with Benito Cereno apparently its center. All is nightmarish

---

[9] This fact was revealed in Harold H. Scudder's article, "Melville's 'Benito Cereno' and Captain Delano's *Voyages,*" *PMLA,* Vol. XLII (June, 1928), 502-32. See also Explanatory Notes, *Piazza Tales,* ed. by Egbert S. Oliver (New York, 1948), 230-34.

and unreal. Cereno is alternately despotic and overindulgent toward his
underlings; toward Delano he is successively friendly, fawning, and
insultingly indifferent. The slaves, in the main docile, have sudden fits
of violence. Several of the Spanish sailors seem to be trying to communi-
cate with Delano but do not make themselves clear. Atufal, a giant black
in chains to which Cereno carries the key, keeps turning up suspiciously
in inconvenient places. Watching Babo shave the Spanish captain, Delano
suddenly fancies that he is seeing a man in the hands of his executioner.

At length the *San Dominick* reaches anchorage, and Delano leaves the
ship. Cereno suddenly leaps overside into his boat as his men commence
to pull away. Immediately three Spanish sailors fling themselves into the
sea, and the servant Babo jumps after Cereno into the American boat,
with drawn dagger. For a moment Delano supposes that the Spaniard is
pretending to be kidnaped, but he is suddenly enlightened by a cry from
one of his boat's crew. Babo is trying to kill his master, not defend him.
The slaves are in full revolt, and Babo is their leader. He is overpowered;
the insurgent slaves are recaptured, not without casualties; and most of
the remaining Spaniards are saved. After some days the *San Dominick*
and the *Bachelor's Delight* set sail together for Lima, to put the case
before the viceregal courts.

At the trial Cereno reveals the true story of the *San Dominick*. The
slaves had revolted, seized the ship, and put to death all of the passengers
and many of the crew. Cereno was kept alive to navigate the vessel to
Senegal. When she encountered the *Bachelor's Delight,* she was trying to
take on water before making the passage to Africa. The servant Babo was
the brains of the revolt, the giant Atufal his lieutenant. Delano was left
unharmed on the *San Dominick* because Babo planned to take his ship
in a surprise night attack and wished to deceive the Americans completely.

Cereno at first promises to regain his health, but then relapses. His
spirit has been broken by the malignant Babo. After the trial he retires to
a monastery, where he dies in three months' time, thus following Babo,
whose eyes look toward Cereno's monastery, his head upon a stake in a
public square of Lima.

The primary theme of "Benito Cereno," determined by Melville's
emphasis, is Delano's struggle to comprehend the action. The first part
of the story is told entirely from his point of view. Later the emphasis
shifts partly to the trial, where the causes of the action are revealed. At
the end two conclusions are made about the meaning of the facts: first,
that reality is a mystery and hard to read, and, second, that evil is real
and must be reckoned with. To which should perhaps be added, there
are some evils that are cureless and some mysteries insoluble to man.
These propositions are related, for the mystery of "Benito Cereno" is a
mystery of evil, contrived by an evil will:

"You were with me all day [says Cereno]; stood with me, sat with me, talked with me, looked at me, ate with me, drank with me; and yet, your last act was to clutch for a monster, not only an innocent man, but the most pitiable of all men. To such a degree may malign machinations and deceptions impose. So far may even the best man err, in judging the conduct of one with the recesses of whose condition he is not acquainted. But you were forced to it; and you were in time undeceived. Would that, in both respects, it was so ever, and with all men."

But Delano is not wholly undeceived. And his speech hints at a corollary: once evil has occurred, it is hard to distinguish between its consequences in the perpetrator and in the victim. So, on the deck of the *San Dominick* Delano comes upon a Spanish sailor, with "a face which would have been a very fine one but for its haggardness. Whether this haggardness had aught to do with criminality, could not be determined; since, as intense heat and cold, though unlike, produce like sensations, so innocence and guilt, when, through casual association with mental pain, stamping any visible impress, use one seal—a hacked one."

Delano, the observer of the action, lacks the sense of evil. Without this key he cannot penetrate the meaning until Cereno forces it upon him, and its deeper implications are permanently closed to him. Consequently, the primary theme opposes the appearance, which Delano sees, to the reality, which Delano does not see. "Benito Cereno" is a story of delusion, of a mind wandering in a maze, struggling but failing to find the essential clue.[10] This theme requires that the reader possess the clue withheld from the character, but the final solution must be no more than generally suggested. The reader takes pleasure in his clear superiority to the baffled character, but he must not take the character for a fool. He must sufficiently participate in the bafflement himself to feel suspense. For this purpose ambiguity is useful: a sense of alternative or multiple interpretations and possibilities, keeping us in indecision. Melville makes full use of ambiguity in "Benito Cereno." Finally, both inward and outward action must have, in addition to complexity, development and firm design. The maze must have a structure.

The structure of Delano's experience aboard the *San Dominick* is most simply projected in the unities of time, place, and action. The time is twelve hours, the place is the ship, the action moves directly toward the climax. A deeper element is the principle of alternation or rhythm, which relates the definite to the complex. The mind of Delano alternates steadily between mistrust and reassurance. It wanders, but wanders in a pattern. The deck of the *San Dominick* strikes him with wonder, with its noisy crowd of blacks, its oakum pickers, its wild Ashantis. But this

[10] Compare Hawthorne, "Rappaccini's Daughter." The observer, Giovanni, has very much the same problem as Delano, and the use of ambiguity in the two stories presents close parallels.

confusion is attributed to abnormal circumstances, in which discipline has naturally slackened. The strangeness of Cereno is explainable from his sufferings. At one point Cereno confers aside with his servant, then asks some highly suspicious questions about the weapons and manning of Delano's ship. But the very crudeness of the questioning disarms suspicion. "To solicit such information openly of the chief person endangered, and so, in effect, setting him on his guard; how unlikely a procedure was that." Delano's misgivings gradually rise in intensity, but, until the end, are allayed. Thus, finally emerging from the Spaniard's cabin to leave the ship, he had got to the point of fearing to be murdered in the passageway. But his fears vanish as soon as he reaches the deck.

This alternation of feeling has a corresponding rhythm in Cereno, who moves consistently between opposite moods. "The singular alternations of courtesy and ill-breeding in the Spanish captain were unaccountable, except on one of two suppositions [both wrong]—innocent lunacy, or wicked imposture." In one phase Don Benito is ceremonious, in the other he withdraws into gloomy indifference, regardless of his guest. At some moments he seems overcome; at others he puts on a rigid self-command.

Critics have commented upon the atmosphere of nightmarish unreality with which Melville invests the *San Dominick*. This atmosphere is in keeping with the theme. The strangeness of the ship is an element of the soul's delusion. Certain motifs and images, however, recur, suggesting that this nightmare has a structure and a meaning. The skill which isolates and focuses the scene is directed toward something more crucial than merely theatrical emphasis:

> Always upon boarding a large and populous ship at sea, especially a foreign one, with a nondescript crew such as Lascars or Manilla men, the impression varies in a peculiar way from that produced by first entering a strange house with strange inmates in a strange land. Both house and ship —the one by its walls and blinds, the other by its high bulwarks like ramparts —hoard from view their interiors till the last moment: but in the case of the ship there is this addition; that the living spectacle it contains, upon its sudden and complete disclosure, has, in contrast with the blank ocean which zones it, something of the effect of enchantment. The ship seems unreal; these strange costumes, gestures, and faces, but a shadowy tableau just emerged from the deep, which directly must receive back what it gave.

The advantages of this effect are obvious enough, but by emphasizing the strangeness and isolation, it also can image the mind which perceives them. Delano is removed from all his customary associations, his supports, his criteria. Some have maintained that his slowness amounts to plain stupidity, seriously damaging the story. Certainly the problem is inherent in the theme, which depends upon a balance of uncertainty and knowledge. The eventual revelation of truth must be inevitable; probably the hero will always seem slow in learning the truth. And if he seems *too* slow, the story is ruined. Therefore it is worthwhile reasserting that Melville has dealt with this difficulty. Delano has one vital disability, clearly stated and essential to the meaning of "Benito Cereno." He is "a person of a singularly undistrustful good nature, not liable except on extraordinary and repeated incentives, and hardly then, to indulge in personal alarms, any way involving the imputation of malign evil in man." He does not understand "of what humanity is capable." Beyond this, the problem is real. It is the creation of a complex and malignant mind, a "hive of subtlety," which has deliberately contrived its confusions.

"Benito Cereno" has a decorative color scheme of white, black, and gray.[11] As in the isolation of the ship, this use of color motifs has both an immediate function of design and along with it a deeper significance in theme. In Delano's search for truth the white is good, the black is evil, the gray the ambiguity between them. The first color is quite fittingly gray, for the *San Dominick* is a ship of mystery.

> The morning was one peculiar to that coast. Everything was mute and calm; everything was gray. The sea, though undulated into long roods of swells, seemed fixed, and was sleeked at the surface like waved lead that has cooled and set in the smelter's mouth. The sky seemed a gray surtout. Flights of troubled gray fowl, kith and kin with troubled gray vapors among which they were mixed, skimmed low and fitfully over the waters, as swallows over meadows before storms. Shadows present, foreshadowing deeper shadows to come.

Out of these vapors comes wandering the fateful *San Dominick*. Against the gray she looks "like a whitewashed monastery after a thunder-storm"; peering over the bulwarks are what seem to be "throngs of dark cowls; while, fitfully revealed through the open port-holes, other dark moving figures were dimly described, as of Black Friars pacing the cloisters." The black is evil; the white is good, since we take the side of the whites and accept the verdict of a white court of law. This symbolism of white and black Matthiessen has called "unfortunate in raising unanswered questions," since the Negroes are the victims of social injustice. The failure to answer these questions makes the tragedy, "for all its prolonged suspense, comparatively superficial." [12]

The charge is a crucial one. It is a true one, if we require that tragedy convey an ideal order. There is none such in "Benito Cereno." Melville's symbols, however, are complex and supply a self-criticism of their own. Melville was certainly conscious of the problem. The white is good, but it is also decay and death—a fate deserved from self-neglect and inertia. "As the whale-boat drew more and more nigh, the cause of the peculiar

---

[11] See Williams. Professor Williams' comments upon the theme of Church and State, upon the interrelationships of Delano, Cereno, and Babo, and upon primitivism in the Negroes are also valuable.

[12] *American Renaissance*, 508.

pipe-clayed aspect of the stranger was seen in the slovenly neglect pervading her. The spars, ropes, and great part of the bulwarks, looked woolly, from long unacquaintance with the scraper, tar, and the brush. Her keel seemed laid, her ribs put together, and she launched, from Ezekiel's Valley of Dry Bones." These images are not accidental. They bear a theme and lead directly to the revelation, the unveiling of the figurehead. At the moment of climax, the slaves cut the cable to flee. The end of it whips off a canvas shroud and reveals a white human skeleton—the skeleton of Don Alexandro Aranda, owner of the slaves and friend of Cereno.

Upon this theme of whiteness the black makes his comment. Beneath the skeleton is chalked the inscription, "Follow your leader!" This is ironically addressed to the white man, but also to the white ship—white with decay. It is not unimportant that the skeleton has been substituted for "the ship's proper figure-head—the image of Christopher Colon, the discoverer of the New World," with its connotation of energy, freedom, youth, and hope. Aranda was killed by the blacks to assure their liberty, and his skeleton was set up to remind the whites to keep their faith—an oath of assistance of course extorted by force and fear. The Negro Babo has his say on whiteness. At the trial Cereno deposes that "the negro Babo showed him a skeleton . . . that the negro Babo asked him whose skeleton that was, and whether, from its whiteness, he should not think it a white's . . . that the same morning the negro Babo took by succession each Spaniard forward, and asked him whose skeleton that was, and whether, from its whiteness, he should not think it a white's; that each Spaniard covered his face." Babo's revenge goes far beyond the provocation. Yet he is partially justified within the theme of whiteness. . . .

If . . . tragedy portrays [an] ideal order, "Benito Cereno" cannot claim to be tragedy. If it is conceived, however, as the realization of mystery, the effective presentment of overwhelming complexity, one's verdict will be different. For the chief virtue of "Benito Cereno" is its sense of an unknown so powerful that it rivals Fate. The man of practical good will, the efficient and officious Delano, can do little to combat it.

Of the orders of the story, Cereno's is the most profound. Melville is Delano as well as Cereno, however, and we see through Delano's eyes. Reality is scanned from the vantage point of the practical, optimistic, liberal nineteenth century.[13] Whatever its shortcomings, it is after all in

---

[13] "In 'Bartleby' and in 'Benito Cereno' we find Melville identifying himself with two figures. The first is the upper-middle-class Anglo-Saxon American, sound in moral principle, mediocre in spiritual development, a successful and respectable citizen. . . . The second figure, the spiritual man, is Bartleby and Benito Cereno" (Chase, *Herman Melville*, 148). Chase goes on to compare the relationship of Delano and Cereno to the Freudian relationship of father and son. It would be profitable to examine the resemblances to Christopher Newman and Claire de Cintré in Henry James's *The American*.

possession; it exists and its efficacious; whatever the virtues of Cereno's order, in the actual world it is fading. The order of the Negroes, if we omit the elements of absolute evil in Babo, raises the question of primitivism. The Negroes are not the primitives of *Typee*'s happy valley, for their problems are more explosive. Crisis arouses in them the same elemental savagery as flashes momentarily in *Typee* in the fierce chief Mow-Mow. In "Benito Cereno," the verdict on the primitive is unfavorable. The rebellious slaves are good and also evil, like other men, but they lack a principle of control. Natural goodness is no better thought of than in *Moby-Dick* in the cook's sermon to the sharks: " 'Your woraciousness, fellow-critters, I don't blame ye so much for; dat is natur, and can't be helped; but to gobern dat wicked natur, dat is de pint. You is sharks, sartin; but if you gobern de shark in you, why den you be angel; for all angel is not'ing more dan de shark well goberned.' " [14] The Negroes are not well governed.

Delano expounds the doctrine of primitivism: the Negro is natural harmony and joy. He has "a certain easy cheerfulness, harmonious in every glance and gesture; as though God had set the whole negro to some pleasant tune." He is, like Hawthorne's Donatello, in tune with nature, a man who has somehow escaped the Fall and the separation. So Delano is delighted by the sight of a young Negress with her child. "There's naked nature, now; pure tenderness and love, thought Captain Delano, well pleased"; and goes on to reflect on the combined tenderness and toughness of savage women, "unsophisticated as leopardesses; loving as doves." But the captain's observations are drawn from the evil Babo, and, as for the women, the court depositions show them crueler than the men. They "would have tortured to death, instead of simply killing, the Spaniards slain by command of the negro Babo."

This harmony and this tenderness really exist, but Delano interprets them too shallowly. The slaves are better and worse than the theory of primitivism. Over them also hangs the shadow of the Fall; and as men they, too, are mysteries. Delano does not know all that human beings are capable of, and he has not allowed for the difficulties of understanding men unlike himself. Without such understanding it is well to be cautious. "However charitable it may be to view Indians as members of the Society of Friends, yet to affirm them such to one ignorant of Indians, whose lonely path lies a long way through their lands, this, in the event, might prove not only injudicious but cruel." [15]

It has been reasonably charged that "Benito Cereno" is insufficiently "worked up" from its source, particularly in its reproduction of Cereno's deposition to the court. The facts of Melville's revision need not be

[14] "Stubb's Supper," chap. 64.
[15] "Containing the Metaphysics of Indian-hating, According to the Views of One Evidently not so Prepossessed as Rousseau in Favour of Savages," *The Confidence-Man*, chap. 26.

reconsidered here. It may not be entirely valueless, however, to reconsider the nature of the story. In "Benito Cereno," the literal, legal truth of fact is a metaphor for truth of the spirit. The search for the one is implicitly the search for the other. Cereno himself, a broken man withholding himself from retirement and death to testify to the facts, is an appropriate symbol for the quest for truth; and his appropriateness is not lessened by the hint that not all has been told. "Benito" is comparable to the quasi-scientific chapters of *Moby-Dick,* which are really an inquiry into the nature, the methods, and the limits of human knowledge.

In the deposition, Melville uses the stately phrases of legal formula to embody a vision of tragic life. Gradually they take on deep cadences, in which Cereno is merged with the public occasion of his testimony, in the frame of his order. "He said that he is twenty-nine years of age, and broken in body and mind; that when finally dismissed by the court, he shall not return home to Chili, but betake himself to the monastery on Mount Agonia without; and signed with his honor, and crossed himself, and, for the time, departed as he came, in his litter, with the monk Infelez, to the Hospital de Sacerdotes." This sentence has the essential quality of "Benito Cereno." Its deepest effects are muted. It has not the life nor the luminiscence of *Moby-Dick.* Cereno is not Ahab, nor Delano, Ishmael—and Babo is smaller than the whale. It is in the sober vein of the later work, well represented by its colors. But after *Moby-Dick* the tale of "Benito Cereno" is Melville's most fully achieved piece of writing.

The Confidence-Man: His Masquerade

by Daniel G. Hoffman

"Strike through the mask!"
—Ahab

I

After *Moby-Dick*, Melville, like Ishmael, managed to survive. Such a survival demanded the Stoic virtues; romantic heroism he had abjured, and the affirmative primitive energies of Eros and Momus were henceforth blighted. In *Moby-Dick* the inner conflicts of the individual and the outer conflicts between the soul and its environment had been magnificently fused. His next two major efforts tried to deal with these problems singly. Emerging from the involuted ambiguities of *Pierre,* Melville turned from that too-personal narrative to one last attempt at a panoramic view of society. Every reader of *The Confidence-Man* is struck by the diminution of the scale of character and action. The confidence man himself deprecates the mode of the book: "Irony is so unjust; never could abide irony; something Satanic about irony. God defend me from Irony, and Satire, his bosom friend." Now there is no mighty hero, no world-mastering whale, no tattooed savages. The great hunters of *Moby-Dick* are replaced, in irony and satire, by these lesser breeds:

> Natives of all sorts, and foreigners; men of business and men of pleasure; parlor-men and backwoodsmen; farm-hunters and fame-hunters; heiress-hunters, gold-hunters, buffalo-hunters, bee-hunters, happiness-hunters, truth-hunters, and still keener hunters after all these hunters.

Melville's main interest is in the last-named hunters. The only Ishmael we can find aboard the riverboat *Fidèle* is a frontiersman—a truth-hunter who, despite his truculent independence and strong mind, is nonetheless duped, as are all the other hunters, by the confidence man.

The balanced encompassing of all the antimonies of experience, which saved Ishmael in *Moby-Dick*, had not proved possible for Herman Melville in life. "Lord, when shall we be done with growing?" Melville had written Hawthorne just after finishing *The Whale;* "As long as we have anything more to do, we have done nothing. So, now, let us add Moby-Dick to our blessings, and step from that. Leviathan is not the biggest fish;—I have heard of Krakens." But this ebullience could not last. Hawthorne gives this account of Melville's state of mind five years later, just after writing *The Confidence-Man:*

> Melville, as he always does, began to reason of Providence and futurity, and of everything that lies beyond human ken, and informed me that he had "pretty much made up his mind to be annihilated"; but still he does not seem to rest in that anticipation; and, I think, will never rest until he gets hold of a definite belief. It is strange how he persists—and has persisted ever since I knew him, and probably long before—in wandering to-and-fro over these deserts, as dismal and monotonous as the sand hills amid which we were sitting. He can neither believe, nor be comfortable in his unbelief; and he is too honest and courageous not to try to do one or the other.[1]

In *The Confidence-Man* Melville wanders to-and-fro over the deserts of an American world in which humane values are impossible and divine laws remain shrouded in mysteries impenetrable to anyone aboard his "ship of fools." This is a despairing book, a bitter book, a work of Byzantine ingenuity. It is as though Melville, denied Ishmael's godlike power to grasp the farthest limits of life, tries, and tries, and tries to spin out of the knotted web of severely limited experience the furtive pattern of truth. In *The Confidence-Man* experience *is* severely limited—to the operations of a swindler on a riverboat, playing, it would seem, for low cash stakes. But each of his diddles demands "full confidence" of his dupe, and each is a "type" of the Fall of Man.

Despairing though it be, *The Confidence-Man* has a wry gusto that carries the reader over its vertiginous argument. Stylistically it is distinguished, and marks a radical departure from both the high rhetoric and the comic palaver of *Moby-Dick*. This style has a new satiric edge. sharpened by images as unexpected as they are apt:

> The miser, a lean old man, whose flesh seemed salted codfish. . . . His cheek lay upon an old white moleskin coat, rolled under his head like a wizened apple upon a grimy snowbank.

[1] Melville to Hawthorne, 17 November 1851; Hawthorne, *The English Notebooks* (20 November 1856), ed. Randall Stewart (New York & London, 1941), pp. 432-3. Hawthorne was then American Consul in Liverpool. Melville, on the verge of a nervous breakdown, had sailed to England for his health.

And there is a new rhythm, whose involutions, even in descriptive passages, dramatize the serpentine twistings of reason proposed by the confidence man:

> Goneril was young, in person lithe and straight. . . . Upon the whole, aided by the resources of the toilet, her appearance at distance was such, that some might have thought her, if anything, rather beautiful, though of a style of beauty rather peculiar and cactus-like.

What is given is taken away; what is removed, lingers. All is equivocal here.

The literary, philosophical, and cultural materials in this book are fused in so enigmatic a fashion that its interpreters have differed as to what the book is really about. Richard Chase, to whose study of Melville in 1949 we owe the discovery of its importance, called *The Confidence-Man* Melville's "second-best book." He sees it as a work of social criticism, drawing on mythical prototypes for satirical intensity. John Schroeder soon rejected Chase's thesis; he reads *The Confidence-Man* as a religious allegory, proving debts to Hawthorne's "Celestial Railroad" and to *Pilgrim's Progress*. And Elizabeth Foster, uncovering still other sources for her critical edition, finds the book to be a tightly organized satire on optimism in its successive historical forms: the Shaftesbury position, the utilitarians, the Deists' faith in Nature, and transcendentalism. Nor are the critics agreed as to the form of the book, although there seems general opinion that it is fiction, and a novel—whether satirical, allegorical, symbolist, or tractarian.[2]

II

Melville's *Confidence-Man*, like Hawthorne's *Blithedale Romance*, is the attempt of a romancer to deal directly with the surfaces of contemporary life while presenting allegorically an ironic criticism of its depths. As was true of Hawthorne's book, the form of Melville's has a baffling intricacy which results both from the complex purposes of the author and from his attempt to assimilate hitherto unmingled literary methods and materials. To judge *The Confidence-Man* we must first understand it; to understand it we must not only read it with the close attention that its style demands, but also we must follow Melville's furtive hints as to the sources, models, and analogues in his mind as he wrote it. Otherwise we may judge the book by standards inappropriate to its achievements. We are about to deal with the confidence man, and,

[2] Chase, *Herman Melville*, pp. 185-209; Schroeder, "Sources and Symbols for Melville's *Confidence-Man*," *PMLA*, LXVI (June 1951), 363-80: Foster, "Introduction" to *The Confidence-Man* (New York, 1954).

as he himself tells us the true book says, "An enemy speaketh sweetly with his lips." We may easily be misled. (His warning, it appears, is only apocryphal, not Gospel.) We may in fact be taken in by the confidence man.

Although Mr. Chase called this work "a book of folklore" and proposed its central character as a portmanteau figure combining attributes of native heroes (Brother Jonathan, Uncle Sam, the Yankee) with those of the heroes of world-historical myths (Christ, Orpheus, Prometheus), later critics have neither verified nor extended his position. Yet Melville in this book transformed in a radical way several of the dominant themes from folklore and myth which Hawthorne had used before him and which he himself had used in *Moby-Dick*. There is witchcraft in *The Confidence-Man*, and demonology. There are the folklore themes of transformation in an egalitarian society, and the contrasting of regional stereotypes; the dominant tension between characters (as well as *i*deas) pits images of the East against those of the West. The confidence man is, among other things, an amalgam of America's popular comic figures: the sly, dupe-bilking Yankee and the frontier sharper. Indeed, the riverboat swindler himself was by 1856 a standard addition to the rogues' gallery of American picaresque lore. In this book he embodies these regional characteristics and tries to fleece persons who embody others—not only the shaggy frontiersman but a Yankee peddler who sits for a savage caricature of what Melville took to be Emerson's fatal shortcomings. There are rituals, too, in *The Confidence-Man*. How else can we regard the recapitulations of Orpheus' descent into hell, the parody of Prometheus' fire-bringing in the con man's extinguishing of the Light of the World? For that matter, as the entire action occurs on All Fools' Day, each episode is a ritual of intensification of the theme of the book, as well as a ritual of initiation for each of the dupes, who trades "full confidence" for the consequences of the Temptation.

What disguises does this confidence man wear in his Masquerade? First (and most ambiguously), a Mute in cream-colors boards the ship, displays mottoes on charity from I Corinthians, begs alms, is abused by some passengers, and goes to sleep. We do not see him again but next observe one Black Guinea, a crippled Negro beggar who lists eight "ge'mman" who can vouch for his character; a minister sets out to find these, but no matter, when he returns the beggar is gone. As the boat stops at wharves and landings various personages debark or enter. Most of black Guinea's references do appear in turn: a Man with a Weed; an agent of the Seminole Widow and Orphan Asylum; the President of the Black Rapids Coal Company. The last becomes before our eyes an Herb-Doctor, peddling Omni-Balsamic Reinvigorator below decks and Samaritan Pain Dissuader in the cabin. Again, he is the Happy Bone Setter. He too would seem to step ashore, and is succeeded by a man from the Philosophical Intelligence Office (an agency that hires out boys). As Man with the Weed he had hinted to a businessman passenger of quick profits to be made in Black Rapids stocks; as Herb-Doctor he spreads word that an officer of that company is on the boat; later, he clandestinely sells the shares. These masquerades take up the first half of the book. A variety of dupes accede, sometimes reluctantly, to the confidence man's pleas, and contribute to his begging, his Indian Orphanage, his Universal Easy Chair, his proposal for The World's Charity ('Missions I would quicken with the Wall Street Spirit'). The Naturopath's herbs find customers—misers are especially vulnerable. Sometimes the con man tells stories to his dupes, or they repeat yarns he has told earlier, or they tell tales of their own. We learn of the cruel wife Goneril, of the Happy Soldier in the Tombs, and, later, tales of Colonel Moredock the Indian-hater, of Charlemont the Gentleman-Madman, and of China Aster who was ruined by requesting a loan. These fictitious characters are discussed: was Goneril cruel or justified? can Moredock's character be believed? In every case the con man's views prevail.

In the latter half of the book the confidence man appears in a bizarre get-up made from the national costumes of every country. This Cosmopolitan, "a true citizen of the world," is involved with several hard-headed and unappealing characters in close arguments on confidence, money-lending, and friendship. At last he descends into the hold of the boat, cheats the barber, and, blowing out the "solar lamp" in the cabin, leads a senile old man away into the darkness.

One can see why the reviewer in the *Literary Gazette* complained of "an uncomfortable sensation of dizziness in the head." Nor could he accept *The Confidence-Man* as a novel, "unless a novel means forty-five conversations . . . conducted by personages who might pass for the errata of creation." We may prepare the way for a better understanding and judgment of this curious book by first determining to which genre of writing it belongs. . . .

The form of Melville's story and the rhythms of its development are determined not so much by characters in action as by the dialectical development of ideas. Lacking the dramatic incidents of *Don Quixote*, *The Confidence-Man* yet resembles that work in its intricate shiftings of the points of view from which reality and appearances are investigated. Perhaps the clandestine analogue and probable model for Melville is the Platonic dialogue, in which the search for truth proceeds through query and reply. As is true in Plato, when Melville reaches the limits of rational (or sophistical) discourse he introduces parables. These, like the Platonic myths, dramatize depths of experience beyond the capacity of the rational premises of the argument to define. But the place of truth-loving, steadfast Socrates is taken by the obscurantist, slippery confidence man. . . .

III

A further demonstration of Melville's originality is his rendering of the American life with which his devilish con man makes such sport. Melville adapts to his own satiric uses a setting and two types of character long familiar in popular culture, where they inevitably appeared affirmatively in comic stories.

The riverboat setting, while it may have been suggested by Melville's youthful trip to Illinois, would seem to owe much to the fictional sketches of Thomas Bangs Thorpe. At the same time it anticipates Mark Twain's *Life on the Mississippi;* but Melville is doubtless truer to reality in his attention to the unsavory characters aboard—an aspect of "Old Times on the Mississippi" which rather slipped Mark Twain's nostalgic mind. Even were Melville unfamiliar with Thorpe's "The Big Bear of Arkansas," he doubtless read that writer's "Remembrances of the Mississippi" in *Harper's New Monthly,* to which he subscribed. Thorpe's sketch appeared in December 1885, in the issue following Melville's own story, "Jimmy Rose," just before he began *The Confidence-Man.* Here, as in "The Big Bear," the passengers are described as a microcosm of the nation's peoples, and the river in terms suggesting Melville's description of "the Mississippi itself, which, uniting the streams of the most distant and opposite zones, pours them along, helter-skelter, in one cosmopolitan and confident tide."

The cosmopolitan confidence man is thus an emblem of the national character, but, like the water of the river, he is made up of its parts. The consistent pattern behind both his masquerade and his clashes with his dupes is the interplay of native regional types. During the first half of the book the con man plays the Yankee peddler to perfection. In fact this role allows him to sidle among the throng in the native image most familiar to them, and most like his own nature. As stock peddler and medicine-doctor he wears Sam Slick's mask, but in philanthropic roles the disguise is that of Johnny Appleseed, the Civilizer in homespun.

Yet, as Mr. Chase points out, the native image is cunningly intermingled with hints and glints of older heroic figures. Intimations of Christ, Orpheus, and Prometheus appear in such inverted forms as to suggest that the con man is an Antichrist, a mock-Orpheus, a false Prometheus. There are omens of his double-dealing nature in the opening chapter. When the mute in cream-colors appears, "It was plain that he was, in the extremest sense of the word, a stranger." Boarding the *Fidèle,* he passes

a placard nigh the captain's office, offering a reward for the capture of a mysterious imposter, supposed to have recently arrived from the East, quite an original genius in his vocation, as would appear, though wherein his originality consisted was not clearly given; but what purported to be a careful description of his person followed.

The crowd, greedy for the captor's reward, on tiptoe reads the placard, while pickpockets work them over and hawkers sell pennydreadful lives of frontier desperadoes, all dead now; "which would seem cause for unalloyed gratulation, and is such to all except those who think that in new countries, where the wolves are killed off, the foxes increase." We are moving into Simon Suggs's territory, whose thought that "IT IS GOOD TO BE SHIFTY IN A NEW COUNTRY" had appeared a decade earlier.

The mute then traces on his placard the words of St. Paul, "Charity thinketh no evil. . . . Charity suffereth long and is kind. . . ." Accordingly, some readers take this fellow to be a Christ figure; his buffeting by the crowd (who don't object to the barber's sign, "NO TRUST") indicates the fate of Christ's message in this world. More likely, he *is* the confidence man himself, a mock-Christ, devilishly quoting Scripture to his purpose. What can be on that placard of "a mysterious imposter . . . from the East" but a description of his own person? In the first of his many masks he walks scot-free through the crowd. He is never what he seems. His parody of Christ's suffering among thieves is a sabotage of Christ's heroism: this "lamb-like" mute lays him down to sleep. Color symbolism also allies the mute with the confidence man. Here he is white; next he is Black Guinea with a coal sifter. Then he is the Man with a Weed, in gray with a mourning band. Later, as Cosmopolitan, he is a sartorial rainbow, suggesting the "colorless all-color of atheism from which we shrink" in "The Whiteness of the Whale."

The East he arrives from is inferentially not only Bethlehem but the American East, traditional home-base of guile and wile. Like the Yankee peddler, the con man is itinerant, crafty, an inveterate prying busybody and thimblerigger. He never gives up; every man has his fatal weakness— be it his vices of greed or gullibility or cynicism, or, better still, his virtues of philanthropy or idealism. The con man will undo him one way if another won't work, and, like the venal peddler, take a virtuoso's delight in his own mendacity.

Here is one of his more obvious Yankee bargains: A consumptive miser (from whom he has already bilked $100) objects to the price of the Omni-Balsamic Reinvigorator:

> "Well, if two dollars a box seems too much, take a dozen boxes at twenty dollars, and that will be getting four boxes for nothing; and you need use none but those four, the rest you can retail out at a premium, and so cure your cough, and make money by it. . . . Cash down. Can fill an order in a day or two. Here now," producing a box; "pure herbs."

The price is as spurious as the arithmetic (he had just sold three boxes at fifty cents apiece). His line of reasoning is the same as that peddler of brooms whose clean sweep in Providence we observed in chapter three.

Melville had often used the traits of Yankee guile, sly trickery, hoaxing, and swift repartee, but never before for satire so disenchanted. Except for Dr. Benjamin Franklin in *Israel Potter* (the most extended forerunner of the "original genius" in this later book), his Yankee tricksters had not been lacking in their "humanities." The first such character in Melville's work is Dr. Long Ghost in *Omoo,* whose practical jokes are not judged adversely since the narrator, in his beachcomber phase, is not far removed from Long Ghost's attitude towards authority. Ishmael had his trickster side, while Stubb "diddles" the French whaler of the precious ambergris by a ruse worthy of any Yankee. In fact their sense of humor, displayed in such jolly hoaxes, makes these sometime rascals appealing in our eyes.

Israel Potter himself is, as Chase maintains, closely modelled on the Yankee of popular lore. He is by turns farmer, batteauxman, surveyor in the wilderness, hunter, peddler, sailor, harpooner on a Nantucket whaler, Revolutionary soldier, and prisoner of war. Escaping from a prison ship to the English shore, he must live a masquerade in earnest now and becomes a royal gardener at the very palace of King George. Then as courier for the Continental underground he is dispatched to Paris with messages in the heel of his boot; he delivers these to Franklin and meets both John Paul Jones and Ethan Allen, before the war's end finds him destitute in the London slums. The rest of his "Fifty Years of Exile" is a testament of sorrows, concluded by his return to his birthplace to find a stranger plowing over "a little heap of ruinous burnt masonry." In Israel Potter we see the Yankee character at its best—upright, manly, opposing first a tyrant father, then a tyrant king; outwitting the enemy in the latter's own gardens, besting even Dr. Franklin—yet defeated by life in the end.

Israel Potter is clearly transitional between *Moby-Dick* and *The Confidence-Man,* and nowhere is this more evident than in the treatment of Yankee character. For if Israel Potter is manly and resourceful, he is hardly shrewd; Melville separates these two aspects of Yankeeism. Franklin is a "household Plato" dressed in "a conjuror's robe," full of complacent saws and prudent counsel; too prudent to be incorrupt. (This conception of Franklin is Melville's own, for Franklin is barely mentioned in Potter's autobiography which Melville used as his source.) On the other hand, Ethan Allen is a stirring portrait of the idealized American character. Melville takes an unusual view of the half-legendary leader of the Green Mountain Boys of Vermont:

> Allen seems to have been a curious combination of a Hercules, a Joe Miller, a Bayard, and a Tom Hyer. . . . Though born in New England, he exhibited no trace of her character. He was frank, bluff, companionable as a Pagan, convivial, a Roman, hearty as a harvest. His spirit was essentially Western, for the Western spirit is, or will yet be (for no other is, or can be), the true American one.

Ethan Allen seems the fulfillment of that creative promise hinted at in *Moby-Dick* in the mysterious character of Bulkington, "full six feet in height . . . chest like a coffer-dam . . . one of those tall mountaineers from the Alleghenian Ridge in Virginia." Perhaps it is significant that in *Israel Potter* we see Ethan Allen only in chains.

In *The Confidence-Man* the shift of sympathy away from Yankee character toward the Westerner is complete. We see this in the only two characters who claim our sympathies as heroes do: Pitch the frontiersman and Colonel Moredock the Indian-hater. The most savage caricature in the book is of a "practical poet" of Yankee cuteness—the con man's hardest touch.

But first, the frontiersman. At midpoint in the book the herb-doctor meets "a rather eccentric person":

> sporting a shaggy spencer of the cloth called bearskin; a high-peaked cap of racoon-skin . . . raw-hide leggins; grim stubble chin; and to end, a double-barrelled gun in his hand—a Missouri bachelor, a Hoosier gentleman, of Spartan leisure and fortune, and equally Spartan manners and sentiments; and, as the sequel may show, not less acquainted, in a Spartan way of his own, with philosophy and books, than with woodcraft and rifles.

This Ring-Tailed Roarer with the Stoic philosophers under his coonskin cap—a backwoods Ishmael—challenges the con man:

> "Nature is the grand cure. But who froze to death my teamster on the prairie? And who made an idiot of Peter the Wild Boy?" . . .
> "Did I hear something about herbs and herb-doctors?" here said a flute-like voice, advancing. . . . "If I caught your words aright, you would seem to have little confidence in nature; which, really, in my way of thinking, looks like carrying the spirit of distrust pretty far."
> "And who of my sublime species may you be?" turning short around him, clicking his rifle-lock. . . .
> "One who has confidence in nature, and confidence in man, with some little modest confidence in himself."

The double-dealer would seem to have met his match. Typically, the confidence man dismisses the woodsman's knowledge as "drollery," and carefully shifts the topic away from his home ground. Seizing a chance remark about the innate bad character of the boys on the bachelor's plantation, the con man asks if he will replace them with a machine, since "Philanthropic scruples, doubtless, forbid your going as far as New Orleans for slaves?" At this moral cant the Missourian snaps, "You are an abolitionist, ain't you?"

> "As to that, I cannot so readily answer. If, by abolitionist you mean a zealot, I am none; but if you mean a man, who, being a man, feels for all

men, slaves included, and by any lawful act, opposed to nobody's interest, and therefore rousing nobody's enmity, would willingly abolish suffering (supposing it, in its degree, to exist), from among mankind, irrespective of color, then am I what you say."

"Picked and prudent sentiments [replies the Missourian]. You are the moderate man, the invaluable understrapper of the wicked man. You, the moderate man, may be used for wrong, but are useless for right."

The bachelor has proved a harder nut than the herb-doctor foresaw. The latter retires with condescending remarks about the eccentric influence of the wilderness on human feelings.

At this point the backwoodsman has won the first victory of any pas-senger over the confidence man. We see him as an Ethan Allen-like image of the West. No longer does Melville envisage "a most imperial and archangelical image of that unfallen western world," as in *Moby-Dick;* the Western character now is tested and tempered in adversity, aware of the evil in the world, and on perpetual guard against it.

But the Devil is not so easily vanquished. Soon after the herb-doctor debarks, the Missourian is accosted by another stranger, a grovelling, obsequious agent of the Philosophical Intelligence Office. The talk turns to boys, and the con man now reverses his former position that the bache-lor should replace them with a machine. He begs to differ with the con-viction that those thirty-five boys, like all boys, were rascals. The bachelor rebuffs him yet again: "My name is Pitch; I stick to what I say." But let it not be said that the boy is father to the man; the man *succeeds* the boy as the butterfly the worm. But, Pitch maintains, "The butterfly is the caterpillar in a gaudy cloak, stripped of which there lies the imposter's long spindle of a body, pretty much worm-shaped as before." This should draw blood, for the grovelling con man is himself the worm, and in his next recrudescence, as Cosmopolitan in a gaudy cloak, he becomes the butterfly of the analogy. Pitch is already half-aware of what none of the others had suspected—that his interlocutor is a masquerader playing many roles.

Pitch, then, has both the hard-won wisdom of experience and the de-termination not to be trapped by the confidence man. To maintain this defensive posture he must resemble "Bruin in a hollow trunk," abjuring the "human-feelings of geniality on which the confidence man trades. There is the real danger in Pitch's attitude that, as the herb-doctor said, "since, for your purpose, you will have neither man nor boy, bond nor free, truly, then, some sort of machine for you is all there is left." Pitch may go too far in his misanthropy. Perceiving the innate depravity of human character, he claims "cider-mill, mowing-machine, corn-husker . . . doing good all their lives long . . . the only practical Christians I know." Truth itself, he says, is "like a threshing-machine." These may be said in only half-earnest, yet such remarks portend two developments.

One is the defeat of the frontiersman by the con man. To withstand him, Pitch would need to give himself completely over to mechanism. But he yet has his humanities, and these are his undoing. The other is the appearance, in the tale of Moredock, of a Western character who *has* become machine-like in his truculent opposition to evil.

Pitch is undone when the con man appeals to his vanity and his latent kindliness. "Ah, sir, permit me—when I behold you . . . thus eccentrically clothed in the skins of wild beasts, I cannot conclude that the equally grim and unsuitable habit of your mind is likewise but an eccentric assumption, having no basis in your genuine soul, no more than in nature herself." The first sign of "a little softening" is all the con man needs to wheedle three dollars and a pledge of confidence in the boy to be sent, sight unseen, in two weeks. Then the Intelligence Officer debarks —at a "grotesque bluff" called the Devil's Joke. At the rail, Pitch ponders his experience.

> He revolves, but cannot comprehend, the operation still less the operator.
> Was the man a trickster, it must be more for the love than the lucre.
> Two or three dirty dollars the motive to so many nice wiles?

It is only then that he thinks of the serpent who tempted Eve. At that moment he is cordially greeted by yet another stranger with a voice "sweet as a seraph's."

The Cosmopolitan, although maintaining that "Life is a picnic *en costume*," has no success in turning Coonskins into a friend. Pitch now knows him for what he is: despite genialities, he sees "Diogenes masquerading as a cosmopolitan." The latter admonishes him: "To you, an Ishmael, disguising in sportiveness my intent, I came ambassador from the human race, charged with the assurance that for your mislike they bore no answering grudge, but sought to conciliate accord between you and them." Pitch, however, is now confirmed in misanthropy, and Melville leaves him "to the solitude he held so sapient." He is indeed an Ishmael, the "wild man [whose] hand will be against every man and every man's hand against him." Unlike the Ishmael of Genesis, however, this frontiersman is curiously cast in a reversal of the Westerner's usual role. Possessing ethical vision without power, he is a paradigm of the ironic role of the intellectual humanist in a philistine culture.

Pitch is now succeeded by an unsavory stranger who, far from rebuffing the ambassador from the human race, comes forward to meet him "with the bluff *abord* of the west." This is Charles Arnold Noble, with a hint of treachery in his middle name: sly and venal, the Western promise rotted from within, he is soon the con man's pal, seeming to believe in what the Cosmopolitan seems to believe. Together they uphold geniality (while trying to get each other drunk), uplift, progress, and free-and-easies. The Cosmopolitan now calls himself Frank Goodman, and

Charlie, having overheard Frank's last exchange with "Coonskins," is reminded of the misanthropy of Moredock, the Indian-hater. But Frank finds it unthinkable that anyone should hate Indians. "I admire Indians . . . finest of primitive races." Charlie sees that he must explain the "Metaphysics of Indian-hating" to make Moredock's career comprehensible, and he begins by describing, as though to an Easterner who had never seen one, what a backwoodsman is.

> The backwoodsman is a lonely man. He is a thoughtful man. He is a man strong and unsophisticated. Impulsive, he is what some might call unprincipled. . . . self-reliance, to the degree of standing by his own judgment, though it stand alone. Not that he deems himself infallible . . . but he thinks that nature destines such sagacity as she has given him, as she destines it to the 'possum. . . . As with the 'possum, instincts prevail with the backwoodsman over precepts. Like the 'possum, the backwoodsman presents the spectacle of a creature dwelling exclusively among the works of God, yet these, truth must confess, breed little in him of the godly mind. Small bowing and scraping is his, further than when with bent knee he points his rifle, or picks its flint. . . . The sight of smoke ten miles off is provocation to one more remove from man, one step deeper into nature. Is it that he feels that whatever man may be, man is not the universe? . . . Be that how it will, the backwoodsman is not without some fineness to his nature. Hairy Orson as he looks, . . . beneath the bristles lurks the fur.
>   Though held in a sort a barbarian, the backwoodsman would seem to America what Alexander was to Asia—captain in the vanguard of conquering civilization.

This ·is of course a portrait of Pitch, raised to a higher power of heroic idealization. Yet in Charlie's story there is already an ominous portent as to Moredock's character. In a world where God's works are godless, what is the fate of the captain of civilization's vanguard who follows his natural instincts to become indistinguishable from the beasts of the wilderness? Melville seems to be saying that, though man is damned, he is more damned in isolation from his fellows than when he acknowledges his humanity. Moredock is an ambiguous case. After Indians slaughter his family he becomes the slave of his unquenchable passion for revenge. Yet he "demonstrates something curious . . . namely, that all Indian-haters have at bottom loving hearts. . . . No cold husband or colder father. . . . He could be very convivial; told a good story . . . with nobody, Indians excepted, otherwise than courteous in a manly fashion; a moccasined gentleman, admired and loved." No doubt Mr. Schroeder is right in presenting the Indians in this tale as devils, as confidence men. Yet Moredock is not, as Schroeder maintains, the ultimate hero of this book. Nor does the opposite view—Roy Harvey Pearce's—acknowledge sufficiently Moredock's human complexity. "The Indian-hater," Mr. Pearce suggests, "can see nothing but the dark side of life [in which] he loses sight of his human self. The issue of blind confidence and blind hatred is in the end identical." [6] But this won't do; Moredock retains his human self, *except with Indians;* and his tragedy is that, still strongly feeling his "humanities," to follow instinctual vengeance—even against red devils—requires that he secede from the human community. He is urged to become the Governor of Illinois: to civilize the district as its chief of state. But how could he "enter into friendly treaties with Indian tribes"? His monomaniacal passion resembles Ahab's, though his enemy is more unequivocally the Adversary than was the whale. Commitment to revenge leads Moredock not to Ahab's self-destruction but into the sterile, mechanical defeat of all his human promise. What "The Metaphysics of Indian-Hating" tells us is that the hero dedicated to extirpating evil must be a lonely isolato. He cannot be a leader of men.

The con man professes not to get the point. "If the man of hate, how could John Moredock be also the man of love?" For Frank there is no such thing as the conflict between the threat and the promise of the Western character—between Mike Fink the retrograde barbarian avenger and Davy Crockett, "Captain in the vanguard of conquering civilization." The confidence man has a contrary metaphysics of his own. For the unfathomable complexity of human nature he substitutes his false synthesis of simplicity; for the true wild rhythms of nature, which Westerners well know, he substitutes avowals of regularity and kindliness. Frank Goodman eulogizes the press as "defender of the faith in the final triumph of truth over error . . . machinery over nature, and the good man over the bad."

Charlie, telling the tale to show man's complexity to Frank, in the end agrees that man is simple. He is therefore unprepared when Frank tests his own avowals of friendship by requesting a loan of fifty dollars. Charlie indignantly spurns him, as "Out of old materials sprang a new creature. Cadmus glided into the snake." In short, Charlie, who has done the devil's office, becomes a human version of the confidence man. But that won't do for Frank, who is a taster, not of devils, but of *man.* With a magic ritual he *enchants* Charlie back to his "best shape," laying down a circle of ten coins "with the air of a necromancer" and "a solemn murmur of cabalistical words." Now that Charlie is human again, Frank is about to renew his request for a loan. Already defeated (for the con man has by now tasted him), Charlie pleads a headache, and retires.

There are coils within the coils of logic in this book, as Melville tries to strike through, or peel away, the masks that hide the truth. And he finds, time and again, that the masks conceal yet other masks. Where then does identity ultimately reveal itself? Charlie's place is taken by yet another stranger in whose person "shrewdness and mythiness" were "strangely jumbled . . . he seemed a kind of cross between a Yankee peddler and a Tartar priest, though it seemed as if, at a pinch, the first

---

[6] Schroeder, p. 379; Pearce, "Melville's Indian-Hater: A Note on the Meaning of *The Confidence-Man*," *PMLA*, LXVII (December 1952), 942-8.

would not in all probability play second fiddle to the last." Having shown us Western character in Pitch as manly but fallible, in Moredock as heroic but doomed, and in Charlie Noble as corrupt and invidious, Melville now turns to the Westerner's opposite as a final foil for the confidence man. And that opposite is in this book what it was in popular culture: the Yankee peddler.

The description of Mark Winsome as half peddler, half Tartar priest certainly resembles Lowell's set piece on the Yankee character in *The Biglow Papers*—and the same author's double-edged view of Emerson in *A Fable for Critics*. It recalls also a comment of Melville's on the Concord sage—"this Plato who talks through his nose." Mark Winsome is his caricature of Emerson, and it would seem that Melville, though spurning orthodoxy himself, was of the same mind as the Reverend Andrews Norton, who, on hearing Emerson's Divinity School Address, had called his transcendental gospel "the latest form of infidelity." Perhaps that is why his cosmopolitan devil, upholding the Emersonian idea of the incompatibility of beauty with evil, not only proposes "confidence in the latent benignity of that beautiful creature, the rattle-snake," but "all but seemed the creature he described." His words echo Milton's when Satan appears before Eve. Expressing this doctrine, the devil reveals his identity. But Winsome is no more concerned to be consistent than is Emerson himself, and rejects the proposal. His mystical air is replaced by "an expression of keen Yankee cuteness" as he obscurely argues the cosmopolitan into a "labyrinth." Winsome, chill and icy in aspect, soon proclaims the spiritual superiority of death to life, and calls in a disciple to take his place and demonstrate his cold philosophy in action.

The disciple Egbert is not so much a smack at Thoreau (as has been maintained) as Melville's caricature of the Emersonian man. Even shrewder-looking than his Master, Egbert is "a practical poet in the West India trade. . . . if mysticism, as a lesson, ever came his way, he might, with the characteristic knack of a true New Englander, turn even so profitless a thing to some profitable account." The action he proposes is to debate with Frank Goodman the compatibility of friendship with the lending of money. They take up Frank's discussion where it broke off with Charlie Noble. Now Egbert *assumes the identity* of "Charlie." In a savage hit at Emerson's "Friendship," Egbert as "Charlie" tells Frank (who assumes the role of "Frank") the fable of China Aster, a tart little allegory on the bloodless ethic of Yankee cuteness. For China Aster was ruined by confidence and a friendly loan.

The tale shows us also the fate of the Promethean creative spirit in a world where the confidence man sets the tone of social intercourse. For China Aster, whose name suggests the Star of the Orient and thus hints at Christ, is allegorically presented also as the Promethean spirit in American life. He is "a young candlemaker . . . whose trade would seem a kind of subordinate branch of that parent craft and mystery of the hosts of heaven, to be the means, effectively or otherwise, of shedding some light through the darkness of a planet benighted. But he made little money by the business." His friend Orchis, winning money in a lottery, insists on lending him money so that he may "hold up the pure spermaceti to the world." The name of Orchis suggests not only the superfluous luxury of the tropical plant (by contrast, the china aster is a common field flower), but also its origin in the Greek word for testicle. Orchis is the confidence man in yet another masquerade. For he is "a shoemaker; one whose calling it is to defend the understandings of men from naked contact with the substance of things." He urges the Promethean spirit to abandon the austerities which dedication to his "mystery" demands, and live in ease and sensuality. China Aster, doomed by his inability to withstand temptation, is ruined in a corrupt world by his virtues too. His honesty is incompatible with success, while confidence is incompatible with his mission of making candles to enlighten a benighted world. And "the root of all was a friendly loan."

When Frank persists in asking a loan, Egbert terminates the "social and intellectual" phase of their acquaintance, for "If you turn beggar, then, for the honor of noble friendship, I turn stranger." His Yankee ethic makes friendship an ideal which cannot be sullied by the claims of compassion. Scornfully turning, the cosmopolitan leaves Egbert "at a loss to determine where exactly the fictitious character had been dropped, and the real one, if any, resumed." In this practical poet of Yankee cuteness who upholds death over life, mind over heart, the ideal over the possible, and the self over the ties of compassion, the confidence man at last has met his match. For how can the Devil catch a creature who *has no soul?* Who, then, is Egbert, and who Winsome? The philosopher himself had asked Frank, "What are you? What am I? Nobody knows who anybody is." And introducing his disciple he had said, "I wish you, Egbert, to know this brother stranger." It was the mute who entered "in the extremest sense of the word, a stranger." The Mystical Philosopher and his Practical Disciple are "brother strangers" with the confidence man. Their faith in heartless self-reliance complements his in indiscriminate confidence. His makes no room in the moral universe for evil, theirs leaves none for good. They show that "defect in the region of the heart" which Melville found so repelling in Emerson's philosophy.

Sophisticated as is the intellectual background of these tortuous arguments, Melville has leavened both sets of confidence men with the common yeast of traditional Yankee character. He found that character seemingly genial, and frigid; ingratiating, and repelling; dealing in abstract ideals, and in shrewd cutpurse bargains. The traditional type of the Yankee peddler gave Melville the master masks in his confidence man's masquerade.

IV

His failure to diddle Egbert does not cast down the Cosmopolitan. A fellow-devil is not his lawful prey; blithely, he goes below decks to finish his work among mankind. The last chapter has occasioned some strange readings of the book. Its final sentence—"Something further may follow of this Masquerade"—leads many critics to assert either that the book as it stands is unfinished (Melville, the argument runs, was so tired out that he quit in the middle of the book and sent an incomplete manuscript off to the printer), or that a sequel is promised, but never was written. The error of such readings may not be obvious, but wrong indeed they are. The chapter is called "The Cosmopolitan Increases in Seriousness," a title which indicates that his masquerade is coming to a close. Let us be serious too; like the old man he meets in the cabin, let us have before us a Bible.

That cabin is curiously described. Many men sleep in berths ranged on the walls; a "solar lamp" swings from the center ceiling. Other lamps hang nearby, "barren planets, which had either gone out from exhaustion, or been extinguished by such occupants of berths as the light annoyed, or who wanted to sleep, not see." The setting is clearly an emblem of the end of a universe in which man is too tired to grope any longer toward moral choices. All of China Aster's little candles are dark now. The one solar lamp has a

> shade of ground glass . . . all round fancifully variegated, in transparency, with the image of a horned altar, from which flames rose, alternate with the figure of a robed man, his head encircled by a halo.

This iconography is certainly allegorical. But we don't as yet know what to make of it; nor does the old man even notice the fanciful images on the lampshade. He is poring over the Book, with a look of "hale greenness in winter." His aspect suggests the beatitude of Simeon beholding the Master of Faith, and one who goes heavenward "untainted by the world, because ignorant of it." These and other hints suggest that the old man, the ultimate dupe in this Masquerade, is America grown old in ignorance of evil—a senile Captain Delano. The Cosmopolitan, seeing him read the Bible, genially assures him, "You *have* good news there, sir—the very best of good news." From a curtained berth a voice objects, "Too good to be true." The Cosmopolitan then professes "a disturbing doubt" concerning the Book. Despite his good opinion of man, he has been told that it is written, "Believe not his many words—an enemy speaketh sweetly with his lips . . . With much communication he will tempt thee." The curtained sleeper interjects, "Who's that describing the confidence-man?" But the innocent old man sets the con man's doubts at rest; the passage came not from the true book but merely the Apocrypha, so it need not be heeded.[7] "What's that about the Apocalypse?" cries the voice from the berth—we by now suspect the curtained sleeper to be a voice from the dead, "seeing visions," as the Cosmopolitan says. The old man now proposes that "to distrust the creature, is a kind of distrusting the Creator." Since the old fellow had "a countenance like that which imagination ascribes to good Simeon" (who beheld the boy Jesus and acknowledged the Christ), we may take a special interest in the sudden appearance of a young boy at the cabin table. Can this oldster possibly have the spiritual perceptivity of the saint he seems to resemble? Not that the boy is the Christ; he is a peddler, dressed in fluttering red and yellow rags "like the pointed flames in the robes of a victim in *auto-da-fé*." From his grimy face sloe-eyes gleamed "like lustrous sparks from fresh coal." He offers door-locks and money-belts; despite the old man's trust of his fellow-creatures, the young peddler sells him one of each, throwing in as bonus a Counterfeit Detector. The lad seems in cahoots with the Cosmopolitan, but the old man does not catch his wink, nor suspect anything at all. Now that the oldster has armed himself against untrustworthy fellows, the con man reminds him of his earlier assertion that such distrust "would imply distrust of the Creator." The old man is confused; unknowingly he has sold his soul to the young devil. Besides, his new counterfeit detector is untrustworthy too—so complicated are the instructions. Completely bamboozled, when he whimpers for a life preserver he accepts what the con man hands him—a tin chamber pot—and takes his proffered arm.

"Ah, my way now," cried the old man . . . "where lies my way to my state-room?"

"I have indifferent eyes, and will show you; but, first, for the good of all lungs, let me extinguish this lamp."

The next moment, the waning light expired, and with it the waning flames of the horned altar, and the waning halo round the robed man's brow; while in the darkness which ensued, the cosmopolitan kindly led the old man away. Something further may follow of this Masquerade.

The awakened voice who asked about the Apocalypse suggests the locus of unstated meaning in this icon. After the seventh seal was opened, John "heard a voice from the four horns of the altar which is before God." This announced the destruction of a third part of mankind by fire, smoke, and brimstone, "And the rest of the men which were not killed by these

[7] The confidence man even *misquotes* the Apocrypha. "This Son of Sirach even says . . . 'Take heed of thy friends,' not, observe, thy seeming friends, thy hypocritical friends, thy false friends, but thy *friends*, thy real friends—that is to say, not the truest friend in the world is to be implicitly trusted." But the verse following the con man's quotation reads, "A faithful friend is a strong defense and he that hath found such a one hath found a treasure" (Ecclesiasticus: 6.13).

plagues yet repented not of the work of their hands, that they should not worship devils" (Rev. 9:13-21). The robed and haloed figure on the lampshade is of course Saint John, who, like the altar of God, wanes into darkness as the confidence man extinguishes the Light. What "may follow of this Masquerade" is no sequel Herman Melville would write; the consequences of man's traduction aboard the *Fidèle* will be revealed in Hell on Judgment Day.

                                    V

One leaves this book feeling as Huck Finn did about one of its sources, *Pilgrim's Progress*—"The statements was interesting, but tough." As a work of fiction *The Confidence-Man* is clearly a desperate experiment; its partial success—the satiric power of individual episodes and characters —was won at the cost of a larger failure. This is the failure of form. Melville had led himself into a maze of nondramatizable speculation to which none of the traditions he could make use of were fitted to give adequate form. His method of uniting ideas with action, as R. P. Blackmur long ago made clear,[8] is largely "putative"; this is especially so in *The Confidence-Man*. He attempts allegory without a superstructure of belief, and dialectic without the possibility of resolution. The traditions of native character, so effectively humanized in *Moby-Dick,* here are separated into the Westerner's independence, pushed to the point of self-damning isolation; and Yankee guile without a saving grace, pushed to the point of demonic inhumanity. A book of brilliant fragments, its method of development is too like a charade in which the clues are perversely half-concealed, or incomplete. . . .

Flawed though it is, *The Confidence-Man* demands comparison with those great picaresque satiric romances whose scope is as ambitious as its own: not only *Gulliver's Travels*, but *Don Quixote, Gargantua and Pantagruel,* and *Candide.* Melville in fact goes beyond them, and beyond Hawthorne's experiments, too, in using the romancer's imaginative freedom for intellectual rather than psychological analysis. Although he satirizes many follies his viewpoint is less satiric than ironical. And irony is the uncomforted refuge of perception without power. The great European satires are works of comic imagination based on the affirmation of man's ideals; Melville's, though their equal in indignation, attacks not only human institutions and human folly, but, as they never do, human nature itself.

Melville's life spanned the century in which the community of Christendom was irreparably broken into chaos. His progress from blithe good humor through the extremities of romantic egoism to the despairing

[8] In *The Expense of Greatness* (New York, 1940).

ironies of *The Confidence-Man* marked both a personal tragedy and the experience of his culture. It was shared by Hawthorne, in whom increasing confusion destroyed the sources of his creative powers. And it is still more clearly exampled in Mark Twain. He suffered as deeply as Melville but, by suppressing *What is Man?* until after his own death, tried to protect himself from the public consequences of his realization that God had abdicated from the universe. That book and *The Mysterious Stranger* seem the naïve fantasies of a village atheist, compared with Melville's merciless apocalypse published sixty years earlier.

After *The Confidence-Man* Melville seemed to have little choice but to follow the fate of the character in his story "Bartleby," and, facing the blank wall, "prefer not to" write any further stories. Like the Scrivener in the Dead Letter Office, Melville spent most of his remaining thirty-five years as an obscure customs inspector on a New York wharf and took no part in the literary life of his country. His great work had been done, but in the era that Mark Twain called "The Gilded Age"—and characterized in Colonel Sellers, who is both dupe and confidence man—nobody heeded Herman Melville. That generation sought a literary hero more congenial than moody Melville with his demonic Ahab and sardonic cosmopolitan. In the platform funnyman who regaled audiences with frontier humor and found no fault with President Grant, post-Civil War America thought to behold its avatar. How much his contemporaries overvalued Mark Twain's lesser talents, how little they understood the depths of his genius, our own generation has sufficiently acknowledged. We can see better than they how closely Mark Twain's greatest work draws on traditions similar to Melville's. The imaginations of both are deeply stirred by the lore of omens and witchcraft, and both respond to the bracing tensions of native character and humor. The conflicts between native and stranger, between truth and deception, between reality and appearance, characteristic of the popular imagination, are intensified both in Melville's romances and *Adventures of Huckleberry Finn*. The signal difference in their handlings of these materials is in their conceptions of an "original character." Although Twain saw perhaps as clearly as Melville the depravity of "the damned human race" who line his Mississippi's shores, he made his hero not only moral, and a human being, but triumphant. In doing so he remained true to the ebullient optimism of the folk traditions which contributed to his view of the American world.

Melville the Poet

by Robert Penn Warren

F. O. Matthiessen has undertaken to give in twenty-two pages[1] a cross section of the rather large body of the poetry of Herman Melville. If he had intended to give merely a little gathering of his poet's best blossoms, his task would have been relatively easy. But he has also undertaken, as he says in his brief but instructive preface, to "take advantage of all the various interests attaching to any part of Melville's work." So some items appear because they present the basic symbols which are found in the prose or because they "serve to light up facets of Melville's mind as it developed in the years after his great creative period."

In one sense all one can do is to say that Mr. Matthiessen, with the space permitted by the series to which this book belongs ("The Poets of the Year"), has carried out his plan with the taste and discernment which could have been predicted by any reader of his discussion of Melville's poetry in the *American Renaissance*. But I shall take this occasion to offer a few remarks supplementary to the preface and to point out other poems and passages in Melville's work which I hope Mr. Matthiessen admires or finds interesting but which could have no place in his arbitrarily limited collection.

First, I wish to comment on Melville's style. It is ordinarily said that he did not master the craft of verse. Few of his poems are finished. Fine lines, exciting images, and bursts of eloquence often appear, but they appear side by side with limping lines, inexpressive images, and passages of bombast. In a way, he is a poet of shreds and patches. I do not wish to deny the statement that he did not master his craft, but I do feel that it needs some special interpretation.

If, for example, we examine the poems under the title "Fruit of Travel Long Ago," in the *Timoleon* volume of 1891, we see that the verse here is fluent and competent. In his belated poetic apprenticeship, he was capable of writing verse which is respectable by the conventional stand-

[1] *Selected Poems of Herman Melville.*

ards of the time. But the effects which he could achieve within this verse did not satisfy him. Let us look at the poem called "In a Bye-Canal." The first section gives us verse that is conventionally competent:

> A swoon of noon, a trance of tide,
> The hushed siesta brooding wide
> Like calms far off Peru;
> No floating wayfarer in sight,
> Dumb noon, and haunted like the night
> When Jael the wiled one slew.
> A languid impulse from the oar
> Plied by my indolent gondolier
> Tinkles against a palace hoar,
> And hark, response I hear!
> A lattice clicks; and lo, I see
> Between the slats, mute summoning me,
> What loveliest eyes of scintillation,
> What basilisk glance of conjuration!

But the next eight lines are very different. The metrical pattern is sorely tried and wrenched.

> Fronted I have, part taken the span
> Of portent in nature and peril in man.
> I have swum—I have been
> 'Twixt the whale's black fluke and the white shark's fin;
> The enemy's desert have wandered in,
> And there have turned, have turned and scanned,
> Following me how noiselessly,
> Envy and Slander, lepers hand in hand.

Then the poem returns to its normal movement and tone:

> All this. But at the latticed eye—
> "Hey, Gondolier, you sleep, my man;
> Wake up!" And shooting by, we ran;
> The while I mused, This surely now,
> Confutes the Naturalists, allow!
> Sirens, true sirens verily be,
> Sirens, waylayers in the sea.
> Well, wooed by these same deadly misses,
> Is it shame to run?
> No! Flee them did divine Ulysses,
> Brave, wise, and Venus' son.

The poem breaks up. The central section simply does not go with the rest. It is as though we have here a statement of the poet's conviction that the verse which belonged to the world of respectability could not accommodate the rendering of the experience undergone " 'Twixt the whale's black fluke and the white shark's fin." [2] Perhaps the violences, the distortions, the wrenchings in the versification of some of the poems are to be interpreted as the result not of mere ineptitude but of a conscious effort to develop a nervous, dramatic, masculine style. (In this connection, the effort at a familiar style in *John Marr and Other Sailors*, especially in "Jack Roy," is interesting.) That Melville was conscious of the relation of the mechanics of style to fundamental intentions is ably argued by William Ellery Sedgwick in *Herman Melville: The Tragedy of Mind* in connection with the verse of *Clarel*. Mr. Sedgwick argues that the choice of short, four-beat lines, usually rhyming in couplets, a form the very opposite to what would have been expected, was dictated by a desire to confirm himself in his new perspective. "The form of *Clarel* was prop or support to his new state of consciousness, in which his spontaneous ego or self-consciousness no longer played an all-commanding role." I would merely extend the application of the principle beyond *Clarel*, without arguing, as Mr. Sedgwick argues in the case of *Clarel*, that Melville did develop a satisfactory solution for his problem.

If we return to "In a Bye-Canal," we may observe that the poem is broken not only by a shift in rhythm but also by a shift in tone. The temper of the poem is very mixed. For instance, the lines

> Dumb noon, and haunted like the night
> When Jael the wiled one slew

introduce a peculiarly weighted, serious reference into the casual first section which concludes with the playful *scintillation-conjuration* rhyme. Then we have the grand section of the whale and the shark. Then the realistic admonition to the gondolier. Then the conclusion, with its classical allusion, at the level of *vers de société*. Probably no one would argue that the disparate elements in this poem have been assimilated, as they have, for example, in Marvell's "To His Coy Mistress." But I think that one may be well entitled to argue that the confusions of temper in this poem are not merely the result of ineptitude but are the result of an attempt to create a poetry of some vibrancy, range of reference, and richness of tone.

In another form we find the same effort much more successfully

---

[2] Can this be an echo of the "wolf's black jaw" and the "dull ass' hoof" in Ben Jonson's "An Ode to Himself" (*Underwoods*)? In both Jonson and Melville, the content is the same: the affirmation of independence in the face of a bad and envious age.

realized in "Jack Roy" in the difference between the two following stanzas:

> Sang Larry o' the Cannakin, smuggler o' the wine,
> At mess between guns, lad in jovial recline:
>
> "In Limbo our Jack he would chirrup up a cheer,
> The martinet there find a chaffing mutineer;
> From a thousand fathoms down under hatches o' your Hades
> He'd ascend in love-ditty, kissing fingers to your ladies!"
>
> Never relishing the knave, though allowing for the menial,
> Nor overmuch the kind, Jack, nor prodigally genial.
> Ashore on liberty, he flashed in escapade,
> Vaulting over life in its levelness of grade,
> Like the dolphin off Africa in rainbow a-sweeping—
> Arch iridescent shot from seas languid sleeping.

Or we find the same fusion of disparate elements in "The March into Virginia," one of Melville's best poems:

> Did all the lets and bars appear
> To every just or larger end,
> Whence should come the trust and cheer?
> Youth must its ignorant impulse lend—
> Age finds place in the rear.
> All wars are boyish, and are fought by boys,
> The champions and enthusiasts of the state:
>
> .   .   .   .   .
>
> No berrying party, pleasure-wooed,
> No picnic party in the May,
> Ever went less loath than they
> Into that leafy neighborhood.
> In Bacchic glee they file toward Fate,
> Moloch's uninitiate;
>
> .   .   .   .   .
>
> But some who this blithe mood present,
> As on in lightsome files they fare,
> Shall die experienced ere three days are spent—
> Perish, enlightened by the volleyed glare;[3]
> Or shame survive, and, like to adamant,
> The throe of Second Manassas share.

[3] Melville's double use of the word *enlightened* here is interesting and effective. The poem "Shiloh, a Requiem" echoes the metaphorical sense of the word in the line, "What like a bullet can undeceive?"

On a smaller scale, Melville's effort to get range and depth into his poetry is illustrated by the occasional boldness of his comparisons. For example, in "The Portent," the beard of John Brown protruding from the hangman's cap is like the trail of a comet or meteor presaging doom.

> Hidden in the cap
> Is the anguish none can draw;
> So your future veils its face,
> Shenandoah!
> But the streaming beard is shown
> (Weird John Brown),[4]
> The meteor of the war.

Or in one of the early poems, "In a Church of Padua," we find the confessional compared to a diving-bell:

> Dread diving-bell! In thee inurned
> What hollows the priest must sound,
> Descending into consciences
> Where more is hid than found.

It must be admitted that Melville did not learn his craft. But the point is that the craft he did not learn was not the same craft which some of his more highly advertised contemporaries did learn with such glibness of tongue and complacency of spirit. Even behind some of Melville's failures we can catch the shadow of the poem which might have been. And if his poetry is, on the whole, a poetry of shreds and patches, many of the patches are of a massy and kingly fabric—no product of the local cotton mills.

But to turn to another line of thought: Both Mr. Matthiessen and Mr. Sedgwick have been aware of the importance of the short poems in relation to Melville's general development. Mr. Sedgwick does give a fairly detailed analysis of the relation of *Battle-Pieces* to *Clarel.* "Even in the *Battle-Pieces,*" he says, "we feel the reservations of this (religious) consciousness set against the easy and partial affirmations of patriotism and partisan conflict." And he quotes, as Mr. Matthiessen has quoted in the preface to the present collection and in the *American Renaissance,* an extremely significant sentence from the prose essay which Melville appended to the *Battle-Pieces:* "Let us pray that the terrible historic tragedy of our time may not have been enacted without instructing our whole beloved country through pity and terror." And Mr. Sedgwick refers to one of the paradoxes of "The Conflict of Convictions," that the victory of the Civil War may betray the cause for which the North was fighting:

---

[4] The depth and precision of the word *weird* is worthy of notice.

> Power unanointed may come—
> Dominion (unsought by the free)
> And the Iron Dome
> Stronger for stress and strain,
> Fling her huge shadow athwart the main;
> But the Founder's dream shall flee. . . .

But even in this poem there are other ideas which relate to Melville's concern with the fundamental ironical dualities of existence: will against necessity, action against ideas, youth against age, the changelessness of man's heart against the concept of moral progress, the bad doer against the good deed, the bad result against the good act, ignorance against fate, etc. These ideas appear again and again, as in "The March into Virginia":

> Did all the lets and bars appear
> To every just or larger end,
> Whence should come the trust and cheer?
> Youth must the ignorant impulse lend—
> Age finds place in the rear.
> All wars are boyish, and are fought by boys,
> The champions and enthusiasts of the state.

Or in "On the Slain Collegians":

> Youth is the time when hearts are large,
> And stirring wars
> Appeal to the spirit which appeals in turn
> To the blade it draws.
> If woman incite, and duty show
> (Though made the mask of Cain),
> Or whether it be Truth's sacred cause,
> Who can aloof remain
> That shares youth's ardour, uncooled by the snow
> Of wisdom or sordid gain?

Youth, action, will, ignorance—all appear in heroic and dynamic form as manifestations of what Mr. Sedgwick has called Melville's "radical Protestantism," the spirit which had informed *Moby-Dick*. But in these poems the commitment is nicely balanced, and even as we find the praise of the dynamic and heroic we find them cast against the backdrop of age, idea, necessity, wisdom, fate. Duty may be made the "mask of Cain" and "lavish hearts" are but, as the poem on the Collegians puts it, "swept by the winds of their place and time." All bear their "fated" parts. All move toward death or toward the moment of wisdom when they will stand, as "The March into Virginia" puts it, "enlightened by the volleyed glare."

Man may wish to act for Truth and Right, but the problem of definitions is a difficult one and solution may be achieved only in terms of his own exercise of will and his appetite for action. That is, his "truth" and the Truth may be very different things in the end. "On the Slain Collegians" sums the matter up:

> What could they else—North or South?
> Each went forth with blessings given
> By priests and mothers in the name of Heaven;
>   And honour in both was chief.
> Warred one for Right, and one for Wrong?
> So be it; but they both were young—
> Each grape to his cluster clung,
> All their elegies are sung.

Or there is "The College Colonel," the young officer who returns from the war, a crutch by his saddle, to receive the welcome of the crowd and especially, as "Boy," the salute of age. But to him comes "alloy."

> It is not that a leg is lost
> It is not that an arm is maimed.
> It is not that the fever has racked—
> Self he has long disclaimed.
> But all through the Seven Days Fight,
> And deep in the Wilderness grim,
> And in the field-hospital tent,
> And Petersburg crater, and dim
> Lean brooding in Libby, there came—
> Ah heaven!—what *truth* to him.

The official truth and the official celebration are equally meaningless to him who has been "enlightened by the volleyed glare"—who has known pity and terror.

The event, the act, is never simple. Duty may be made the mask of Cain. In "The Conflict of Convictions," it is asked:

> Dashed aims, at which Christ's martyrs pale,
> Shall Mammon's slaves fulfill?

And in the same poem, in the passage which Mr. Sedgwick quotes, Melville conjectures than the Iron Dome, stronger for stress and strain, may fling its huge, imperial shadow across the main; but at the expense of the "Founders' dream." But other dire effects of the convulsion, even if it involves Right, may be possible. Hate on one side and Phariseeism on the other may breed a greater wrong than the one corrected by the conflict. The "gulfs" may bare "their slimed foundations," as it is phrased in the same poem in an image which is repeated in "America." The allegorical female figure, America, is shown sleeping:

> But in that sleep contortion showed
> The terror of the vision there—
> A silent vision unavowed,
> Revealing earth's foundations bare,
> And Gorgon in her hiding place.
> It was a thing of fear to see
> So foul a dream upon so fair a face,
> And the dreamer lying in that starry shroud.

Even if the victory is attained, there is no cause for innocent rejoicing. As, in "The College Colonel," the hero looks beyond the cheering crowd to his "truth," so in "Commemorative of a Naval Victory," the hero must look beyond his "festal fame":

> But seldom the laurel wreath is seen
> Unmixed with pensive pansies dark;
> There's a light and shadow on every man
> Who at last attains his lifted mark—
> Nursing through night the ethereal spark.
> Elate he never can be;
> He feels that spirits which glad had hailed his worth,
> Sleep in oblivion.—The shark
> Glides white through the phosphorous sea.

There is more involved here than the sadness over the loss of comrades. The shark comes as too violent and extravagant an image for that. The white shark belongs to the world of the "slimed foundations" which are exposed by the convulsion. It is between the whale's black fluke and the white shark's fin that wisdom is learned. He is the Maldive shark, which appears in the poem by that name, the "Gorgonian head" (the "Gorgon in her hiding place" appears too in the bared foundations of earth glimpsed in the dream of "America"), the "pale ravener of horrible meat," the Fate symbol.

We may ask what resolution of these dualities and dubieties may be found in Melville's work. For there is an effort at a resolution. The effort manifests itself in three different terms: nature, history, and religion.

In reference to the first term, we find the simple treatment of "Shiloh":

> Foemen at morn, but friends at eve—
> Fame or country least their care:
> (What like a bullet can undeceive!)

But now they lie low,
While over them the swallows skim
And all is hushed at Shiloh.

Mortal passion and mortal definition dissolve in the natural process, as in "Malvern Hill":

We elms of Malvern Hill
Remember everything;
But sap the twig will fill:
Wag the world how it will,
Leaves must be green in Spring.

The focal image at the end of "A Requiem for Soldiers Lost in Ocean Transports" repeats the same effect:

Nor heed they now the lone bird's flight
Round the lone spar where mid-sea surges pour.

There is, however, a step beyond this elegiac calm of the great natural process which absorbs the human effort and agony. There is also the historical process. It is possible, as Melville puts it in "The Conflict of Convictions," that the "throes of ages" may rear the "final empire and the happier world." The Negro woman in "Formerly a Slave" looks

Far down the depth of thousand years,
And marks the revel shine;
Her dusky face is lit with sober light,
Sibylline, yet benign.

In "America," the last poem of *Battle-Pieces,* the contorted expression on the face of the sleeping woman as she dreams the foul dream of earth's bared foundations, is replaced, when she rises, by a "clear calm look."

. . . It spake of pain,
But such a purifier from stain—
Sharp pangs that never come again—
And triumph repressed by knowledge meet,
And youth matured for age's seat—
Law on her brow and empire in her eyes.
So she, with graver air and lifted flag;
While the shadow, chased by light,
Fled along the far-drawn height,
And left her on the crag.

"Secession, like Slavery, is against Destiny," Melville wrote in the prose Supplement to *Battle-Pieces*. For to him, if history was fate (the "foulest crime" was inherited and was fixed by geographical accident upon its perpetrators), it might also prove to be redemption. In *Mardi*, in a passage which Mr. Sedgwick quotes in reference to the slaves of Vivenza, Melville exclaims: "Time—all-healing Time—Time, great philanthropist! Time must befriend these thralls." Melville, like Hardy, whom he resembles in so many respects and with whose war poems his own war poems share so much in tone and attitude, proclaimed that he was neither an optimist nor a pessimist, and in some of his own work we find a kind of guarded meliorism, like Hardy's, which manifests itself in the terms of destiny, fate, time; that is, in the historical process.

The historical process, however, does not appear always as this mechanism of meliorism. Sometimes the resolution it offers is of another sort, a sort similar to the elegiac calm of the natural process: the act is always poised on the verge of history, the passion, even at the moment of greatest intensity, is always about to become legend, the moral issue is always about to disappear into time and leave only the human figures, shadowy now, fixed in attitudes of the struggle. In "Battle of Stone River, Tennessee," we find the stanzas which best express this.

> With Tewksbury and Barnet heath,
> In days to come the field shall blend,
> The story dim and date obscure;
> In legend all shall end.
> Even now, involved in forest shade
> A Druid-dream the strife appears,
> The fray of yesterday assumes
> The haziness of years.
>> In North and South still beats the vein
>> Of Yorkish and Lancastrian.

. . . . .

> But Rosecrans in the cedarn glade
> And, deep in denser cypress gloom,
> Dark Breckinridge, shall fade away
> Or thinly loom.
> The pale throngs who in forest cowed
> Before the spell of battle's pause,
> Forefelt the stillness that shall dwell
> On them and their wars.
>> North and South shall join the train
>> Of Yorkist and Lancastrian.

In "The March into Virginia" the young men laughing and chatting on
the road to Manassas are "Moloch's uninitiate" who "file toward Fate."

> All they feel is this: 'tis glory,
> A rapture sharp, though transitory
> Yet lasting in belaurelled story.

The glory of the act ends in legend, in the perspective of history, which
is fate. Human action enters the realm where it is, to take a line from
"The Coming Storm."

> Steeped in fable, steeped in fate.

Nature and history proved the chief terms of resolution in *Battle-
Pieces*. Only rarely appears the third term, religion, and then in a conventional form. For instance, there is "The Swamp-Angel," which deals
with the bombardment of Charleston:

> Who weeps for the woeful City
> Let him weep for our guilty kind;
> Who joys at her wild despairing—
> Christ, the Forgiver, convert his mind.

It is actually in the terms of nature and history that the attitude which
characterizes *Clarel* first begins to make itself felt. Mr. Sedgwick has
defined Melville's attitude as the result of a "religious conversion to life."
In it he renounced the quest for the "uncreated good," the individualistic
idealism of *Moby-Dick*, the "radical Protestantism." Mr. Sedgwick continues: "Behind *Clarel* lies the recognition that for ripeness, there must
be receptivity; that from the point of view of the total consciousness it
is not more blessed to give than to receive. One receives in order to be
received into life and fulfilled by life. . . . Melville's act was toward
humanity, not away from it. He renounced all the prerogatives of in-
dividuality in order to enter into the destiny which binds all human
beings in one great spiritual and emotional organism. He abdicated his
independence so as to be incorporated into the mystical body of humanity." There is the affirmation at the end of *Clarel*:

> But through such strange illusions have they passed
> Who in life's pilgrimage have baffled striven—
> Even death may prove unreal at the last,
> And stoics be astounded into heaven.
>
> Then keep thy heart, though yet but ill-resigned—
> Clarel, thy heart, the issues there but mind;

That like the crocus budding through the snow—
That like a swimmer rising from the deep—
That like a burning secret which doth go
Even from the bosom that would hoard and keep;
Emerge thou mayst from the last whelming sea,
And prove that death but routs life into victory.

Or we find the same attitude expressed by the comforting spirit which appears at the end of "The Lake":

She ceased and nearer slid, and hung
In dewy guise; then softlier sung:
"Since light and shade are equal set,
And all revolves, nor more ye know;
Ah, why should tears the pale cheek fret
For aught that waneth here below.
Let go, let go!"

With that, her warm lips thrilled me through,
She kissed me while her chaplet cold
Its rootlets brushed against my brow
With all their humid clinging mould.
She vanished, leaving fragrant breath
And warmth and chill of wedded life and death.

And when, in the light of these poems we look back upon "The Maldive Shark" we see its deeper significance. As the pilot fish may find a haven in the serrated teeth of the shark, so man, if he learns the last wisdom, may find an "asylum in the jaws of the Fates."

This end product of Melville's experience has, in the passage which I have already quoted from Mr. Sedgwick, been amply defined. What I wish to emphasize is the fact that there is an astonishing continuity between the early poems, especially *Battle-Pieces*, and *Clarel*. Under the terms of nature and history, the religious attitude of *Clarel* and "The Lake" is already being defined.

Billy Budd, Foretopman

by F. O. Matthiessen

Home art gone and ta'en thy wages . . .
Quiet consummation have.
> —marked by Melville in *Cymbeline.*

Then in the circuit calm of one vast coil,
Its lashings charmed and malice reconciled
> . . . High in the azure steeps
Monody shall not wake the mariner.
> —from Hart Crane's "At Melville's Tomb."

Judging from the dates on the manuscript,[1] Melville worked on this final story off and on from the fall of 1888 to the spring of 1891; and even then he did not feel that he had attained "symmetry of form." But though many of its pages are still unfinished, it furnishes a comprehensive restatement of the chief themes and symbols with which he had been concerned so long ago. And he had conceived the idea for a purer, more balanced tragedy than he had ever composed before.

He stated explicitly once again that his was a democratic stage, and affirmed the universality of passion in common men as well as in kings.

"*Billy Budd, Foretopman.*" From *American Renaissance: Art and Experience in the Age of Emerson and Whitman* (New York: Oxford University Press, 1941) by F. O. Matthiessen. Copyright 1941 by Oxford University Press, Inc. Reprinted by permission.

[1] The only edition of *Billy Budd* so far is that prepared by Raymond Weaver for *The Collected Works,* London, 1924, and somewhat corrected by him in *The Shorter Novels of Herman Melville,* New York, 1928. The problem of editing Melville's one extant major manuscript was an exacting one, since, in addition to the general difficulty of the novelist's handwriting, these particular pages contain many insertions by no means easy to decipher; and even the order of pagination is not always certain. It is not surprising that Weaver fell into many inaccuracies. A more thoroughly detailed study of the manuscript, which is now in the Harvard College Library, has led F. B. Freeman to undertake a new edition. By Freeman's courtesy I have had the great benefit of using this edition, which should soon be in print, and I have thus been able to adopt the true readings in two or three crucial passages quoted below. The need of making corrections both in Weaver's edition and in his biography should not cause us to forget that we are indebted to his enthusiastic and devoted pioneering for the first-full-length study of Melville.

Just as, when dealing with Ahab or with Israel Potter, he had remarked on the outer contrast between his material and Shakespeare's, so now he asserted that "Passion, and passion in its profoundest, is not a thing demanding a palatial stage whereon to play its part. Down among the groundlings, among the beggars and rakers of the garbage, profound passion is enacted." He chose for his hero a young sailor, impressed into the King's service in the latter years of the eighteenth century, shortly after the Great Mutiny at the Nore. By turning to such material Melville made clear that his thought was not bounded by a narrow nationalism, that the important thing was the inherent tragic quality, no matter where or when it was found.[2] As he said in one of the prefaces to his verse: "It is not the purpose of literature to purvey news. For news consult the *Almanac de Gotha*."

Billy is suggestive of Redburn in his innocence; but he is not so boyish, and not at all helpless in dealing with the other men, among whom he is very popular. He combines strength and beauty, and thereby shares in the quality of Jack Chase himself, as well as in that which Pierre inherited from his grandfather. But no more than Pierre does Billy have any wisdom of experience. Melville's conception of him is Blakean. He has not yet "been proffered the questionable apple of knowledge." He is illiterate, and ignorant even of who his father was, since he is a foundling, in whom, nevertheless, "noble descent" is as evident as "in a blood horse." He is unself-conscious about this, as about all else, an instinctively "upright barbarian," a handsome image "of young Adam before the Fall." How dominantly Melville is thinking in Biblical terms appears when he adds that a character of such unsullied freshness seems as though it had been "exceptionally transmitted from a period prior to Cain's city and citified man." He had made a similar contrast between the country and the city in *Pierre*; and he had thought of unspoiled barbarism at every stage of his writing since *Typee*. Here he focuses his meaning more specifically and submits "that, apparently going to corroborate the doctrine of man's fall, a doctrine now popularly ignored, it is observable that where certain virtues pristine and unadulterate peculiarly characterise anybody in the external uniform of civilization, they will upon scrutiny seem not to be derived from custom or convention, but rather to be out of keeping with these."

This reflection dovetails in with many passages that struck Melville in Schopenhauer, the newly acquired volumes of whom, along with several in the Mermaid series of Elizabethan dramatists, quickened his interest

---

[2] Melville also refers to a similar story of a hanging for an alleged mutiny on board the U.S. brig-of-war *Somers* in 1842. Though Melville does not mention it, his cousin Guert Gansevoort was the Lieutenant on the *Somers* at that fateful time. As. C. R. Anderson has suggested, in "The Genesis of *Billy Budd*" (*American Literature*, November 1940), the retelling of "The Mutiny on the *Somers*" in *The American Magazine* in June 1888 may very well have been what stimulated Melville to give his interpretation of the same theme.

most in these last years. He was impressed by Schopenhauer's frequent declaration that Christianity presents a significant truth in its claim that human nature is fundamentally corrupt. He also scored in *Studies in Pessimism* (1891): "Accordingly the sole thing that reconciles me to the Old Testament is the story of the Fall. In my eyes, it is the only metaphysical truth in that book, even though it appears in the form of an allegory." This preoccupation of Melville's with the Fall can be traced back to some of his markings in *The Marble Faun,* and even further. For he noted in *Henry V* the King's belief that the monstrous ingratitude of Cambridge and Scroop against his trust was like "another fall of man." He underlined likewise, in *Richard II,* the Queen's agonized question to the old gardener who had reported the evil news of her Richard's deposition:

> What Eve, what serpent, hath suggested thee
> To make a second fall of cursed man?

Melville also added there that this same thought was "to be found in Shelley & (through him) in Byron. Also in Dryden." As far as the last is concerned, Melville might have been thinking of *The State of Innocence, and Fall of Man,* Dryden's theatrical version of *Paradise Lost.* We shall find evidence that he was thinking of Milton directly while envisaging the tragedy of Billy Budd.

One thing to be noted is that whiteness is no longer ambiguous as it was in *Pierre,* or terrifying as in *Moby-Dick.* It has been restored its connotations of purity and innocence, such as it had in *Redburn,* such as were attributed to it more specifically when Melville remarked in *Typee* that "white appears to be the sacred color among the Marquesans," and when he caused the narrator of *Mardi* to be mistaken by the natives for the demigod, White Taji. The accretions and variations in Melville's symbolic handling of light and dark could form a separate essay in themselves. How ingrained a part of his imaginative process their contrast became can be judged from a single instance in those self-revelatory notes for the story about Agatha, which he sent to Hawthorne just after finishing *Pierre.* He conceived that this story of a girl who was to be deserted by her sailor husband should open with a shipwreck, and that "it were well if some faint shadow of the preceding *calm* were thrown forth to lead the whole." That, incidentally, is the theoretical corroboration of what had been his successful practice in *Moby-Dick,* the intensification of his dramatic effects by making them burst out of just such moments of delusive calm. The contrast between light and shade that he is cultivating here is a peculiarly subtle one, as effective as his symbolical use of the amaranth in *Pierre.* Filled with meditations, the girl reclines along the edge of a cliff, and gazes seaward.

Suddenly she catches the long shadow of the cliff cast upon the beach a hundred feet beneath her; and now she notes a shadow moving along the shadow. It is cast by a sheep from the pasture. It has advanced to the very edge of the cliff, and is sending a mild innocent glance far out upon the water. There, in strange and beautiful contrast, we have the innocence of the lamb placidly eyeing the malignity of the sea (All this having poetic reference to Agatha and her sea-lover, who is coming in the storm . . .).

This extraordinary way of presenting good and evil has not really carried us far from *Billy Budd*, where innocence is as inevitably foredoomed by black malice. Billy does not have the spiritual insight of Dostoevsky's Idiot, some share of which came to Pip in his madness. "With little or no sharpness of faculty or any trace of the wisdom of the serpent, nor yet quite a dove, he possessed that kind and degree of intelligence going along with the unconventional rectitude of a sound human creature." But his simplicity was completely baffled by anything equivocal; he had no knowledge of the bad, no understanding even of indirection. Honest and open hearted, he concluded everyone else to be likewise. In such an undeveloped nature the only overt flaw was a blemish in his physical perfection, a liability to a severe blockage in his speech under moments of emotional pressure. Melville deliberately recurred in this detail to his memory of "the beautiful woman in one of Hawthorne's minor tales," that is to say, to "The Birthmark," and thus resumed another element from his past. He found his hero's defect to be "a striking instance that the arch-interpreter, the envious marplot of Eden still has more or less to do with every human consignment to this planet."

From the day when Billy was suddenly transferred by impressment from the homeward-bound merchantman *Rights-of-Man* to H.M.S. *Indomitable* —the names of the ships provide an ironic commentary on the act —he came into the sphere of Claggart, the master-at-arms, a type of character whose lineage also goes back to the beginning of Melville's experience. Melville dwells on his striking appearance, on the fact that his features were as finely cut "as those on a Greek medallion," except for a strangely heavy chin. His forehead "was of the sort phrenologically associated with more than average intellect." His silken black hair made a foil to the pallor of his face, an unnatural complexion for a sailor, and though not actually displeasing, seeming "to hint of something defective or abnormal in the constitution and blood." Everything in his manner and education seems incongruous with his present position as a naval chief of police and, though nothing is known of his life on shore, the sailors surmise him to be a gentleman with reasons of his own for going incognito. He is about thirty-five, nearly double Billy's age, and in character his opposite. His skill as master-at-arms is owing to his "peculiar ferreting genius"; and as Melville probes his cold-blooded superiority, he is led to formulate its essence by way of an allusion to Plato's conception of "natural depravity":

> A definition which though savoring of Calvinism, by no means involves Calvin's dogma as to total mankind. Evidently its intent makes its applicable but to individuals. Not many are the examples of this depravity which the gallows and jail supply. At any rate, for notable instances,—since these have no vulgar alloy of the brute in them, but invariably are dominated by in-tellectuality,—one must go elsewhere. Civilization, especially if of the austerer sort, is auspicious to it. It folds itself in the mantle of respectability. It has its certain negative virtues serving as silent auxiliaries. . . . There is a phenomenal pride in it. . . .
>
> But the thing which in eminent instances signalises so exceptional a nature is this: though the man's even temper and discreet bearing would seem to intimate a mind peculiarly subject to the law of reason, not the less in his heart[3] he would seem to riot in complete exemption from that law, having apparently little to do with reason further than to employ it as an ambidexter implement for effecting the irrational. That is to say: toward the accomplishment of an aim which in wantonness of malignity would seem to partake of the insane, he will direct a cool judgment sagacious and sound.

Melville's growing interest in this story seems to have lain in such elaboration of the types to which his characters belonged, since nearly all the longer passages of abstract analysis appear to have been added after the first draft. In this formulation Claggart takes on some of the attributes of Ahab's monomania; he possesses also the controlled diabolic nature of a Chillingworth. Melville sums up his spiritual dilemma by saying that, "apprehending the good," Claggart was "powerless to be it"; and though Iago *is* not mentioned, the two seem cast in the same mould. Melville had made an earlier sketch of this type in Bland, the subtle and insinuating master-at-arms in *White-Jacket;* but a nearer likeness was Jackson, whose malevolence had so terrified Redburn. The extraordinary domination that this frail tubercular sailor had also managed to exercise over all the rest of the crew was due solely to his fiendish power of will. He was "a Cain afloat," with even more of contempt than hatred towards life; and as this quality burned still in his dying eyes, he seemed consumed with its infernal force.

Just as the presence of Redburn's virtue and health had served to stimu-late Jackson's bitterest cruelty, so Billy affected Claggart. But Redburn had at least perceived something of what Jackson was, whereas Billy's open good-nature has not even that defense. In a passage that takes us back to a variant of his observations on the power of an Edmund and the helplessness of unaided virtue, Melville reflects that "simple courage lack-ing experience and address and without any touch of defensive ugliness, is of little avail"; since such innocence "in a moral emergency" does not

---

[3] An earlier reading for "heart" was "soul's recesses."

"always sharpen the faculties or enlighten the will." In pushing farther than he had in *Redburn* his analysis of how antipathy can be called forth by harmlessness, Melville contrasted Billy's effect on Claggart with what it was on all the others. The Master of the *Rights-of-Man* had hated to lose him, since "a virtue went out of him, sugaring the sour ones" in its tough crew. He is a natural favorite in any group, a fact that helps condition Claggart's perverse reaction. To characterize what Claggart feels, Melville has recourse to the quotation, "Pale ire, envy, and despair," the forces that were working in Milton's Satan as he first approached the Garden of Eden. Melville also jotted down, on the back of his manuscript, some remembered details about Spenser's Envy[4]; and in his depiction of Claggart's inextricable mixture of longing and malice, he would seem to be recurring likewise to the properties he had noted in Shakespeare's conception of this deadly sin. The necessity of elucidating Claggart's subtlety thus called to Melville's mind the major portrayals of evil that he knew. For all his intellectual superiority, Claggart, like Satan, is incapable of understanding the innocent heart. He cannot conceive of "an unreciprocated malice"; and therefore coming to believe that Billy must also hate him, he is provoked into bringing about the boy's downfall by reporting him to the captain on a framed-up charge of plotting mutiny.

My account thus far of Melville's antagonists may make this work sound like a metaphysical discourse rather than a created piece of fiction. The abstract elements do break through the surface much more than they did in *Moby-Dick,* yet the characters are not merely stated, but are launched into conflict. A condensed scene brings out the ambiguous mixture of attraction and repulsion that governs Claggart's actions concerning Billy. This is one of the passages where a writer to-day would be fully aware of what may have been only latent for Melville, the sexual element in Claggart's ambivalence. Even if Melville did not have this consciously in mind, it emerges for the reader now with intense psychological accuracy.[5] The scene is where Billy at mess has just chanced, in a sudden lurch of the ship, "to spill the entire contents of his soup-pan upon the new-scrubbed deck."

> [Claggart,] official rattan in hand, happened to be passing along the
> battery in a bay of which the mess was lodged, and the greasy liquid
> streamed just across his path. Stepping over it, he was proceeding on his
> way without comment, since the matter was nothing to take notice of under
> the circumstances, when he happened to observe who it was that had done
> the spilling. His countenance changed. Pausing, he was about to ejaculate

---

[4] "Spenser depicts her (Envy) as a ghastly hag forever chewing a venomous toad."

[5] E. H. Eby has remarked (*Modern Language Quarterly,* March 1940) on the extraordinary symbols of gestation that run throughout "The Tartarus of Maids." If, on one level, Melville was writing about the social injustices produced by the factory system, on another he was contrasting the biological burdens of women with the easy lot of the men in his companion piece, "The Paradise of Bachelors."

something hasty at the sailor, but checked himself, and pointing down to the streaming soup, playfully tapped him from behind with his rattan, saying, in a low musical voice, peculiar to him at times, "Handsomely done, my lad! And handsome is as handsome did it, too!" and with that passed on. Not noted by Billy as not coming within his view was the involuntary smile, or rather grimace, that accompanied Claggart's equivocal words. Aridly it drew down the thin corners of his shapely mouth.

Everybody laughed as they felt bound to at a humorous remark from a superior, and Billy happily joined in. But entirely out of his observation was the fact that Claggart, as he resumed his way, "must have momentarily worn some expression less guarded than that of the bitter smile and, usurping the face from the heart, some distorting expression perhaps, for a drummer-boy heedlessly frolicking along from the opposite direction, and chancing to come into light collision with his person, was strangely disconcerted by his aspect. Nor was the impression lessened when the official, impulsively giving him a sharp cut with the rattan, vehemently exclaimed, 'Look where you go!' "

Preoccupied as Melville was throughout his career by the opposition between the generous heart and the ingrown self-consuming mind, he never made the merely facile contrast. He had presented the atheistic Jackson as "branded on his yellow brow with some inscrutable curse; and going about corrupting and searing every heart that beat near him." Yet he had concluded, through Redburn's own thoughts, that "there seemed even more woe than wickedness about the man; and his wickedness seemed to spring from his woe; and for all his hideousness there was that in his eye at times that was ineffably pitiable and touching; and though there were moments when I almost hated this Jackson, yet I have pitied no man as I have pitied him." These feelings were what kept Redburn from becoming an Ishmael. Such compassion for life, matched with the facing of evil in its fullness, makes likewise, as we have seen, the briefest description of the elements that composed Melville's tragic vision.

In Claggart again he does not portray a monster. For when the master-at-arms' "unobserved glance happened to light on belted Billy rolling along the upper gun-deck in the leisure of the second dog-watch, exchanging passing broadsides of fun with other young promenaders in the crowd, that glance would follow the cheerful sea-Hyperion with a settled meditative and melancholy expression, his eyes strangely suffused with incipient feverish tears. Then would Claggart look like the man of sorrows. Yes, and sometimes the melancholy expression would have in it a touch of soft yearning, as if Claggart could even have loved Billy but for fate and ban." Evanescent as that tenderness was, it shows that Claggart is not wholly diabolic, and that the felt recognition of its miserable isolation by even the warped mind partakes in the suffering of the Christ.

Thus Melville's vision tended always to be more complex than the posing of a white innocence against a very black evil. In *Moby-Dick*, and drastically in *Pierre*, the symbolical values of this contrast began so to interchange that they could not always be followed. In "Benito Cereno" they became distinct again, but the embodiment of good in the pale Spanish captain and of evil in the mutinied African crew, though pictorially and theatrically effective, was unfortunate in raising unanswered questions. Although the Negroes were savagely vindictive and drove a terror of blackness into Cereno's heart, the fact remains that they were slaves and that evil had thus originally been done to them. Melville's failure to reckon with this fact within the limits of his narrative makes its tragedy, for all its prolonged suspense, comparatively superficial. In *Billy Budd* he has progressed far from any such arbitrary manipulation of his symbols. Furthermore, he has added another dimension through the character of Captain Vere, whose experienced and just mind puts him in contrast with both Billy and Claggart. Melville indicates how this captain, though not brilliant, is set apart from his fellow officers by "a marked leaning toward everything intellectual," especially for "writers who, free from cant and convention, like Montaigne, honestly, and in the spirit of common sense, philosophise upon realities." It reinforces our knowledge of what Melville meant by "realities" to observe that this last phrase originally read "upon those greatest of all mysteries, facts."

The central scene of the drama takes place in Vere's cabin. The captain has an instinctive mistrust for Claggart, but deems it necessary to summon Billy to answer the charge just brought against him. A familiar strain of Melville's imagery asserts itself as Claggart fixes Billy with his eyes, which now become "gelidly protruding like the alien eyes of certain uncatalogued creatures of the deep. The first mesmeric glance was one of surprised fascination; the last was as the hungry lurch of the torpedo-fish." The unsuspecting sailor is so amazed by the suddenness of the accusation that he is speechless, seized by one of his paroxysms of stuttering. Desperate to break its spell and to assert his innocence, he strikes out, and the force of his blow over Claggart's temple is such that it not only fells him to the deck, but kills him. With a single insight Vere grasps the whole situation: "Struck dead by an angel of God. Yet the angel must hang!" In the court-martial that he summons, he points out to his less intelligent and less rigorous officers that they must not let themselves be swayed by their feelings, that the recent great mutiny in the fleet will not permit now any swerving from the strictest discipline. He argues that they do not owe their allegiance to human nature, but to the king, that martial law can deal only with appearance, with the prisoner's deed; and he fears how appearances will affect the crew if a murderer is not executed. "But I beseech you, my friends, do not take me amiss. I feel as you do for this unfortunate boy. But did he know our hearts, I take him to be of that generous nature that he would feel even for us on whom in this military necessity so heavy a compulsion is laid." Yet the heart is "the feminine in man, and hard though it be, she must here be ruled out."

In such manner the struggle between Claggart and Billy is re-enacted on a wholly different plane within the nature of Vere himself. He has the strength of mind and the earnestness of will to dominate his instincts. He believes that in man's government, "forms, measured forms, are everything." But his decision to fulfil the letter of his duty is not won without anguish. He holds to it, however, and thereby Billy, who had been defenseless before the evil mind of Claggart, goes to defeat before the just mind as well. It does not occur to him to make any case at his trial. He is incapable of piecing things together, and though certain odd details that other sailors had told him about the master-at-arms now flash back into his mind, his "erring sense of uninstructed honor" keeps him from acting what he thinks would be the part of an informer against his shipmates. So he remains silent, and puts himself entirely in his captain's hands.

The final interview between them, in which the captain communicates the death-sentence, is left shrouded by Melville as not having been witnessed by a third party. He conjectures, however, that Vere,

> in the end may have developed the passion sometimes latent under an exterior stoical or indifferent. He was old enough to have been Billy's father. The austere devotee of military duty, letting himself melt back into what remains primeval in our formalized humanity, may in the end have caught Billy to his heart, even as Abraham may have caught young Isaac on the brink of resolutely offering him up in obedience to the exacting behest. But there is no telling the sacrament—seldom if in any case revealed to the gadding world—wherever, under circumstances at all akin to those here attempted to be set forth, two of great Nature's nobler order embrace.

Here the search for a father, if latent in all Melville's Ishmaels, and in all the questings of his homeless spirit for authority, is enacted in an elemental pattern. Following out the Biblical parallels that have been suggested at crucial points throughout this story, if Billy is young Adam before the Fall, and Claggart is almost the Devil incarnate, Vere is the wise Father, terribly severe but righteous. No longer does Melville feel the fear and dislike of Jehovah that were oppressing him through *Moby-Dick* and *Pierre*. He is no longer protesting against the determined laws as being savagely inexorable. He has come to respect necessity.[6]

He can therefore treat a character like Vere's with full sympathy. As the two emerge from the cabin, the captain's face is a startling revelation to the senior lieutenant, since it is transfigured for a moment with "the

---

[6] In that extremely popular nineteenth century fantasy, Adelbert von Chamisso's *Peter Schlemihl*, which he owned in the translated edition of 1874, Melville checked the following statement and underscored its last phrase: "Afterwards I became reconciled to myself. I learnt, in the first place, to respect necessity."

agony of the strong." In contrast Billy appears serene. He had been shocked to the roots of his being by his first experience of the existence of evil; but that tension has been relaxed by the mutual trust that he found in his captain. During his last night, when he is kept under guard on the upper gun-deck, his white jumper and duck trousers glimmer obscurely against the cannon surrounding him, "like a patch of discolored snow in early April lingering at some upland cave's mouth." Other images of whiteness rise repeatedly through the final pages, as they alone can express Billy's essence.

He slept for several hours as peacefully as a child. "Not that like children Billy was incapable of conceiving what death really is. No, but he was wholly without irrational fear of it, a fear more prevalent in highly civilized communities than those so-called barbarous ones which in all respects stand nearer to unadulterate Nature." And it was as a barbarian that he received the ministrations of the chaplain, with a native courtesy though with no response to the awfulness of death to which the priest sought to awaken him. But this man possessed "the good sense of a good heart," and "since he felt that innocence was even a better thing than religion wherewith to go to judgment, he reluctantly withdrew." Though he realized that he could not convert Billy to dogma, he did not for all that fear for his future.

At the climax of the story, the "fervid heart" asserts its transcendent power, in the one passage that takes on the full body of the great passages in *Moby-Dick*. At the scene of his execution,

Billy stood facing aft. At the penultimate moment, his words, his only ones, words wholly unobstructed in the utterance, were these—"God bless Captain Vere!" Syllables so unanticipated coming from one with the hemp[7] about his neck—a conventional felon's benediction directed aft toward the quarters of honor; syllables, too, delivered in the clear melody of a singing-bird on the point of launching from the twig, had a phenomenal effect, not unenhanced by the rare personal beauty of the young sailor, spiritualized now through late experiences so poignantly profound.

Without volition, as it were, as if indeed the ship's populace were the vehicles of some vocal current-electric, with one voice from alow and aloft, came a resonant sympathetic[8] echo—"God bless Captain Vere!" And yet at that instant Billy alone must have been in their hearts, even as he was in their eyes.

At the pronounced words and the spontaneous echo that voluminously rebounded them, Captain Vere, either through stoic self-control or a sort of momentary paralysis induced by emotional shock, stood erectly rigid as a musket in the ship-armorer's rack.

The hull, deliberately recovering from the periodic roll to leeward, was just regaining an even keel, when the last signal, the preconcerted dumb

---

[7] An alternative reading: "ignominious noose."
[8] Weaver omitted this word.

one, was given. At the same moment it chanced that the vapory fleece hanging low in the East, was shot through with a soft glory as of the fleece of the Lamb of God seen in mystical vision, and simultaneously therewith, watched by the wedged mass of upturned faces, Billy ascended; and ascending, took the full rose of the dawn.

In his steady handling here of his old distinctions between earthly truth and heavenly truth, between horologicals and chronometricals, Melville has gained a balance that was lacking to his angry defiance in *Pierre* and *The Confidence-Man*. Vere obeys the law, yet understands the deeper reality of the spirit. Billy instinctively accepts the captain's duty, and forgives him. Melville affirms the rareness of such forgiveness by means of the double image in which the sudden raising of Billy on the halter becomes also his ascension into heaven, an identification even more complete in an earlier variant of the final clause: "took the full Shekinah of that grand dawn," that is to say, received the divine manifestation by which God's presence is felt by man. How carefully Melville is holding the scales, how conscious he is of the delicacy of the equilibrium he has created, is shown by the fact that the crew, swept in the moment of high tension into echoing Billy's words, reacts in the next with a murmur that implies a sullen revocation of their involuntary blessing, a murmur that is cut short by the command, "Pipe down the starboard watch, boatswain, and see that they go."

Appearances were against Billy even after his death. The only report of the event in an official naval chronicle recorded how Claggart, "in the act of arraigning the man before the captain was vindictively stabbed to the heart by the suddenly drawn sheath-knife of Budd." Praising the master-at-arms' fidelity to his thankless function, it reflected on "the enormity of the crime and the extreme depravity of the criminal." Yet one of Billy's shipmates kept his name alive in some fashion by a doggerel ballad on his tragic end. And Melville added, in a note to his manuscript, "Here ends a story not unwarranted by what sometimes happens in this incomprehensible world of ours—Innocence and infamy, spiritual depravity and fair repute." [9] The "contraries" were still ever present to him, and in the pages dealing with the chaplain he broke again into what had been one of his themes in *White-Jacket:* the incongruity that Christianity should lend the sanction of its presence to a battle cruiser. In his hatred of war he felt that the *Athéiste*, with which the *Indomitable* fell into engagement shortly after Billy's execution, was, "though not so intended to

[9] This note is one of the hardest passages to decipher. What I have taken to be an abbreviation for "incomprehensible," Weaver read as "incongruous" and though that reading does not seem to correspond to the shapes of the letters, "incomprehen" may be "incompeten[t]." Weaver first printed "infamy" as "infirmary," but since this was meaningless in the context, he changed it to "infirmity" in 1928, though he then unaccountably omitted "by what sometimes happens." In his version "repute" appears as "respite."

be, the aptest name . . . ever given to a warship." In that engagement Captain Vere received a mortal wound, and in his dying hours was heard to murmur the words, "Billy Budd," but not in "accents of remorse." Melville could now face incongruity; he could accept the existence of both good and evil with a calm impossible to him in *Moby-Dick*. In one of his *Battle-Pieces* he had already expressed the conclusion that

> No utter surprise can come to him
> Who reaches Shakespeare's core;
> That which we seek and shun is there—
> Man's final lore.

In creating *Lear* or *Macbeth* Shakespeare did not seek good and shun evil. He sought and shunned one and the same thing, the double-faced image of life. It is hardly too much to say that Melville's quatrain is one of the most comprehending perceptions ever made of the essence of tragedy.

Throughout *Billy Budd* Melville gave testimony that he had grown into possession of what he had perceived in those lines. He showed too what he had meant by calling his age shallow. He knew, as he had known in *The Confidence-Man*, that something more than mere worldly shrewdness was necessary for understanding such characters as those of his villain and hero. We have observed how often in his final story he reinforced himself at critical instances by Biblical allusions. His concern with both Testaments, pervasive throughout his work, now gave rise to his laconic statement that the great masters of legal policy, Coke and Blackstone, "hardly shed so much light into obscure spiritual places as the Hebrew prophets." Melville believed that he could probe Claggart's depravity only by means of the illumination gained in meditating on the Scriptural phrase, "mysteries of iniquity." And only by profound acceptance of the Gospels was he able to make his warmest affirmation of good through a common sailor's act of holy forgiveness.

At the time of Captain Vere's announcement of Billy's sentence, Melville remarked that it "was listened to by the throng of standing sailors in a dumbness like that of a seated congregation of believers in Hell listening to their clergyman's announcement of his Calvinistic text." At that point Melville added in the margin of his manuscript the name of Jonathan Edwards. The rectitude of Vere seems to have recalled to him the inexorable logic, the tremendous force of mind in the greatest of our theologians. Melville might also have reflected that the relentless denial of the claims of ordinary nature on which Edwards based his reasoned declaration of the absolute Sovereignty of God had left its mark on the New England character, on such emotionally starved and one-sided figures as Hawthorne drew, on the nightmare of will which a perverted determinism had become in Ahab. Without minimizing the justice of

Vere's stern mind, Melville could feel that the deepest need for rapaciously individualistic America was a radical affirmation of the heart. He knew that his conception of the young sailor's "essential innocence" was in accord with no orthodoxy; but he found it "an irruption of heretic thought hard to suppress." [10] The hardness was increased by his having also learned what Keats had, through his kindred apprehension of the meaning of Shakespeare, that the Heart is the Mind's Bible. Such knowledge was the source of the passionate humanity in Melville's own creation of tragedy.

How important it was to reaffirm the heart in the America in which *Billy Budd* was shaped can be corroborated by the search that was being made for the drift of significance in our eighteen-eighties and nineties by two of our most symptomatic minds. John Jay Chapman was already protesting against the conservative legalistic dryness that characterized our educated class, as fatal to real vitality; while Henry Adams, in assessing his heritage, knew that it tended too much towards the analytic mind, that it lacked juices. Those juices could spring only from the "depth of tenderness," the "boundless sympathy" to which Adams responded in the symbol of the Virgin, but which Melville—for the phrases are his— had found in great tragedy. After all he had suffered Melville could endure to the end in the belief that though good goes to defeat and death, its radiance can redeem life. His career did not fall into what has been too often assumed to be the pattern for the lives of our artists: brilliant beginnings without staying power, truncated and broken by our hostile environment. Melville's endurance is a challenge for a later America.

[10] Freeman's edition places this significant comment in its proper context for the first time. Weaver's inaccurate placing of it made it refer to the way that Christianity is distorted by a chaplain's lending its sanction to a man-of-war.

Chronology of Important Dates

1819	Herman Melville born to Allan and Maria Gansevoort Melville in New York City.
1830	Allan Melville suffered severe business losses and died in 1832. Meanwhile the family had moved to Albany, where Melville went to school, later clerking and teaching in the vicinity.
1839	Sailed on the *St. Lawrence*, a merchant ship, for Liverpool.
1841	Sailed from Fairhaven, Massachusetts, on the whaler *Acushnet*. After undergoing many of the experiences described in *Typee*, *Omoo*, and *White-Jacket*, returned on the frigate *United States* in the fall of 1844.
1846	*Typee.*
1847	*Omoo.* Married Elizabeth Shaw of Massachusetts and settled in New York City.
1849	*Mardi* and *Redburn.* Traveled in Europe.
1850	*White-Jacket.* Moved to "Arrowhead," a farm near Pittsfield, Massachusetts. Formed friendship with Hawthorne.
1851	*Moby-Dick.*
1852	*Pierre.*
1855	*Israel Potter.*
1856	*The Piazza Tales.* Left for Europe and the Near East, apparently on the verge of a nervous breakdown.
1857	*The Confidence-Man.* Returned to the United States.
1863	Settled with family in New York City.
1866	*Battle-Pieces and Aspects of the War.* Became an Inspector of Customs, a position he held until 1887.
1876	*Clarel.*
1891	Died, September 28.
1924	*Billy Budd* first published.

Notes on the Editor and Authors

RICHARD CHASE teaches at Columbia. He is the author of such works as *Herman Melville, Walt Whitman Reconsidered, The American Novel and Its Tradition,* and *The Democratic Vista.*

NEWTON ARVIN, long an eminent professor and critic, is the author of *Hawthorne* and *Whitman.*

MARIUS BEWLEY is the author of *The Complex Fate* and numerous essays in the literary magazines.

RICHARD P. BLACKMUR is the author of such influential volumes of criticism as *The Expense of Greatness* and *Form and Value in Modern Poetry.* He is a professor of English at Princeton.

RICHARD HARTER FOGLE, of the department of English at Tulane University, is the author of *Hawthorne's Fiction.*

DANIEL G. HOFFMAN, poet, critic, and professor, teaches at Swarthmore.

ALFRED KAZIN is the author of such notable works as *On Native Grounds* and *The Inmost Leaf.*

D. H. LAWRENCE, the famous English novelist who wrote *Sons and Lovers* and *The Rainbow,* often interested himself, as a critic, in cultures other than his own.

F. O. MATTHIESSEN, a pioneer in modern American literary studies, wrote, besides *American Renaissance, The Achievement of T. S. Eliot* and *Theodore Dreiser.*

HENRY A. MURRAY, psychologist and critic, has long been interested in Melville.

ROBERT PENN WARREN is well known as a poet and critic, and also as the author of such novels as *Night Rider* and *All the King's Men.* He teaches at Yale.

Selected Bibliography

Newton Arvin, *Herman Melville* (1950). The best critical biography, although it somewhat underplays certain of Melville's later works.

Richard Chase, *Herman Melville* (1949). This book contributes to our knowledge of Melville's use of folklore and mythic archetypes.

Leon Howard, *Herman Melville* (1951). A factual biography.

Jay Leyda, *The Melville Log: A Documentary Life of Herman Melville*, 2 vols. (1951). An imposing mausoleum of data, relevant and irrelevant.

Charles Olson, *Call Me Ishmael* (1947). Oracular in the D. H. Lawrence manner. Makes interesting comparisons of Melville and Shakespeare.

Edward H. Rosenberry, *Melville and the Comic Spirit* (1955).

William Ellery Sedgwick, *Herman Melville: The Tragedy of Mind* (1944). A sensitive study of Melville's thought.

Raymond Weaver, *Herman Melville: Mariner and Mystic* (1921). The pioneering biography, still of interest though necessarily in some ways outmoded.

Among general works on American literature which contain valuable passages on Melville are Charles Feidelson, *Symbolism and American Literature* (1953); Leslie Fiedler, *Love and Death in the American Novel* (1960); D. H. Lawrence, *Studies in Classic American Literature* (1923); R. W. B. Lewis, *The American Adam* (1955); F. O. Matthiessen, *American Renaissance* (1941); and Yvor Winters, *In Defense of Reason* (1947).

TWENTIETH CENTURY VIEWS

American Authors

TWENTIETH CENTURY VIEWS

British Authors

TWENTIETH CENTURY VIEWS

European Authors

BAUDELAIRE, edited by Henri Peyre (S-TC-18)
SAMUEL BECKETT, edited by Martin Esslin (S-TC-51)
BRECHT, edited by Peter Demetz (S-TC-11)
CAMUS, edited by Germaine Brée (S-TC-1)
CHEKHOV, edited by Robert Louis Jackson (S-TC-71)
DANTE, edited by John Freccero (S-TC-46)
DOSTOEVSKY, edited by René Wellek (S-TC-16)
EURIPIDES, edited by Erich Segal (S-TC-76)
FLAUBERT, edited by Raymond Giraud (S-TC-42)
GOETHE, edited by Victor Lange (S-TC-73)
HOMER, edited by George Steiner and Robert Fagles (S-TC-15)
IBSEN, edited by Rolf Fjelde (S-TC-52)
KAFKA, edited by Ronald Gray (S-TC-17)
LORCA, edited by Manuel Durán (S-TC-14)
MALRAUX, edited by R. W. B. Lewis (S-TC-37)
THOMAS MANN, edited by Henry Hatfield (S-TC-36)
MOLIÈRE, edited by Jacques Guicharnaud (S-TC-41)
PIRANDELLO, edited by Glauco Cambon (S-TC-67)
PROUST, edited by René Girard (S-TC-4)
SARTRE, edited by Edith Kern (S-TC-21)
SOPHOCLES, edited by Thomas Woodard (S-TC-54)
STENDHAL, edited by Victor Brombert (S-TC-7)
TOLSTOY, edited by Ralph E. Matlaw (S-TC-68)
VIRGIL, edited by Steele Commager (S-TC-62)
VOLTAIRE, edited by William F. Bottiglia (S-TC-78)